About The Cover

The cover of this book includes the following images:

1. Cleveland Press columnist and television personality Dick Feagler with singer Eric Carmen in 1981. Cleveland Public Library Photograph Collection.
2. The Plain Dealer presses in 1954. Cleveland Public Library Photograph Collection.
3. Plain Dealer television critic and columnist George Condon in 1954. Cleveland Public Library Photograph Collection.
4. Journalist Terence Sheridan at the Sarajevo airport in 1993. Photograph by Elizabeth Sullivan.
5. Cleveland City Council President George Forbes tosses journalist Roldo Bartimole out of special council meeting in March 1981. Special Collections, Cleveland State University Library.
6. Plain Dealer journalists, from left, Jack Hagan, Don Bean, and Robert McAuley. Courtesy of Robert McAuley.
7. Louis B. Seltzer reads an issue of The Press in the city room in 1960. Special Collections, Cleveland State University Library.
8. Actress Jayne Mansfield poses with Plain Dealer photographers. Back row, from left, Bill Ashbolt, Dudley Brumbach, Marvin Greene, Bill Wynne. Front row, from left, Karl J. Rauschkolb, Mansfield, Ray Matjasic. Special Collections, Cleveland State University Library.
9. A "Save the PD" rally in 2013 in front of the PD offices at E. 18th Street and Superior Avenue. Photograph courtesy of Harlan Spector.
10. Robert McGruder, The Plain Dealer's first black reporter, pictured in 1969. McGruder rose to become the PD's managing editor before leaving for the Detroit Free Press, where he became executive editor. Cleveland Public Library Photograph Collection.
11. Reporter Harlan Spector with deskmate John Petkovic in The Plain Dealer newsroom in the 1990s. Courtesy of Harlan Spector.
12. Dennis Kucinich stopped by The Plain Dealer on Nov. 8, 1977, the evening he was elected Cleveland mayor. Kucinich, once a Plain Dealer copy aide, sent the story of his election up the pneumatic tube to the composing room. Plain Dealer photograph by William "Bill" Wynne. Special Collections, Cleveland State University Library.
13. Plain Dealer copy editor Robert Manry entering the harbor in Falmouth England, Aug. 17, 1965. Manry was completing a 78-day trip across the Atlantic in *Tinkerbelle*, a 13 ½-foot sailboat. Special Collections, Cleveland State University Library.
14. The Plain Dealer city room in 1947. The PD's daily circulation stood at 220,618 two years earlier, ranking it second highest behind The Press. Cleveland Public Library Photograph Collection.
15. Plain Dealer photographer William "Bill" Wynne. Special Collections, Cleveland State University Library.

Cover Image:

　　Dave Davis and Joan Mazzolini

Cover Image Infographic:

　　Justin Grogan-Myers and Donna Stewart
　　Systems Division, Michael Schwartz Library, Cleveland State University

Plain Dealing:
Cleveland Journalists Tell Their Stories

Dave Davis and Joan Mazzolini

Plain Dealing:
Cleveland Journalists Tell Their Stories

Dave Davis and Joan Mazzolini

An ebook version of this book can be accessed from
http://engagedscholarship.csuohio.edu/msl_ae_ebooks/6/
This book is brought to you for free and open access at EngagedScholarship @ Cleveland State University. It has been accepted for inclusion in MSL Academic Endeavors eBooks by an authorized administrator of EngagedScholarship @ Cleveland State University.
For more information, please email an administrator at library.es@csuohio.edu.

2018 MSL Academic Endeavors

Imprint of the Michael Schwartz Library at Cleveland State University

Plain Dealing: Cleveland Journalists Tell Their Stories by Dave Davis and Joan Mazzolini is licensed under a Creative Commons Attribution-NonCommercial-NoDerivatives 4.0 International License, except where otherwise noted.

Published by:

MSL Academic Endeavors

Cleveland State University

Michael Schwartz Library
2121 Euclid Avenue
Rhodes Tower, Room 501
Cleveland, Ohio 44115

https://engagedscholarship.csuohio.edu

ISBN 13: 978-1-936323-65-4

ISBN 10: 1-936323-65-6

This book was produced using Pressbooks, and PDF rendering was done by PrinceXML.

Dedication

On behalf of our authors and contributors, we dedicate this book to Cleveland, the city that we love, and to journalism, our calling. Our stories, for what they're worth.

~Joan and Dave

Acknowledgements

Special thanks to our authors and contributors:

Tom Andrzejewski	Michael O'Malley
Roldo Bartimole	Michael D. Roberts
Margaret Bernstein	Louis B. Seltzer
Carrie Buchanan	Mary Anne Sharkey
Gary Clark	Terence Sheridan
George E. Condon	Harlan Spector
Dick Feagler	Kaye Spector
Janet Beighle French	Scott Stephens
Jack Hagan	Gail Stuehr
Leslie Kay	Evelyn Theiss
Susan Condon Love	Stuart Warner
Robert McAuley	William "Bill" Wynne

Contents

Introduction	1
Twenty-Five Stories	
Adventures in journalism	9
Dig deep, stick to the facts, no cheap shots: A reporters' editor talks about The PD newsroom	25
Strength, beauty, power - covering Cleveland's long-ignored black community	35
A daughter remembers Cleveland's real best-kept secret	42
A three newspaper family	48
Shooting from the heart	56
Why the Press used "all its editorial artillery" against Dr. Sam Sheppard	65
A backstage pass to momentous events	72
How I became a newspaper woman against all odds	76
A muckraker comes to Cleveland and founds Point of View	83
Confessions of a wayward reporter	95
The cop shop	102
Precision journalism and uncovering disparities in the courts	111
Catching a ride into the newsroom - and history	121
The ladies of the press	125
Stop the presses (for the very last time)	131
The magic of a city and newsroom full of characters	140
The road to a big-city daily and life at Ohio's largest newspaper	146
Health care, the "sleeve," and life in The PD newsroom	155
Covering Cleveland neighborhoods: these streets talk - if only we'd listen	161
Welcome to The Plain Dealer	167
A prize-winning columnist leaves The PD	172
Those were the days in Rubber City ... but they had to end	175

Newsgathering in the new millennium: boom and then bust	188
Misfit	192

Photographs

Covering Cleveland - 1946 to 2013	201
About Our Authors And Contributors	219
Resources	233

Introduction

DAVE DAVIS

I wanted to title this book "Misfits." But co-editor Joan Mazzolini wouldn't allow it. "Let's think of something else," she counseled. Though I use the term with affection and admiration, truth be told there are only 16 misfits in this book. Maybe 17. As for the other contributors, the label would be inaccurate, perhaps even offensive, at least as it's commonly used.

But although my original title may have been a bit much, I think it captures two important points that I want to make in this introduction. The first is that I believe that good journalism usually is not the product of consensus, of committee, but rather comes from individuals. Reporter driven, as our contributors say. Television commentator David Brinkley bluntly acknowledged the power of the individual in news gathering when he stated, "News is what I say it is."

Additionally, I believe that good journalists are honest and fair but willing to take risks and pursue the truth no matter where it takes them or who it offends. They aren't part of the status quo. They question it. They don't always comfortably fit into the world around them, and often that's by choice. They are outsiders, to a degree. It's an important characteristic, I think. That and a sense of humor.

Plain Dealer columnist George E. Condon, in his piece "Adventures in journalism," put it this way:

> *Newspapers traditionally have served as havens for men and women who were not completely understood by the outside world; they have provided sanctuary to those who were harassed and pursued by the keepers of the conventions, carefully keeping alive in the editorial rooms the last spark of individuality in a society that grows more regimented by the hour. Sometimes, ... the behavior of newsmen may seem anti-social, or irrational to the outside world. It is not. It is simply a manifestation of the creative spirit at work in material surroundings.*

Condon penned those words in 1967, and I believe they are true today.

So I let the question of a title roll around in my head for a few weeks. I needed to find something that fit everyone, and that wouldn't require a long explanation such as the one I just gave. I cracked open a few reference books, talked to Joan and others and even got on the computer and Googled it. Outcasts. Award winners. Truthtellers. Nah. Storytellers. Hellraisers. Straight talkers, hummm, straight talkers. How 'bout plain dealers.

We settled on "Plain Dealing."

It's not as sexy or provocative as "Misfits," but works well on a couple of different levels. We're using the title "Plain Dealing" in the original, old-timey sense of the term. A "plain dealer" is a straight shooter, someone who tells it like it is – arguably the most important quality in a journalist. All of our contributors are "plain dealers."

And yes, everyone in this book – except Louie Seltzer, the legendary and sometimes controversial editor of The Cleveland Press – worked at The Plain Dealer, the newspaper that was my home for 24 years. So, there is that connection as well. For some, their time at the PD was just a matter of months, while for others it was most or all of their career.

What we're offering you is simply a book of stories, many never told before. These stories begin in the 1950s and go up to 2013, covering the post-World War II era through the days when Cleveland was a three daily newspaper city, then two, then one. The book ends with the mass layoffs and resulting decline that ushered in the digital-first age.

Our stories are first-person accounts of life in the newsroom, the issues and events we covered, the characters we worked with and met and ultimately, I believe, journalism in Cleveland. Yes, the spotlight is on The Plain Dealer, but there is substantial ink devoted to The Cleveland News, The Press, The Akron Beacon Journal, and Point of View, the muckraking newsletter published by Roldo Bartimole. (Yes, even Roldo worked at The PD).

So that's what we have here, for better or worse.

Today – July 31, 2018 – marks the 200th anniversary of the first edition of Cleveland's first newspaper, the Cleaveland Gazette & Commercial Register. This book is being published by Cleveland State University to celebrate those first plain dealers, who established our profession in what was then a 22-year-old township. Even though Cleveland had fewer than 600 people then, they felt the need for a newspaper. Obviously, someone had something to say.

Since that time, journalism has changed a lot in many ways and not at all in others. Obviously, the means of delivering the news and the tools journalists used to do that have evolved and in this digital age are the topic of much hand-wringing and discussion. But I would argue that the basic principles – accuracy, fairness, thoroughness – are as important today as they were when the first edition of the Gazette & Commercial Register appeared on that hot summer day in 1818. In the end, we are storytellers, the public's eyes and ears. We tell people what they need to know, entertain them, chronicle their hopes and dreams and stick up for them.

The Cleveland area has a rich and long journalistic history, from the radio and television stations, to the feisty Akron Beacon Journal, the Knight Newspaper Company's flagship newspaper, to The Plain Dealer, The Cleveland Press, The News, The Call & Post, the Catholic Universe Bulletin, and some very fine community newspapers. Writing a meaningful account of them would take volumes.

Each of these news organizations, at times, has been outstanding. And each has fallen down on the job. And even in the worst times, good journalists have continued to do good work. It's in our blood.

In working on this book, I've concluded that it's too simplistic to dismiss any of these publications based on our bad experiences, though it's important to learn from those experiences and do better. As my friend and contributor Michael O'Malley points out, The Plain Dealer missed what were arguably the two biggest stories of the 19th century – the surrender of Robert E. Lee (April 9, 1865), effectively ending the American Civil War, and the assassination of President Abraham Lincoln (April 15, 1865).

That happened when publication was suspended for nearly two months in 1865 during a family dispute over the direction of the newspaper after the death of its publisher, William Gray, three years earlier.

And then there was the time that The Plain Dealer stumbled in covering its own story – the 78-day, 3,200-mile voyage by PD copy editor Robert Manry, who sailed from Falmouth, Massachusetts, into the hearts of an adoring public and a gaggle of reporters and photographers when he entered the harbor in Falmouth, England, on Aug. 17, 1965. Manry made the trip in a 13 1/2-foot sail boat named *Tinkerbelle*. The PD finally showed up to cover it, but it was late to recognize the story.

And the newspaper's biggest and most shameful journalistic lapse involved coverage of former Teamster boss Jackie Presser. On Sunday, Oct. 10, 1982, a front-page story on federal officials closing an investigation into allegations of criminal wrongdoing by the Teamster boss appeared in The Plain Dealer. (The story did not carry a byline and it was later learned that it had been written by Executive Editor David Hopcraft). The investigation was based on reporting a year earlier by Walt Bogdanich that revealed that Presser had taken kickbacks and was an FBI informant.

What the story didn't say was that federal officials had determined that the statute of limitations had run out on any possible wrongdoing, and so they closed the investigation. Still, the story was widely viewed as a retraction of the earlier reporting. Presser hailed it as "vindication," and it cleared the way for him to become president of the International Brotherhood of Teamsters, whose rank-and-file members would not have liked the idea that he was a snitch.

Later, Bogdanich's reporting was found to have been completely accurate, Presser was acknowledged to have been a longtime federal informant, and his crime associates testified in 1988 before Congress that the Plain Dealer story had been arranged by the mob. Plain Dealer reporters, through the Newspaper Guild, immediately spoke out against their employer's action, setting up an informational picket in front of their own newsroom the day the story appeared, publicly shaming the newspaper for not standing up for the good reporting. Once again, the power of the individual at work. (See the Resources section in the Back Matter of this book to watch coverage of the controversy by Don Webster at WEWS-TV5).

But there was a lot of outstanding reporting on Presser, too, and all of the problems over the years combined don't amount to much when compared with the solid reporting that appeared in the newspaper day in and out. There have been hundreds of thousands of stories published since the PD's first edition 176 years ago.

And then there are my highlights:

- The Plain Dealer's 1861 coverage – and its editorial support of – Sara Lucy Bagby, the last person prosecuted under the Fugitive Slave Act. Johnson was an 18-year-old slave who

escaped to Cleveland, only to be captured and sent back to Virginia just days before the Civil War began. The newspaper covered events as they unfolded, which rallied support for her among residents. On the day she was forced to return to captivity, N.A. Gray, brother of The Plain Dealer's founder, traveled with her on the train in a show of support.
- The remarkable deadline coverage of the Collinwood school fire in 1908, a tragedy that claimed the lives of 172 students and teachers and led to fire safety reform.
- The 1969 publication, the first by any news organization, of the pictures by former Army combat photographer Ronald Haeberle documenting the My Lai massacre and helping to change the course of the Vietnam War.
- The 1971 exposé on the abuse of patients at the Lima State Hospital for the Criminally Insane by William Wynne, Ned Whelan, and Richard Widman. Stories and photographs documenting horrifying abuses ran for days on the front page of the Plain Dealer and eventually resulted in nearly 30 hospital employees going to prison.
- The ground-breaking precision journalism project in 1978 by Leslie Kay and Tom Andrzejewski, who exposed unfairness in the Cuyahoga County court system by analyzing every single county court case from the early to mid-70s.
- A five-day series by Mary Anne Sharkey and W. Steve Ricks in 1984 that played a major role in bringing down Ohio Supreme Court Chief Justice Frank Celebrezze, who had turned the high court into his own fiefdom, awash in partisanship, patronage and political manipulation.
- A 2002 series of stories by Connie Schultz on Michael Green, a black man who spent 13 years in prison after wrongly being convicted of rape. The stories were so moving that the man who actually committed the crime turned himself in after reading them.
- Joan Mazzolini's work exposing life-threatening shortcomings in the VA health system and the care given to military veterans, and Rachel Dissell's more recent relentless coverage on untested rape kits, reporting that has led to hundreds of indictments in previously unsolved rape cases, closure for many victims and their families, and a change in the way that law enforcement agencies handle rape kit testing.

And there are literally hundreds more.

Many thanks to our contributors, who opened themselves up and wrote about their lives and careers with honesty and detail. Not everyone here agrees on everything, as you will see. But that's as it should be. As news people, we don't often write about ourselves and some of our contributors have never done it. I think it's fair to say that it made them uncomfortable and, at times, it was painful process. The other thing you should know is that for everyone involved in this project this was simply a labor of love, which is a nice way of saying that no one got paid. Our authors and the others involved gave generously of their time because they believed in the project, and they had a story to tell.

We are hoping that the book will be of value to other journalists, students, educators and people who love Cleveland history and journalism. To that end, we are making it available for free as an e-book on CSU's website (See http://bit.ly/PlainDealing2018). It also can be downloaded for free as a PDF or in other formats that will allow you to read it on a smart phone or tablet. You can pay to get actual printed copies of the book at cost through CSU's print-on-demand service.

Please use it, share it, enjoy it. All we ask is that you do so for noncommercial purposes, meaning that you don't try to make money off of our work, and that you give us proper credit.

Thanks to Bill Barrow at Cleveland State University, the force behind the Cleveland Memory Project. Bill is head of Special Collections at CSU's Michael Schwartz Library. He is a close friend to many Cleveland journalists, most notably the late George E. Condon, and he has worked tirelessly to preserve their work. This book would not have been published if it weren't for Bill's determination. He's a journalist at heart.

Thanks, too, to Joan Mazzolini, my co-editor. Her will is strong.

Molly Callahan and Doug Kramer lifted this project up.

I also would like to recognize the contributions by: the talented and hard-working team at CSU, including Barbara Loomis, Justin Grogan-Myers and Donna Stewart; Ryan Donchess, a broadcast engineer at Youngstown State University, where I teach; historian John Vacha, who shared his ideas and research; Brian Meggitt and Adam Jaenke, caretakers of Cleveland Public Library's photography collection; Lisa Lewis at the Northeast Ohio Broadcasting Archive at John Carroll University; Cleveland Magazine Editor Steve Gleydura and Lute Harmon Jr., its president and publisher; Jim Strang, Tom Suddes, Wendy Carr McManamon, David Gray, Dave Tabar and Marcia Wynne Deering.

As I'm writing this introduction, I've just learned of the death of Dick Feagler, perhaps the single most important person in this era of Cleveland journalism. We are honored to republish his 1982 column for Cleveland Magazine on the closing of The Press, a piece he likened to an obit, where journalists often overlook the bad in favor of the good. (An editor once sent an obit I wrote back to me saying nicely, very nicely, "We try not to kick people in the ass on the way out"). I didn't know Dick personally, but Joan was a friend whom he frequently invited to appear on his television show, "Feagler & Friends." She saw him recently and, as always, he was full of stories. They caught up and, after a couple of hours, he told her that the Indians game was about to start; she would have to watch it with him or leave.

On her way out, she told Dick, "I'll come back and see you soon." With a glint in his eye and a mischievous grin, he responded, "Don't threaten me."

In thinking about this book, I find his words in "Stop the presses (for the very last time)" prophetic:

> *I notice, too, to my dismay, that the truth of the Cleveland Press – all of it – is not captured in this obit. What is captured here, in part – in small part – is my truth. All of us have our own truth and those of us who are left will carry our own versions of the feel and history of the newspaper with us to our own graves. Each one of us will call his version the truth, but none of us will have it all because you don't get it all. In journalism or in life.*

Equally important are two other stories we are republishing by Cleveland journalism giants who are gone – The Plain Dealer's television critic and columnist George E. Condon and Louis B. Seltzer, the editor of The Press.

Lastly, the strength of this book is in its essays, the work of our contributors. Any flaws or limitations you see are my own.

There are a million reasons why this book might not have happened, and only 25 why it did. I offer you those 25 reasons, my colleagues.

TWENTY-FIVE STORIES

Adventures in journalism

GEORGE E. CONDON

The world was bemused, if not startled, in 1965, when a newspaper copy editor from Cleveland sailed the Atlantic Ocean, from Falmouth, Massachusetts, to Falmouth, England, in a 13-½-foot sailboat. The intrepid amphibious newsman was Robert Manry of the Plain Dealer, and his tiny craft was named *Tinkerbelle*.

It was a daring, puzzling feat – a voyage of 78 days' duration over 3,200 miles of ocean in a craft that could be classified somewhere halfway between waterwings and a rowboat. The significance of this admirable derring-do was obvious, certifying as it did that man had not lost entirely his zest for adventure, or the courage to challenge the eternal elements. What puzzled many people was that a newspaperman from inland Cleveland – a copy editor, at that! – should have been such a marine adventurer.

There would not have been such puzzlement had the world known Cleveland newspapermen better, for theirs is a long, outstanding record of adventurous thrusts into the unknown, usually in the face of staggering odds. Sometimes, just to keep the record straight, the newsmen did a little staggering themselves, but that's neither here nor there.

The Manry sea voyage recalls to the mind the earlier, valiant attempt by a group of Cleveland journalists to cross the Cuyahoga River – which offhand does not sound like the kind of feat that should be mentioned in the same book with Manry's heroism until one considers all the facts and the hazards attached thereto.

One has to know, for instance, about Cleveland's High Level Bridge.

The Detroit-Superior High Level Bridge, a major east-west connection over the Cuyahoga Valley, is a two-deck structure which was the largest double-deck, reinforced concrete bridge in the world when it was opened in 1917. It is still an imposing – if overburdened – span with its old-fashioned bulk covering a distance of 3,112 feet in length, with 12 concrete arches and one 591-foot steel arch. The top deck is used for regular traffic vehicles, while the lower deck – now sealed off – was reserved for use by streetcars.

To traverse the bridge, the streetcars had to drive down into a subway on either side of the river. There were two subways on the West Side; one having an entrance on West 25th Street, near Franklin Avenue, and the other on Detroit Avenue at West 28th Street. The entrance on the East Side was on Superior Avenue at West 6th Street.

The subways and the bridge together made streetcar riding in Cleveland highly worthwhile. They formed the grand climax to a trip downtown, and they gave the trip west a smashing, exciting beginning. Upon approaching the bridge, the streetcars suddenly left the bright street and dipped down into a dark, steeply graded tunnel at what seemed to be excessive speed, swaying and rocking as they hurtled downward, while the white-knuckled passengers fearfully eyed the concrete walls of the tunnel a finger's length away. There was always the unspoken fear, too, that the streetcar's brakes had failed and that this was a runaway vehicle.

At the bottom of the East Side incline, leading down into the subway, the streetcars had to make a sharp turn, causing the steel wheels to press against the rails with a piercing, screeching sound that added just the right note to the growing apprehension.

Just as the passengers were adjusting to the dim, yellow lights of the streetcar in the dark tunnel, the car would emerge abruptly in the day light of the open deck, and this was the most thrilling part of the entire ride. Nothing more than a short iron railing guarded the side of the deck, hardly sufficient to keep a streetcar from toppling over. The tracks were laid on a bed of wooden ties, but you could see between the ties to the yellow river below – 196 feet below. This perilous ride, or so it seemed, did not last long; just long enough to scare the bejabbers out of the passengers, and then suddenly the streetcar was back in the dark tunnel on the other side, the walls were rushing past again, and you could tell that it was twisting and fighting its way back up to street level once again.

Now the question that had bothered virtually nobody except the curious newsmen was whether an automobile could drive down the ramps, maneuver through the tunnel, cross the open main section of the deck, and still emerge safely at the other side. At first it was merely a kind of intellectual speculation worthy of being discussed in the friendly setting of a downtown pub, as it was one night until one of the newspapermen, a natural leader named Jimmy Lanyon, who was sports editor of The Plain Dealer at the time, rose to his feet and announced that he was prepared to meet the challenge head-on by driving his car across the bridge's streetcar deck that very moment.

"Let us be done with the talk," cried Lanyon. "Let us have some action!" Some of his stouthearted colleagues jumped to join him, and in a twinkling the adventurous newsmen were on their way. Their car roared down Superior Avenue, lunged down the ramp like an escaped fury, twisted through the dark tunnel, passing an eastbound streetcar whose motorman jumped up and down on his bell in panic as he stared out with disbelieving eyes, and finally shot out on the open deck where, its tires slashed by the tracks, its innards shaken loose by the jolting drive, it finally wheezed and pitched to a stop.

All streetcar traffic between downtown and the West Side was halted for several hours while transit workers and police effected a rescue of the valiant newsmen and pulled their car out of the way. The incident was reported in terse style by the newspapers the next day. Nowhere in print was there any editorial commendation of the attempted crossing.

Newspapers traditionally have served as havens for men and women who were not completely understood by the outside world; they have provided sanctuary to those who were harassed and pursued by the keepers of the conventions, carefully keeping alive in the editorial rooms the last spark of individuality in a society that grows more regimented by the hour. Sometimes, as in the gallant attempt to drive the streetcar deck, the behavior of newsmen may seem anti-social, or irrational to the outside world. It is not. It is simply a manifestation of the creative spirit at work in material surroundings.

For the first 22 years of its existence, Cleveland was without its own newspaper. What little journalistic attention the town received was from a publication called the Ohio Patriot, published in New Lisbon, Ohio, southwest of Youngstown, beginning in 1808.

At last, on July 31, 1818, the first Cleveland newspaper, the Gazette and Commercial Register, appeared. It was better than nothing, but it followed a fitful schedule of publication, with intervals of up to three weeks between issues. The following year, 1819, the Herald was established. From that time on, there was wild confusion on the newspaper front, with new publications springing up left and right even as old ones were going out of business.

In today's (1967's*) Cleveland, with a metropolitan population approaching the 2 million mark, there are two large dailies, the afternoon Press and the morning Plain Dealer. There is but one Sunday paper, that published by the Plain Dealer.

In January 1842, when the Plain Dealer came into being, Cleveland had been a city only a few years and its population, combined with that of Ohio City, was about 7,500. Serving this handful of people was the new paper, the Plain Dealer, the Herald, the Morning Mercury, the Eagle-Eyed News Catcher, the Commercial Intelligencer, and the Cleveland Gatherer (a weekly); six newspapers in all.

The pity of it all, of course, is that the Eagle-Eyed News Catcher was not able to survive. It had a name that deserved to live.

The Plain Dealer grew out of the Independent News-Letter, started in 1827. It was rechristened the Cleveland Advertiser in 1832. When two brothers, Admiral Nelson Gray and Joseph William Gray took over the Advertiser at the end of 1841, they gave the paper the unusual name which makes out-of-towners cock their head in puzzlement when they first hear it. Archer H. Shaw, onetime chief editorial writer for the Plain Dealer and author of the definitive biography of the newspaper, "The Plain Dealer – One Hundred Years in Cleveland," recalled that there had been a short-lived New York Plain Dealer started in 1836 by William Leggett, who had been one of the editors and a part owner of the New York Evening Post. J. W. Gray, who had lived in New York, and who was an avowed admirer of Leggett, presumably was influenced in his choice of the name by the New York publication.

The name traces in origin to an old English expression. A "plain-dealer" was an honest, straightforward type of person, and "plaindealing" was to be desired. Shakespeare frequently used the words within that frame of reference and another playwright, William Wycherley, was the author of a play called "The Plain Dealer" late in the 17th century.

"So handy and expressive a title could not long be neglected in other fields," wrote Shaw. "In 1712 a publication named the Plain Dealer was started in London, but only a few issues appeared. Boswell, in his great biography of Samuel Johnson, mentions another Plain Dealer, an English monthly devoted to 'select essays on several curious subjects.' The last number appeared in 1725.

Adventures in journalism | 11

It had a successor of the same name and similar character, which appeared in 1763, but soon went the way of the rest."

Winston Churchill, when visiting Cleveland as a young man, spotted the name. "Oh," he said, "there's the Cleveland Plain Dealer. I think that by all odds, the Plain Dealer has the best newspaper name of any in the world."

In his editorial salutatory, Gray acknowledged the curiosity about the change in name from the Advertiser to the Plain Dealer:

"We offer no apology for changing the name of this paper," he wrote, "but the Scripture command – 'Put not new wine into old bottles, lest they break.'

"This paper is now in the hands of a new editor, with new publishers and proprietors. It is soon to be printed on new type and furnished with new exchanges and correspondents and we hope with new patrons also. This is the 'new wine' that would *burst* the old Advertiser and not leave a trace of its well-earned fame.

"We think the good taste of our readers will sanction the modest selection we have made. Had we called it the Torpedo timid ladies never would have touched it. Had we called it the Truth Teller no one would believe a word in it! Had we called it the Thunder Dealer or Lightning Spitter it would have blown Uncle Sam's mail bags skyhigh. But our democracy and modesty suggest the only name that befits the occasion, the Plain Dealer."

Shaw recalled that President Woodrow Wilson used to say he could tell a Clevelander by the way he pronounced Plain Dealer. Clevelanders pronounced the name as one word, with the accent on the first syllable. Non-Clevelanders pronounced the two words separately, with the accent on the first syllable of the second word.

In those days when open partisanship was such an important part of journalism, Gray left no doubt where he and the Plain Dealer stood. He was a Democrat and the Plain Dealer was a Democratic newspaper and it continued to be such without wavering until 1940 when, after a century in the Democratic lineup, the Plain Dealer switched positions and endorsed Wendell Willkie.

There was, in fact, such an intermingling of partisan politics and journalism in the mid-19th century that the two were inseparable. Gray, for example, was chairman of the Ohio delegation to the Democratic National Convention in Baltimore in 1852. It is worth mentioning because one of the strangest contradictions in political history pivoted on Gray's action at that convention. Had it not been for this editor of a Cleveland newspaper, one of Gray's fellow Clevelanders undoubtedly would have been elected President of the United States instead of Franklin Pierce of New Hampshire.

Among the strong dark horse possibilities at the convention was Governor Reuben Wood of Ohio, a resident of Cleveland, and, like Gray, a native of Vermont. When the favorites for the nomination were unable to win the necessary 49 ballots, the convention turned its attention to Governor Wood.

All that Governor Wood needed for the nomination was the support of his own state delegation which, by all the rules and traditions of politics, he should have had in his hip pocket. But Editor Gray balked at voting for his own townsfellow because, he explained later, the governor was a "Hunker."

A Hunker, in the political lexicon of that day, was an ultra-conservative Democrat, and Gray didn't like that wing of the party. Some of the political experts of the day interpreted the editor's refusal to vote for Wood as Gray's revenge on the Hunkers for their part in engineering the defeat of New York's Governor Silas Wright in his 1846 bid for re-election. Wright and Gray were lifelong friends, and Editor Gray suspected Governor Wood of having been too friendly with the Hunkers.

When the Ohio delegation led by Gray stunned the party by its incredible refusal to support Governor Wood, the convention immediately passed by the Ohio governor and chose Pierce as its candidate. He was elected President.

Governor Wood accepted an appointment as consul in Valparaiso the following year, 1853, but he held the post only briefly. He retired from politics a year later and withdrew to his estate on Ridge Road in Rockport Township, now Cleveland's far West Side, presumably to ponder what-might-have-been; perchance to dream of the political perfidy of his own townsman.

Editor Gray did not go unrewarded for his part in frustrating the rise of a fellow Clevelander to the nation's highest office. He was named postmaster of Cleveland by a grateful President Pierce in 1853 and he held that political plum until 1858.

One of the most interesting of Cleveland's 19th century editors, and undoubtedly the most powerful, was Edwin Cowles, who came to Cleveland in 1825 from the little Ohio town of Austinburg, in Ashtabula County to the east of Cleveland.

Cowles is remembered for a variety of achievements. Perhaps he should be regarded mainly as the perfect issue of the crossbreeding of politics and journalism. As the editor of the Leader, a morning newspaper he is to be credited with having made that journal the most influential in the city in his time. As a politician, he surely should be remembered as one of the founders of the Republican Party.

The Leader grew out of the merger of two newspapers, the True Democrat, which was begun in the nearby town of North Olmsted (now a Cleveland suburb) around 1852, and the Forest City, which began publication in Cleveland the same year. The owners of the Forest City were two brothers from Coshocton, Ohio – Joseph and James Medill. They consolidated their newspaper with the True Democrat in 1853 and the result of the merger was the Forest City Democrat. George Bradburn and John C. Vaughn had owned the True Democrat, and in the merger, Vaughn joined with Joseph Medill and Edwin Cowles in a partnership that lived only a short time – just one year. Cowles became the sole owner of the newspaper in 1854, and one of his first acts was to change its name to the Leader. His former partner, Joseph Medill, went to Chicago and started there a newspaper called the Chicago Tribune, which is publishing to this very day, according to reports reaching the East.

Cowles, a fiery, outspoken man, was an outstanding catalyst in the civic life of Cleveland during one of the most important formative periods in the city's history. He swung his newspaper as a political club, as did the other editors of the day, but he swung his club faster and fiercer. His running feuds with his competition, especially Gray of the Plain Dealer, brought personal-political journalism to its all-time peak in Cleveland. As a matter of fact, Cowles succeeded Gray as postmaster of Cleveland, receiving his appointment from the newly elected President Lincoln.

The Plain Dealer did not let that appointment go by without comment. Its editorial said:

"To select so obnoxious an individual personally on the score of being a ruffian Republican is more than even Clevelanders can bear. The appointment of Cowles, personally unfit, simply because connected with a sheet owned and used by the irrepressibles to slaughter the conservatives and put down the liberal sentiments of the party look so much like 'rule or ruin' that the masses are indignant."

The Plain Dealer did not always approach the subject of Editor-Postmaster Cowles so subtly. It once said of him, simply:

"The editor of the Leader is the original ass that Balaam mounted."

At another time, the Plain Dealer described Cowles as "a catiff wretch . . . one of the most base and infamous of creatures, who, wearing the garb of a human, has nearly all the elements of a demon .... A fellow whose fruitful brain can produce a whole catacomb of lies in one single night resembles so much the prince of the regions of Pluto that if he be not his Satanic Majesty in person, he is worst still, being one of his dastardly and treacherous imps . . . "

Other Cleveland editors, caught in this crossfire, still managed to get in occasional potshots at both Gray and Cowles. The Cleveland Times, for example, dismissed Editor Gray as a lying bank pimp – a liar both by instinct and choice."

Even the out-of-town papers, attracted by the noise of all the fun in Cleveland, and perhaps even a trifle envious, tried to get in on the act. James Gordon Bennett of the New York Herald declared that "Western editors are all whiskey bottles, their reporters are bottles of whiskey and their papers have all the fumes of that beverage without any of its strength."

The Cincinnati Enquirer made an admirable attempt to top everybody when, speaking of W. W. Armstrong, who succeeded Gray as the editor-owner of the Plain Dealer, it said:

"When the snarling, ill-conditioned editor of the Cleveland Plain Dealer gets drunk and falls out of the third story window of his boarding house, people in the street who catch a glimpse of his florid face and sanguinary hair cry out: 'Behold, that blazing meteor!' They afterward gather up the quivering, glutinous, odorous mass on the pavement, sweep it up and carry it into the house and put it to bed."

Cowles established himself, editorially, as an enemy of the Democratic Party, an enemy of slavery, and an enemy of the Catholic Church. He was outspoken and vitriolic on each one of those subjects.

"The war between Cowles of the Leader and the Catholic interests in Cleveland, presided over by that fine old ecclesiastic and citizen, Bishop Richard R. Gilmour, was very lurid and uncompromising," Charles E. Kennedy, later manager-editor of the Plain Dealer, recalled in his memoirs, "Fifty Years in Cleveland."

Kennedy, a Unitarian, wrote:

"Cowles hammered away at the Pope and all his works on the editorial page, but not against individual Catholics, some of whom were on his payroll . . . [he] was front man and head of the Order of the American Union, chief mission of which was the prevention of public office holding by members of the Catholic Church . . . It died some years before the A.P.A., working along similar lines, came into existence.

"While it thrived, the O.A.U. played quite a big part in politics, especially here in Cleveland, where, in the spring of 1877, the entire Republican local ticket, most of them members of the order, and led by William G. Rose, the candidate for mayor, was elected.

"This ticket was framed up in Cowles' private office in the rear of the Leader's business office...."

Ironically, Cowles' daughter became a Catholic while on a trip to Paris, France, as a direct result, it was said, of her father's opposition to her marriage with a titled French suitor.

The really impressive feature of Cowles' success as an editor was that he managed to fight his way to the top in Cleveland journalism despite an inability to hiss. As even little school children are aware, an editor who cannot hiss is like a praying mantis that cannot pray, or a humming bird that cannot hum. Editors depend on their ability to hiss as an aerial acrobat depends upon his trapeze. In some newspapers, the editor's voice never has been heard – only the sound of his hissing as he stalks the halls like a restless steam radiator. It's all part of the game, as they say, and it is likely that if some reporters were not hissed at, they would never produce.

Cowles' deficiency would have been more of a handicap except that he did not *know* he could not hiss during his early career. He didn't find out about it until he was 23 years old, when, presumably, it finally dawned on some of his friends – not to mention his reporters – that they never had known a hiss to escape the editor's lips.

A distinguished elocutionist of the day, a Professor Kennedy, was called into the case to determine what was holding Cowles back at a time when competing editors were hissing in such strength that the sound could be heard five miles out in Lake Erie by passing mariners.

Henry Howe, a distinguished historian, reported that a thorough examination by Professor Kennedy revealed that Cowles had "so peculiar an impediment of speech that no parallel case was to be found on record."

"It was found," wrote Howe, "that he [Cowles] had never heard the hissing sound of the human voice, and consequently had never made that sound. Many of the consonants sounded alike to him. He never heard the notes of the seventh octave of the piano or organ, never heard the upper notes of a violin, the fife in martial music, never heard a bird sing, and has always supposed that the music of the birds was a poetical fiction."

Once it was known just why the editor never hissed, of course, it was possible to take some remedial action. Which is exactly what Prof. Kennedy did. He spent hours coaching the editor and Howe the Historian is the authority for the word that it produced gratifying results.

"After much time spent in practicing under Prof. Kennedy's tuition," said Howe, "he [Cowles] was enabled to learn arbitrarily how to make the hissing sound, but he never heard the sound himself, although he could hear ordinary low-toned conversation."

All that is left to the imagination is the picture of what pandemonium must have ensued in the Leader city room on the day that Cowles walked in and, without warning, hissed at his staff for the very first time. What a truly historic hiss that must have been!

The nationwide Scripps-Howard chain of newspapers had its beginning in Cleveland in 1878, when Edward W. Scripps founded the Penny Press, the forerunner of today's (1967's*) Cleveland Press.

Scripps, a picturesque six-footer with a bright red beard and a cast in his right eye that gave him such a baleful look as to frighten friend and foe alike, came to Cleveland from Detroit, where he had been city editor of the Detroit Evening News, owned by his half-brother James E. Scripps. With him, to assist in launching the new paper, was his cousin, John Scripps Sweeney, who served as business manager.

The capitalization of the Penny Press was ten thousand dollars. Investors in the venture, besides the active proprietors, Scripps and Sweeney, were James and George Scripps, the latter being another half-brother.

The new journal was greeted with ridicule and derision from the established publications because of its smaller, unorthodox size and a generally unkempt appearance. Some called it "the Frankfort Street Handbill," after the street where it had its office. But Scripps, nevertheless, had hit on a successful formula that would lead to a newspaper empire. Not only was his publication only half the price of the other papers, he pinpointed the editorial policy in the direction of the so-called working class, as distinguished from his competitors' preoccupation with the moneyed elite. Within a year, the penny dreadful was on a self-supporting basis and within three years it had more circulation than all its rivals combined.

The determination to begin the Cleveland newspaper came to Scripps while he was in Paris, France, traveling with his brother George.

"I determined to be my own boss and run a newspaper of my own, subject to orders from no one," he wrote in his autobiography, "Damned Old Crank," adding: "I had never been in the city of Cleveland, but that city was only a short distance from Detroit, where I first entered the news business. I knew the size of it and some of its character. I determined I would make my first newspaper venture there."

It was, in a limited sense, a return to ancestral ground because his grandfather on his mother's side, Timothy Osborn, was a wanderer who had settled near Cleveland, on the Chagrin River, where he operated a grist mill and held the office of justice of the peace.

An odd coincidence is that Scripps, the 13th child in the family, was born on a farm near Rushville, Illinois, in Cuyahoga County. There he gloried in the title of laziest boy in Cuyahoga County: When he undertook to publish the Penny Press in Cleveland, he must have been the busiest boy in Ohio's Cuyahoga County. And it very well may have been that he also was the busiest drinker in the county, too, because it is his own assertion that until he reached middle age, he consumed daily "enough whiskey to keep three or four men drunk all the time." He estimated his input at a gallon of whiskey a day.

It is understandable that the staid citizens of the community chose to regard this fearsome-looking newcomer with a wary eye. They were apprised very quickly of his casual, if not utterly disrespectful attitude toward the ruling class, and of his disinclination to play the journalistic game of the day according to the established rules.

The best intimation of this came when one of the city's leading citizens, Leonard Case, who also was one of the wealthiest men in town, committed suicide by chloroforming himself in his bed. While the other papers were politely skirting the cause of Case's death and were devoting their columns to the generous terms of the dead man's will, which made a bequest of his considerable fortune for the founding of Case School of Applied Sciences (today's Case Institute of Technology – now Case Western Reserve University*), the Penny Press was reciting the unhappy details about the suicide and the causative factors.

This was followed by a sensational episode involving a Press reporter named Maurice Perkins, Scripps, and one of Cleveland's most prominent industrialists, Henry Chisholm.

When he came to tot up his life in his autobiography, Scripps chose to tell this story under the dramatic chapter heading: "I Kill Henry Chisholm."

Perkins, while checking the police rounds one night when Scripps was in Detroit, had come across a story involving the arrest of a young man who had been in a street brawl with a woman of questionable repute. The police identified the youth as Stuart H. Chisholm, and Perkins used the name in his story.

The principal owners of the Cleveland Rolling Mills in Newburgh were two brothers, Henry and Stuart Chisholm. Each had a son named Stuart. Henry's son was named Stuart H. Chisholm. Stuart's son was named Stuart Chisholm; no middle initial.

The youth actually involved in the scrape was Stuart (no middle initial) Chisholm, and Henry Stuart was infuriated when the Penny Press wrongly involved his son, Stuart H. He sent a messenger to request Perkins to come to his office at the roiling mills to talk over the matter next day. The reporter, a thin, cadaverous type, obligingly presented himself to the industrialist.

Instead of the man-to-man chat he had expected, Perkins was set upon by some of Chisholm's employees who tore off his clothes and painted him from head to feet with black paint, climaxing their brush work by dumping what was left in the paint can on top of his head. Thereupon, their artistic passion spent, they gave him the heave-ho out of the building. He was picked up by a good Samaritan and taken to his home.

Scripps by this time had returned to Cleveland and had just gotten the news of his newspaper's erroneous identification when he received word of the dreadful experience of Reporter Perkins. He hastily summoned a doctor, fearing that the paint would harden on Perkins and bring about a fatal suffocation. When that danger had been averted and Perkins was quietly hiccupping his way back to recovery, Scripps returned to his office and further excitement.

A mob of men, whom he alleged were drawn from the ranks of the roiling mill employees, had gathered in front of the Press office and were threatening trouble. Scripps stood up in his carriage, whipped out a pistol and, florid-faced, turned on them his most baleful look; a wild-eyed expression which startled even him one day when he happened to look at himself in the mirror.

The mob parted, allowing Scripps access to his small plant, and then departed without causing any damage. But shortly a worse threat presented itself – a deputy sheriff with warrants for the arrest of Scripps and Sweeney on the charge of criminal libel.

The two men posted bond and returned again to the Press, where they found that all work had been suspended and where another deputy sheriff was waiting to serve a warrant "by attachment" for fifty thousand dollars in damages claimed by Chisholm in a civil suit.

Scripps was told he could not touch the Press property until it had been inventoried by court-appointed appraisers and until he had given the court his bond for one hundred thousand dollars – double the amount of the damages sought. The appraisers who showed up turned out to be Edwin Cowles, owner and editor of the Leader, and William Gleason, a former Plain Dealer employee. Neither felt kindly toward their maverick colleague and insisted on a thorough, time-consuming inventory – which served, incidentally, to delay the Press in its attempt to publish.

Scripps' major problem, though, was finding somebody who would stand behind his bond for a hundred thousand dollars. He called a number of wealthy Clevelanders who had made protestation of their friendship previously, but all turned him down.

"These men liked my paper and frequently came to me to praise me for my honesty and fearlessness," he wrote later. "Naturally I turned to them for help. Naturally enough, they deserted me in my hour of need. All of them, every last one of them."

It suddenly occurred to Scripps that if he could find an enemy of the Chisholms, he likely would find a friend of E. W. Scripps. He asked his attorney, Judge R. R. Paine, for help. Paine was the father of a youngster on the Press staff, Robert F. Paine, who would become editor of the Press and serve in that capacity for thirty years.

Judge Paine took the editor to a shabby house in a not-too-reputable neighborhood and introduced him to an old, wizened man named Samuel C. Baldwin, who must have been quite a remarkable character in his own right. He made a living as a professional bondsman for thieves and prostitutes and owned approximately a half-million dollars' worth of property in the red-light district. Baldwin, some years before, had testified in a lawsuit in which Henry Chisholm was one of the principals. Whatever it was that Baldwin said on the witness stand, Chisholm did not approve of it, and he allegedly had slapped Baldwin on the face as he stepped down from the witness chair. Baldwin was the bona fide Chisholm enemy that Scripps had hoped to find, and he was more than happy to go bond for the editor, thereby restoring to Scripps his newspaper and his freedom.

It was the moment Scripps had been waiting for. It was late Saturday afternoon, and the Press missed its usual edition time, but it didn't matter to Scripps; now he was at last on the offensive. By 6 o'clock Saturday evening, his newspaper was on the street with the story of "The Shame of Chisholm," and the team of Scripps and Sweeney saw to it that enough extra copies were run off the presses to blanket the city with the story.

That wasn't enough for Scripps. His odd eye was hot with the glare of a righteous man who had been wronged, and he published the story, in condensed form, at the top of the editorial column day after day through the week that followed.

Word came to him that the fury of his attack had had such devastating effect on the great industrialist that his health had been affected, and that Chisholm, indeed, had taken to his bed. Scripps was visited by Chisholm's doctor and one of his friends, the president of a Cleveland bank, who begged the editor to relent in his attack.

"I replied bitterly," Scripps said later, "that Chisholm had shown no mercy to the poor weakling Perkins and was entitled to no mercy from Perkins' employer and friend."

The terms of surrender laid down by Scripps was that Chisholm withdraw his civil suit for damages and pay five thousand dollars, which would be given to Perkins, who was still on his sickbed, hiccupping away through all the turmoil.

Chisholm agreed to the terms, through his attorney, and the celebrated case was settled, but not without a tragic anticlimax. Chisholm died only a few weeks later, and his death generally was attributed to the controversy with the Press.

"I was shocked by the event," wrote Scripps later. "I believed then, and believe now, that had Chisholm's attack on Perkins killed Perkins, and had Chisholm been successful in suppressing my publicity and hence avoided public contumely, he would have lived many years longer, a leading and respected citizen of the city of Cleveland.

"I may be mistaken, but I never believed that simple remorse killed Mr. Chisholm. But neither have I ever had any doubt that Chisholm's death was caused by me. Had I taken a pistol and shot him to death, I would have felt no more and no less responsibility for that death than I have ever since felt.

"It is true that I did not know I was killing Chisholm when I was killing him. Nonetheless I believe that had I known that I was killing him at the time, I would have pursued the same course. I believe I would have felt no more remorse, no more guilt, under those circumstances than I have since felt, and I have felt none.

"I believed then that I was not only doing what was right, but that I was actually performing a public duty."

As for Perkins, he quit hiccupping the minute that Scripps handed him his five thousand dollars, rose from his sickbed, and went off on a "frolic" that lasted several weeks and cost him half of the money.

Aside from Scripps himself, and Robert F. Paine, no single man personified the Cleveland Press more than Louis B. Seltzer, the slight, dapper editor who ruled the paper for 37 years, until his retirement in 1966. He joined the Press in 1917 and became editor in 1928. His tenure in that office was the longest in the newspaper's history. He was succeeded by Thomas L. Boardman.

When Seltzer was in his cub years at the Press, he wrote under the byline of "Looey, the Office Boy." Long after he moved past the office boy level he continued to be known as Looey by his friends and even his casual acquaintances. He also was known as "Little Bromo" (Seltzer), usually among his critics, of whom there were more than a few, and "Mr. Cleveland," among those who admired him excessively.

There was a Cleveland legend that Louis Seltzer really ran the city, and there were times when that was no overstatement. He moved the Press from its dilapidated old building at East 9th Street and Rockwell Avenue to a glistening new glass-and-white-brick structure two blocks north, at East 9th Street and Lakeside Avenue in 1959. In this new site, the Press is just across the street from City Hall, and some political insiders guessed that the Press move was to make it easier for Seltzer to run the city by centralizing operations, so to speak.

Until recently, the Press had nominal, if not minimal, competition in the afternoon field, but the Forest City Publishing Company, which owned both the afternoon Cleveland News and the Plain Dealer, inexplicably sold the News to the rival Press in 1960. By this move, the Press was given the afternoon monopoly and picked up some 80,000 former News subscribers. The circulation battle between the Plain Dealer and the Press had been relatively even until that time, but the death of the News shot the Press far ahead of the P.D., 390,000 to 310,000. The Plain Dealer, put under the direction of a young editor-publisher, Tom Vail, in 1962, has wiped out that imposing lead. Since 1965 the two rivals have been on the fifty-yard line, circulation just about even, glaring at each other again.

As the competition waxes keener between the two newspapers, the city inevitably is reminded of some of the titanic circulation battles that were fought in Cleveland in the past. What makes the comparison even more apt is that both editors, Vail and Boardman, are as fascinated by politics as were the editors of the earlier years when even a homicide was secondary to a political speech – except, of course, when the victim in the homicide happened to be a politician.

Politics and journalism are intertwined in the genealogy of many Cleveland leaders. For example, Louis Seltzer's father, Charles Alden Seltzer, besides being a novelist, was the longtime mayor of North Olmsted. Tom Vail's father, Herman L. Vail, now president of the Forest City Publishing Company, served as a state representative in his younger years. The editor-publisher's grandfather, Harry L. Vail, was himself a newspaperman turned politician. He had been editor of the Sunday Morning Voice before he chose to enter politics as a popular county commissioner.

A lot of the fun and glamor went out of newspapers as they matured financially and adopted the cautious, conservative attitude which is almost always the concomitant condition where the money stakes are high. Then editors tend more and more to straddle the editorial fence in the name of objectivity. Not only does such impartiality leave the readers fumbling in the dark as they try to tell the good guys from the bad guys in any specific election campaign, but the modern, unemotional, balanced reporting that is featured in today's newspaper is about as exciting to read as the annual report of an agricultural test station.

A member of the Cleveland journalism scene, briefly, was Time magazine, which published out of the Penton Building at West 3rd Street and Lakeside Avenue from 1925 to 1927. It was a very young magazine at that time, an experiment in journalism that was still scratching for a foothold. Henry R. Luce and Briton Hadden had launched the enterprise in 1923, but the results after two years of publication were something short of sensational. The circulation at the beginning of 1925 was 34,100.

Cleveland seemed to offer several important advantages over New York, where the magazine was published at the outset: lower costs for printing and office expenses and better distribution. Mailed from New York, as second-class matter, it had experienced embarrassing delays in delivery to subscribers in the populous Midwest, and often did not reach readers in the Far West until a week or more after publication. Time, being a newsmagazine, naturally held the timeliness of its product in high regard, and Cleveland, because of its central location, offered the probability of a more effective radius of distribution. More than 60 percent of the nation's population lived within five hundred miles of Cleveland at that time.

Time made its move to Cleveland in August 1925, and the prime mover was Henry Luce. Hadden was in Europe on vacation at the time, but the magazine did not wait for his return. One day in August a notice appeared on a bulletin board in the Time office, notifying all employees that they were dismissed as of Aug. 16. They were informed, further, that all who applied for a job at the magazine's new address, the Penton Building in Cleveland, on Aug. 19 would be rehired.

In his biography, "Briton Hadden," Noel F. Busch wrote of Time's Cleveland adventure:

"While the advantages of centralized distribution amply justified it, the Cleveland move was by no means in all respects an unmitigated triumph. Grave difficulties developed, of which the most dramatic were Hadden's private reactions to his new and strange environment. For Luce, who had spent nearly half of his previous life in China, the differences between one American city and another were relatively small. The salient quality of all of them was that they differed so markedly from the cities he had known in Europe or the Orient, and thus, like most other things about the U.S., tended to excite his approval. Luce was also, by this time, a married man whose comfortable home and diverse social interests enabled him to get along compatibly with the young married set of Cleveland, with whom he had no marked temperamental disaffinity. With Hadden the case was otherwise.

"For the born New Yorker, other metropoli may be interesting, exciting or admirable but there can be only one place in the world that really defines the word city. For an extremist New Yorker, brought up in Brooklyn, this was doubly true. If Cleveland had combined the grandeur of Rome, the charm of Paris and the solidity of London with the exotic glamor of the casbah in Alexandrian

Bagdad, Hadden would doubtless have found it a poor substitute for Brooklyn Heights. In point of fact, it seemed to him to lack these charms and to substitute for them what were, in his estimation, defects almost as grave as that of not being Brooklyn in the first place. x x x In Cleveland, he made what was to him a horrifying discovery. This was that Babbitts were not in fact amusing freaks at all but rather, just as Sinclair Lewis had suggested, the backbone of U.S. population . . ."

But if Cleveland did not offer sophisticated pleasures to the urbane Hadden, it did give him a superior opportunity to pursue his big hobby, baseball. He organized a sandlot team, equipped it, and appointed himself manager, captain, and shortstop. The pleasure he found in this sport was not enough, however, to make up for Cleveland's other deficiencies as the headquarter city for Time. Most of all, the magazine missed the New York Times, the source of so much grist for the Time mill. The publishers also missed the wealth of young, intellectual talent then available in New York. And so it came about in spring of 1927, when Luce this time was in Europe on vacation, that Hadden moved Time magazine from Cleveland and returned it to its ancestral home in New York. The two-year sojourn in Cleveland had not been without beneficial effect, entirely. Time's circulation had risen to 140,000 by 1927, there was money in the bank, and distribution problems had lessened. Cleveland, baseball, and Babbitry to one side, could take some of the credit for the improvement in the health of the young magazine.

The threat of physical violence hovers over the head of almost every newspaperman at one time or another during his career. The world is full of crackpots and angry people who, for want of a better target perhaps, choose to direct their wretched tempers at the honest men of the press. The history of journalism in Cleveland is replete with incidents of violence attempted on the persons of editors, reporters, and cameramen. There were numerous invitations to the duel at dawn and so many attempts to waylay editors and writers that it is not surprising many of the old-time newsmen, through necessity, were schooled in the use of cane swords and pistols. Edwin Cowles, for example, retired to a backroom in his editorial offices for target practice whenever he had any spare time. The thunderous roar of his blunderbuss was as familiar a sound to the staff of the Leader as the clanking of the old job press.

It remained for modern times, however, to bring forth the most tragic realization of violence in the cold-blooded murder of the president and general manager of the Forest City Publishing Company, John S. McCarrens, who directed the fortunes of two daily newspapers, the Plain Dealer and the Cleveland News.

McCarrens had joined the Plain Dealer executive staff in 1914 as advertising manager, becoming general manager in 1933, the same year that Paul Bellamy, one of the nation's most respected journalists, was named editor. It was a formidable team. Bellamy went on to become the president of the American Society of Newspaper Editors, while McCarrens in 1939 was named president of the American Newspaper Publishers Association; two of the highest honors in the American newspaper business.

Then, on the sunny morning of Thursday, July 22, 1943, McCarrens received a telephone call from a man named Herbert L. Kobrak, asking for an appointment that day. McCarrens agreed to see his caller in his office at two-thirty in the afternoon.

Kobrak was well-known to McCarrens, as he was to most publishing executives in Cleveland. He was a Hungarian native who had come to the United States in 1908, moving from Chicago to Cleveland in 1917 to become general manager of a Hungarian-language daily, the Szabadsag. He frequently identified himself as a Hungarian baron and he was obsessed, according to one of his acquaintances, "with the dream of becoming the William Randolph Hearst of the foreign language press."

Kobrak (he also went under the names of Louis Rosenfeld and Louis Racz) in time became general manager of the Consolidated Press & Printing Company, publisher of the Szabadsag and the German-language paper, Waechter und Anzeiger. In 1939, however, Consolidated went into bankruptcy and Kobrak was unemployed. From that time on, he talked almost incessantly to friends and possible financial backers of starting another newspaper in Cleveland. Among those whom he importuned for assistance in beginning a daily picture newspaper slanted toward the foreign element in Cleveland was John S. McCarrens.

Kobrak arrived at the Plain Dealer Building shortly before two-thirty. A tense, dark man, he attracted attention on the elevator with his erratic behavior. He clutched a briefcase to his chest and his chin trembled. He was admitted to the publisher's inner office a few minutes after his arrival. The secretary, Miss Jane Hammond, heard voices raised and then Kobrak closed the door to McCarrens' office. At 3:10 p.m. four shots were heard in the outer office, the door swung open, and the publisher staggered out.

"Get an ambulance," he said hoarsely. "I've been shot by a madman!"

C.C. McConkie, comptroller of the newspaper, and two secretaries, Miss Hammond and Miss Florence Anthony, helped the wounded executive to the nearby office of Joseph V. Madigan, Plain Dealer circulation director and son-in-law of McCarrens.

When they returned to McCarrens' office, they found Kobrak slumped in a chair, near death. He had shot himself in the temple with a .32-caliber revolver, which had fallen to the floor near his outstretched fingers. He died a half-hour after being taken to the hospital.

McCarrens had been shot three times, once in each arm and once in the abdomen. A police ambulance took him to St. Vincent Charity Hospital. On his arrival there, in a moment of consciousness, he told the Plain Dealer's advertising manager, Sterling E. Graham: "I'm sorry for that fellow. He's crazy."

The publisher clung to life from that Thursday afternoon until the following Saturday morning. One of the notes left by his assassin indicated that Kobrak had planned to kill McCarrens for several months. Another letter left by the murderer was addressed to "Gentlemen of the Press," and adjured them to consult the records for his history and promised them further big news. It told of his association with well-known newspapers, including the Chicago Tribune, and rambled incoherently into speculation over the location of newspapers in heaven and hell, with specific allusions to commentary by Swedenborg and George Bernard Shaw. He concluded by describing himself as a good hunter and fisherman and by revealing that he trained his own bird dogs.

It was the kind of communication that is familiar to newspapermen everywhere. Sick letters from sick people seem to be a fixed part of a newspaperman's life. In the case of Herbert Kobrak and John McCarrens, the sickness led to death.

*Editor's note

~This piece was originally published in "Cleveland: the best kept secret" by George E. Condon, Doubleday, 1967. We thank the Condon family for allowing us to use it. (See https://tinyurl.com/CLEBestKeptSecret).

Dig deep, stick to the facts, no cheap shots: A reporters' editor talks about The PD newsroom

GARY CLARK

I entered journalism by going to war.

My job as a Marine in Vietnam was to write stories about Marines. Those stories would be sent to their hometown papers. The stories would often be the only acknowledgement those Marines would get for performing a dangerous job during an unpopular war.

I would hitchhike by plane, helicopter, truck or jeep during 1968 and 1969 to 1st Marine Division firebases and outposts throughout I-Corps, the most northern combat zone in Vietnam. Like civilian reporters, we would often arrive after a battle or firefight. In other cases, I would be with Marines when shit happened.

My entry into the Marines in 1966 was delayed by about a month. My brother, Brian, a Marine rifle squad leader and the oldest of the five Clark brothers, was killed in a firefight in October 1966, and the Marines gave me a month to grieve with my family.

I returned to the states in 1969 determined to be a reporter and to write stories people would want to read. I earned a journalism degree at the Ohio State University (OSU), worked for a 40,000-circulation daily for four years, and returned to OSU to earn a masters' degree.

I met my wife, Caryn, at that first paper. Caryn got a job painting house interiors for extra cash while I attended grad school. I still remember her, pregnant and in white painters' bib overalls.

Our daughter, Jessica, was born in Columbus in January 1978 between two massive snowstorms.

Later that year, I was hired at The Plain Dealer by Bob McGruder, a smart and respected city editor.

I think newspapers are special. Their mission – to inform readers and reveal the truth – is critical to a democracy.

The Plain Dealer was also my hometown newspaper. I loved working there. I worked at The PD from 1978 to 2000, the last 10 years or so as managing editor.

Those last 10 years were also dramatic, dynamic and very, very hard. Alex Machaskee became publisher in 1990 and frequently fought with the two men who consecutively served as editor of the paper during the 1990s. As managing editor, I had a front row seat. That period has been covered by various alternative papers, newsletters and blogs in Cleveland. But what follows is a view from my perch.

I worked at The Plain Dealer with lots of hard-working, talented people. I helped hire and promote many of them. I promoted aggressive investigative reporting and computer-assisted reporting. I was an advocate for ethical journalism: Report deeply, stick to the facts, and no cheap shots.

I also quickly learned from other reporters and editors that The PD carried some baggage: It had been a target of criticism over the years for a top leadership that was cautious and uninspired, for publishing editorials backing downtown taxpayer-financed development schemes, for a pro-business stance and for a tough labor-relations posture.

But my first few months at the paper were exciting. Dennis Kucinich had been elected the mayor of Cleveland the previous year. When I arrived at the paper, he was involved in a slugfest with the Cleveland Electric Illuminating Co. (CEI) over the future of Muny Light, the city's electric utility and a CEI competitor.

The coverage was tough and in-depth, including a take-out on the directors of major banks and corporations who also served on CEI's board of directors. I wasn't part of that coverage, but I learned much about city politics from it.

My first personal experience with the city's willingness to help corporate Cleveland came a couple of years later.

British Petroleum (Sohio) in 1981 wanted to build a headquarters building on Public Square. George Forbes, the powerful president of Cleveland City Council, hinted a couple of times that he had a public financing package for BP, but he wouldn't disclose it and instead set a private executive session at a local hotel to brief City Council.

My partner at City Hall and I worked the phones and wrote what the financing package might entail.

McGruder asked me to cover the meeting, but to leave if Forbes insisted since we had no legal right to be on private property uninvited.

Forbes was in a foul mood that morning, and wanted the media out. I talked to Roldo Bartimole, the editor of Point of View, a newsletter that explored the relationships between corporate Cleveland and City Hall, and we agreed to argue that we should be allowed to stay because the project was the public's business – but that we would leave if Forbes insisted.

Forbes suddenly exploded and pushed both of us into a line of TV cameramen. The tape of that incident has been re-broadcast many times on Cleveland TV, generally accompanying stories about Forbes and his power. I wish I received royalties.

It also wasn't long before I got my own up-close look at the PD's willingness to use its own power improperly, in my view.

In 1982, The Plain Dealer quietly arranged to publish a lawyer-brokered front-page story that retracted a two-part series authored the previous year by reporter Walt Bogdanich.

The series said that then-Ohio Teamster boss Jackie Presser had taken kickbacks from a public relations firm and that he had been a government informant for years.

Caryn and I were scheduled to attend a staff event the night before publication with Steve Hatch and his wife, Diane. Hatch was executive secretary of the Cleveland Newspaper Guild, Local 1.

Instead, we spent the night at Hatch's apartment with Bogdanich and his wife, reporter Stephanie Saul, while Hatch tried unsuccessfully to have the retraction pulled.

Newspaper Guild members scheduled an informational picket line for the next day. The intent of the picket line was to bring attention to the truth.

One of the things burned into my memory that day was an editor on the city desk answering every call he received with a booming, "The Plain Dealer. We apologize."

Bogdanich eventually left The PD and went on to win three Pulitzer Prizes at the Wall Street Journal and the New York Times.

I continued at The PD, covering the administration of Mayor George Voinovich and Forbes. Covering Forbes was tough – he normally liked doing business in private and was even more difficult with reporters who wrote stories he didn't like.

I was still able to get my share of good stories by working documents or sources – clerks were a great help. I generally got good Page One play, although Bartimole once told me he thought I would do better if The Cleveland Press had a more aggressive reporter covering city hall to motivate me. I thought I was working pretty hard, but I paid attention.

The Press was struggling at the time. Its circulation was dropping – the victim of a tough afternoon rush-hour delivery schedule and the competition from evening television news. The Press didn't start a Sunday paper until late in its existence.

The Press closed in 1982. I was an officer in the Cleveland Newspaper Guild by then, and a senior executive at The Plain Dealer asked me to attend a meeting of Press employees at a local hotel. It was my job to tell them that The Plain Dealer had no openings. It wasn't hiring.

It was heartbreaking to stand in front of all those journalists and tell them that the only other major outlet in Cleveland for their talents was essentially slamming the door.

During those first years at The Plain Dealer, I was "socialized" into the newsroom through my work with Local 1 of the Cleveland Newspaper Guild as a member, PD unit chair and Local president, and from listening to reporters and others tell stories about The PD's past, either in the newsroom or at the Headliner, a newspaper bar down the street.

I worked with the Guild on grievances staff members had with their bosses, and helped bargain contracts. I remember my wife and young daughter one year helping to clean a dusty warehouse the union had rented for a strike headquarters. (The strike was called off after a late-night request from a federal mediator to resume talks.)

Later, I would also bring my son, Brian, to the newsroom on occasional Saturdays. He would watch TV or play with my computer while I worked.

In the mid-1980s, City Editor Bob Samsot asked me to join the city desk as an assistant city editor. Samsot was a good story editor with a calm demeanor and a good relationship with reporters.

I thought twice about going on the desk. Assistant city editors worked long and late hours, including weekends. But I agreed.

After all, with Samsot and McGruder at my back, what could go wrong?

Samsot and McGruder left the paper shortly thereafter. Samsot had quickly learned that newsroom editors could face rough treatment and unfair criticism from top executives at the paper.

McGruder had become managing editor, but was concerned the paper would never select a black as editor.

The editor and publisher at the time was Tom Vail, a scion of a wealthy family.

Vail was rarely in the newsroom. He left operations to Executive Editor David Hopcraft, and my only experience with Vail was on the rare occasions when he did visit the newsroom.

Bill Woestendiek, the paper's editorial director, replaced Hopcraft in 1984.

Woestendiek and McGruder didn't mesh. At one point, McGruder was told in the Headliner by a reporter close to Woestendiek that Woestendiek was planning an investigative team that would include the reporter.

It was the first McGruder had heard of the plan. He quietly turned and walked out. He left The PD in 1986 and went to Detroit, where he was named deputy managing editor of the Detroit Free Press and, eventually, executive editor. I stayed in touch on and off until he died of cancer in 2002.

At The PD, it seemed like a revolving door.

In my 22 years at The Plain Dealer, five different editors headed the paper, in addition to Vail.

I don't know if that's unusual, but it did create uncertainty and turmoil. The turnover, including the continuing, sudden departures of others in divisions throughout the building, prompted some people to recommend never going to lunch with your boss on Friday – because you might not come back.

In 1986, Thom Greer, the paper's sports editor, was named managing editor and eventually replaced Woestendiek as editor.

Greer could be fun and gregarious in a social setting, but he could be abrupt and combative in the newsroom.

I was city editor by then and Greer could be difficult to work with. We often had to fight for our stories, including a running investigation by reporters Jim Parker and John Griffith about a drug dealer who was allowed by Cleveland cops to sell drugs on the streets of Cleveland while the cops tried to develop him as an informant.

Possibly because of the fights over stories, Greer began to act as if the city desk was an underground cell trying to thwart him. City desk editors generally were only sticking up for reporters and their stories. After a particularly ugly meeting, where one of my assistants detailed a frustrating and convoluted editing process, a top editor threatened to put my "dick in the dirt."

Greer launched a purge of the city desk. Nearly every editor on the desk was forced into a new assignment. Most reporters on the city desk signed a petition asking Greer to keep me as City Editor, but he refused.

I was fortunate enough to land on the state desk. Mary Anne Sharkey, the chief of the Columbus bureau, had assembled a seasoned staff that broke lots of news and investigative stories.

The state desk also included Dick Ellers, a roving reporter in northeast Oho, and Bill Sloat in Cincinnati. Sloat was one of the best and most versatile reporters I ever worked with.

My state desk assignment was a wonderful experience, but it didn't last.

Greer moved me to the National Desk, and Sharkey eventually became editor of the editorial and opinion pages, reporting to Vail.

In a major surprise, Greer asked me about a year later to be managing editor. I was confused about the offer since he had kicked me off the city desk.

I said yes, but I often thought afterwards whether I should have more carefully considered that request.

I worked for Greer and, later, for Editor David Hall, as managing editor for nearly 10 years.

Much of it was great. We tried to improve the number and quality of investigative stories and projects, be more aggressive on government beats, and get better writing into the paper. We sent a reporter who was a former Vietnam combat photographer to cover the start of the Gulf War in 1990. We began to get good reviews on our investigative work from judges at Pulitzer and Investigative Reporters & Editors conferences.

The publisher also approved an expensive request to buy a computer for computer-assisted reporting projects. And we named an editor to oversee and promote computer-assisted reporting.

We were Pulitzer Prize finalists three times during the 1990s, twice for investigative reporting and once for beat reporting. We won lots of other awards.

I also made mistakes as managing editor that I still regret.

- Greer had made threats to remove a reporter from an important beat because of a weekly column he wrote for the editorial pages that Greer thought was routinely unfair. I had defended the reporter but, after another of those columns, I agreed with Greer to take him off his beat. It was wrong. I fault myself for not continuing to defend the reporter aggressively enough.
- During a prison riot in Ohio, one of the reporters covering the story said sources were saying that inmates had killed several guards. The reporter was concerned about using the information, but I pushed to use it to be competitive. The next day, we learned the sources – not the reporter – were wrong. I was deeply troubled that my decision had added even more fear and anxiety to the lives of the guards' families.
- I also refused to let a reporter grant anonymity the night before publication to a Supreme Court justice who was the lead critic in a story about another justice. Our legal counsel was concerned that the move would make the story dangerously under-sourced. The reporter resigned without warning the next morning. He was a good reporter who had mentored me, and I wish I could have come up with a solution.

In 1990, Machaskee, who was general manager and who had worked in marketing, labor relations and as Vail's assistant, became publisher. Things began getting tense almost right away.

Machaskee was a tough, driven leader. But he could be snide and accusatory in his frequent memos to Greer and I, and to our department heads. He also seemed to like making people squirm at meetings of his division heads.

I was generally the one who had to research and write the memos explaining to Machaskee why we had done what we did.

Shortly after I became managing editor, Machaskee and the Newhouse family, which owned The Plain Dealer, proposed we zone the paper. It was an extraordinary proposal.

Zoning is the process of hiring additional staff to cover surrounding suburban communities in an effort to add circulation and advertising. It also involves the difficult and time-consuming process of re-working every page in the Metro section on deadline to make them unique to each zone.

I was told to immediately put together an editorial team to develop a zoning proposal – even though we were in the middle of an important mayoral primary between Forbes and Mike White, a council colleague. White won, but I was already knee-deep in zoning plans by the time of the general election.

While zoning is a good way to add news coverage, thus improving the paper for readers, expectations soon became more than we could deliver.

In our proposal, the editorial team advised Greer and Machaskee that zoning seldom increased circulation or advertising. Quoting editors at the New Orleans Times-Picayune, another Newhouse paper, we said zoning is less an offensive strategy than a defensive one – to protect the core circulation area. That advisory seemed to slip people's minds.

And Greer cut our staffing request.

We still hired a remarkable number of people. As zoning evolved from four to six zones, including requirements that each zone have a completely local Metro cover AND a page one story, we added close to 100 staffers – reporters, photographers, bureau chiefs, secretaries, copy editors and page designers.

Those hired were good journalists, who added much to the paper and would eventually move to other areas of coverage. They strengthened the paper.

But it was zoning hell. Tracking all those zones and stories turned editors into score keepers. We received monthly tallies of the number of stories we had produced in each zone, often with a critical note from Machaskee.

On occasions, those memos accused us of being "lazy" or "stupid." I was also threatened in at least one memo from Machaskee with "discipline, up to and including discharge" after weekend editors forgot to alert senior editors and Machaskee that they were working on a story that mentioned previously published Plain Dealer editorial positions on the Middle East.

Machaskee should have been notified. But discharge?

Most editors weren't fearful of Machaskee's complaints or threats at that point, but it added to the pressures.

And Greer would make sudden staffing or other changes, adding to the chaos. At one point, Greer and Machaskee moved Sharkey from editorial director to Metro editor, and Metro editor Ted Diadiun was named sports editor. I doubt either wanted the reassignments at that point in their careers, but we weren't asked.

The dueling memos, reassignments and negative atmosphere mainly affected the management group, but it also affected the staff. They didn't understand the changing mandates and probably thought we were all nuts.

And it added to a growing schism between Greer and I, and between Machaskee and the two of us.

At one point, Machaskee called Greer and I to his office to complain about a story in the paper. I defended the story and myself.

Machaskee exploded and hurled the newspaper over our heads and into a corner of his office.

Greer later told me I wouldn't get a salary increase that year.

The atmosphere had become toxic and I was convinced it couldn't last. I became concerned about my job – as was my wife, although she was supportive through it all.

I also knew that Machaskee's priorities and demands concerning zoning were taking my attention from other areas of news coverage. Zoning was a major cost and coverage initiative, and I knew that Machaskee had to answer to the Newhouses for it.

But planning was suffering, and too many reporters and editors were left to sort things out on their own. Zoning was important, but other important coverage issues were being ignored.

Machaskee removed Greer as editor in 1992 and named him a vice president, moving him to an office far from the newsroom.

David Hall, who had worked at the Chicago Daily News and the Chicago Sun Times, replaced Greer. Hall had been executive editor of the St. Paul Pioneer Press and editor of the Denver Post and the Bergen Record in New Jersey.

I thought I would be replaced as managing editor, but Hall kept me on and treated me well. I thought his hiring would calm Machaskee and it seemed to – for a brief period.

But the same pressures from Machaskee returned. Hall would keep most of his relationship and discussions with Machaskee private, but as the years passed I could see he was becoming stressed and brooding.

Some thought the relationship soured because Hall's hiring had the blessing of the Newhouse family, but didn't have Machaskee's approval. Hall never confirmed that to me.

I, too, was becoming angry and exhausted. After working from 9 a.m. until 8 and sometimes 9 p.m., I would often go to the Headliner to decompress. I had become a regular during my reporting days.

While a few editors complained to Machaskee that newsroom business was conducted at the bar to the exclusion of others, it really wasn't the case. Bartimole also once wrote that the Headliner was a reason the paper wasn't better.

I thought the complaints were disingenuous. Every major newspaper has a nearby newspaper bar, where reporters and editors socialize. Anyone was welcome at the Headliner, although Greer and some senior editors preferred a nicer joint near Public Square. Some politics and government reporters preferred a joint on E. 9th Street.

At some point, I did stop going to the Headliner. A small number of us stopped at another bar for a period, but it wasn't the same.

But the damage had been done. Not to the paper, but to Caryn.

Caryn was raising two kids almost on her own, plus often baby-sitting other kids for extra cash. While I was able to make many of my kids' school events, I was often not home.

Caryn was hurt by the many nights I was away. She was lonely and angry that I seemed to prefer the company of people at the paper. The issue affected our marriage. She still reminds me of it.

Through all of these years, I was fortunate to have the strong support of many of the reporters and editors at the paper.

Among them were Griffith and Parker. John was a bulldog reporter who at one point covered the federal beat, where he broke stories nobody else could get. Later, I would ask him to be city editor and then projects editor, where he helped the paper win lots of awards, including those two Pulitzer Prize finalists for investigative reporting.

Parker was a Special Forces veteran of Vietnam and one of the best writers I ever met. He was a reporter and, as a columnist, developed a following. But he hated Greer and fought him. He eventually was forced out.

I knew by the late 1990s that the conflict between Hall and Machaskee was negatively affecting the paper. It was certainly affecting me. Coverage was affected. Some editors became worried that their careers might be on the line.

People would stop by my office just to ask me the latest on Machaskee and Hall. A few would make appointments to talk to Machaskee to promote themselves or to criticize others. I occasionally heard about those complaints from Hall or Machaskee.

It prompted some on the city desk to suggest people were panicking because "they didn't know whose ass to kiss."

Hall was clearly exhausted – and angry, too. He had a run-in or two with Mayor Mike White about White's refusal to be open with our reporters. It apparently turned ugly.

I later read that Machaskee was furious about the meeting because he was friendly with White, but I was never told that.

In early 1999, Hall left the paper. I applied for the job. The interview was short. Machaskee accused me of delaying a management training plan proposed months earlier by Hall, but I actually had little to do with it.

Machaskee hired Doug Clifton, who had led the Miami Herald.

A few months later, I returned from vacation and Clifton took me to lunch. I thought he wanted to discuss coverage, but he said he wanted to name his own managing editor and offered me the job of managing editor for administration. (It wasn't even Friday!)

On the drive back from lunch, he also asked whether I had ever considered leaving the paper and trying fresh at another newspaper.

I remember Caryn and I standing on our front porch on a lovely evening and talking about what to do. I really didn't want to be an administrative editor – I liked news.

I told Clifton I would leave. (As a last act, I introduced Clifton to David Kordalski, a designer who had applied for a job before Clifton arrived. Kordalski would turn the paper into a visual powerhouse.)

Clifton seemed to have a good relationship with Machaskee.

That was good. I had firmly come to believe that newspapers worked better if the publisher and editor were not at war.

I still think about my years at The Plain Dealer. I think I improved the paper – with the help of lots of others. I have dozens of emails from people I worked with, thanking me for doing just that and for helping their careers. A PD section editor years later said the staff still talked respectfully about my time at the paper.

But maybe that's all defensiveness on my part. I also recognized my failures to better manage up, to rise above the open warfare and to better focus on important issues instead of nasty memos.

I do miss The Plain Dealer.

And if anyone should ask, I'm willing to do it all over again.

Postscript

After I left The Plain Dealer:

~The paper began dismantling the zoning operation; staff reductions would follow.
~John Griffith, who was concerned he would be targeted because he was my friend, asked to be moved to a bureau to get away from the newsroom. He was later laid off. (My dear friend, Jim Parker, died in 1998).
~Arlene Flynn, who was my administrative assistant and a wonderful friend who would "mother" my kids when they called me at the office, died in 2003, leaving a hole in my heart.
~Machaskee was named by the Press Club of Cleveland in 2006 to the Cleveland Journalism Hall of Fame.
~Greer died in 2011.

As for me, I first interviewed at a couple of Cleveland PR firms, but nobody offered me a corner office with a view of Lake Erie. And I avoided applying for government jobs. I didn't want to work for people we had covered.

I first went to work at The Columbus Dispatch as city editor.

After two years, I jumped at the opportunity to join The Denver Post as managing editor. The Post had a fine history. I loved the paper, the staff and Denver, which is a wonderfully vibrant city.

But I had some disagreements with the top leadership and was axed after six years.

I spent a very lonely year unemployed, trying to find another job in newspapers, but the newspaper recession was in full bloom and nobody was hiring.

We sold our house, found a place to rent, and I eventually found a job at the Department of Veterans Affairs, editing for a small office that ran health care programs for the widows and children of deceased or disabled veterans.

I worked with nice people, but the VA Inspector General forced two consecutive directors of the agency into retirement for nepotism and contract illegalities. The agency also had a very difficult time properly spending taxpayer dollars. As a former newspaperman, it made me feel awful.

I retired in 2016.

Strength, beauty, power - covering Cleveland's long-ignored black community

MARGARET BERNSTEIN

"Margaret Bernstein, your columns are so sickeningly sweet that they make my teeth hurt," came the email from a reader.

"Yeah, well, the dental pain is mutual," I retorted, in print. "Feels like I'm pulling teeth as I try to motivate Clevelanders to do something other than complain about this city's problems."

Just being myself– the black writer with the Jewish name who often wrote about minority issues, poverty and those working to make a difference – I managed to trigger a lot of readers.

Long before the dawn of anonymous comments on Cleveland.com, it felt like the mere appearance of my byline could ignite PD readers who wished like hell they could return to the prosperous, and mostly white, Cleveland that they remembered. They wrote me unsigned letters and sent emails, or they called, freshly ticked off after reading something I'd written and ready to unload. When The PD's voicemail system would cut callers off after 2 or 3 minutes, there were those who'd call back over and over again, just to squeeze out every bit of their rant.

I arrived at The Plain Dealer in 1989, hired by Living Editor Michael Bennett. I loved the not-so-hurried pace of being a feature writer and thought I would stay there forever. But my career's been a journey. After 20 years in Features, editors moved me downstairs to Metro to take on the philanthropy beat.

And from there, I hammered out a new role as a metro columnist who was trying out this new thing called solutions-oriented journalism. Twice a week, I tried to shine a light on ways to move Cleveland off the poorest big city list. But the pushback to my efforts was surprising, and intense. This was especially true in articles where I attempted to humanize the poor. "They're the problem!" was the general outcry.

One of my all-time favorite calls came from an older woman who was all worked up about poor people gaming the system. "When I'm driving on I-90, I can see that new Food Bank that they built. I've seen all the fancy cars in the parking lot," she railed. "They're driving Benzes and BMWs to go get their handouts!"

I was like, "Ma'am, the Food Bank doesn't even work like that. No one picks up their free food at that location. All the food there gets sorted and then trucked out to pantries and soup kitchens across the region. What you don't realize is the Cleveland Food Bank has a very big and devoted volunteer base. What you're looking at are the cars of the volunteers."

"You might want to get out of your car next time you drive by, and consider volunteering," I told her, sensing I had silenced her and won the battle.

I don't think the Food Bank gained a helper that day, but I thoroughly enjoyed needling her as I made my point.

I used to just consider it part of my job description to have to engage in some pointless jousting with intolerant readers. Such is the lot of reporters who are determined to show there are more facets to black life than thugs, criminals and athletes, I figured.

And that was something I was determined to do, since the day I arrived at The Plain Dealer. I could see that Cleveland was a profoundly segregated town. Yet The PD had one of the highest readership rates, especially on Sundays, of any newspaper in the country.

And so, I reasoned that if Clevelanders were deliberately choosing to live their separate lives, steeped in their stereotypes, then I was working at what had to be the most important stereotype-fighting weapon in town – the daily newspaper.

My first writing job had been at a black paper in my hometown, Los Angeles, so I guess advocacy journalism was already running through my veins. Then I was hired by Gannett, where there was a heavy emphasis on fair and balanced coverage of minorities. At Gannett properties, the editorial staff was trained to "mainstream" minorities into daily news coverage, and every paper took part in a quarterly contest where they were judged on how well they plied those diversity principles. At Gannett, I'd earned a name corporation-wide for helping boost diversity scores at the two papers where I worked.

When I arrived at The PD at age 30, I was surprised to see there were no similar guidelines and expectations. At Gannett, you were expected to go the extra mile every day to make sure women and people of color were depicted on section fronts, and to add a minority perspective to stories. At The PD, such representation simply wasn't much of a priority.

My training kicked in as soon as I arrived. I immediately started proposing feature stories on subjects of interest to Cleveland minorities. In my first months, I profiled some of newly elected Mayor Michael R. White's appointees for top city jobs, many of whom were people of color or women. For my first King holiday in Cleveland, I wrote a piece tracing Martin Luther King Jr.'s visits to the city during the 1960s.

I certainly wasn't the only reporter making sure people of color and their concerns were being reflected in the newspaper. In the early 1990s, The Plain Dealer had a healthy and growing stable of minority reporters – Dick Peery, Alan Seifullah, Olivera Perkins, Paul Shepard, Dana Canedy, Roxanne Washington, Laura Yee, Frances Robles, Roger Brown, just to name a few.

We were all contributing our perspectives to the daily product, and providing coverage of minorities when feasible.

But The Plain Dealer had no formal policy on diversity. And it needed one.

I remember suppressing a smile one spring day in the 1990s when a group of Native Americans brought their annual Chief Wahoo protest right to us to 1801 Superior. Their beef wasn't just with the Indians, but also with The Plain Dealer for not rejecting the offensive mascot. (Just for contrast: Our sister paper, the Portland Oregonian, announced in 1992 it would no longer refer to the Indians, Braves or Redskins in print.)

So, on the day of the Indians home opener, a crowd of Native Americans had come over to express their feelings to PD brass. And "somehow" more than a dozen of the visitors managed to get through the secure door into the newsroom, where they sat down for a peaceful protest among our rows of desks and computer terminals. (We all knew who let them in.)

That was a good day.

As the years rolled by, I had a variety of roles in Features: columnist, everywoman editor, consumer writer. But no matter my title, I still found myself pitching and writing stories about Cleveland's black community. One year I even asked for a merit raise using the argument that I spent most of my waking hours, even off duty, serving as The PD's de facto ambassador to the black community. It wasn't a role that I set out to fill, especially not during my private time. But because black Clevelanders' impression of the paper was never especially high during the time I worked there, I found that folks increasingly would seek me out and give me story tips.

Within Cleveland's black community, I had gained a reputation as someone at the paper who would actually pick up my phone, return messages and be generally accessible.

I took that responsibility seriously. Like when R&B singer Gerald Levert was found dead in his bed, at his Geauga County home on a Friday in 2006.

I called the arts editor at home and offered to write something special for the weekend. I was told to wait until Monday and pitch the story then.

OK I thought to myself. "You guys have no idea what a megastar he is."

On Monday, music writer John Soeder and I banded together to inform editors of Levert's popularity. We wrote a series of great stories, including coverage of the memorial ceremony at Public Hall, attended by a stage full of black music superstars including Stevie Wonder and Usher, as well as athletes and other celebrities.

Black readers loved and appreciated the heavy coverage. But there was an outright rebellion from white readers who didn't like it at all.

Ted Diadiun had to write a column to address all the reader complaints: "*I don't know that I've ever seen a greater disconnect between two major segments of our audience than in the wake of this newspaper's coverage of Levert and his legacy….It is always dangerous to generalize about race, but it is impossible not to note the reaction separated along racial lines: Black readers were complimentary and grateful that the paper acknowledged Levert's passing with such sensitive and vigorous coverage. White readers were puzzled – some even stunned – at the fuss over somebody many of them had never heard of.*"

Just another day at work, as far as I was concerned. Trying to explain to Plain Dealer readership about the life of an extraordinary person of color who white folks never knew existed.

I considered that part of my mission.

As the years went on, I didn't even have to hunt for stories. People would just call me with them. I absolutely fell in love with some of the characters I wrote about, and considered it an honor to work on some of the projects that I did.

I wrote most of my feature pieces in the dark days before Google, and so I enumerate some of my favorites here just because I fear they won't ever be read again:

- My profile of Odessa Salvant, a fair-skinned woman who could pass for white. Yet she volunteered her entire adult life for the Cleveland NAACP.
- I reported on a meeting of the Minority Women With Breast Cancer United group. These formidable women won grants to pay for mammograms for uninsured women and got University Hospitals to send its mammography van to low-income black neighborhoods. They saved a lot of lives.
- Through interviews I recreated the 1963 night that Malcolm X came to dinner at the Shaker Heights home of Morris and Adrienne Jones.

Once I tangled with fellow feature writer Fran Henry when we both showed up, notebook in hand, to cover the same event at the Fatima Family Center in Hough.

We had both heard about the extraordinary work that poet Honey Bell-Bey was doing with teen and preteen boys, teaching them to recite poetry in unison. Unbeknownst to each other, we were both there ready to introduce Cleveland to the Distinguished Gentlemen of Spoken Word.

I can't stand confrontation and I dearly love Fran, but I would have engaged in fisticuffs on Hough Avenue to win the right to have my byline on that story.

It had Black Excellence flowing all through it.

I wanted it bad, and I told her so. It had become so obvious by then: Those rose-growing-through-the-concrete stories had become my signature.

Thankfully she relented.

Langston Hughes once wrote: "Perhaps the mission of an artist is to interpret the beauty of a people – the beauty within themselves."

During my features heyday, I was pretty sure that this was my mission. To show off the strength, beauty and power within Cleveland's black community.

I would say my greatest moment covering Black Excellence happened at the Lancer restaurant on Nov. 4, 2008.

I was part of the team covering the presidential election. I was posted up at the Lancer with reporter April McClellan-Copeland, as nearly 1,500 people gathered outside along Carnegie for the NAACP's election party. A mix of black leaders and everyday folks were mingling inside and outside the restaurant, watching CNN's election coverage on huge monitors. The evening was dragging on as election nights do. And then suddenly everyone went absolutely bonkers when the race was called for Barack Obama. April and I hugged and then went right back to trying to file on deadline.

Charlie Bibb of East Cleveland gave us the best soundbite that night. "Hands that picked cotton now picked the president," he said.

Occasionally during my feature writer years, I got recruited to do stories and work on special projects for Metro. In 2001, I was invited to be on a team of reporters who would each write a profile of the 10 political hopefuls lining up to succeed retiring Mayor Michael White.

On Sept. 11, 2001, I was up super-early for a breakfast interview with the candidate I would be writing about. I had been firmly instructed to question him about his extramarital affairs. "When he divorced his first two wives, he always had his next wife waiting in the wings. Ask him about that," I was told.

I knew it would be an uncomfortable question to ask. But I didn't want the Metro editors to think I was too soft to ask the hard questions, so I resolved to bring it up. As the last question, of course.

I got to the restaurant at 7 a.m. Everything went fine until the last question. He got so angry that his body trembled. He told me his marriages had nothing to do with his fitness to be Cleveland's mayor, then stood up and left. Nothing surprising here. We both played our parts predictably.

I got in the car and arrived in the newsroom a little after 8 a.m. The TV was on in the features department and I could see smoke pouring from the World Trade Center. As we gathered around the TV, everything seemed to be unraveling. It was scary. We didn't know if our country would soon be at war. We didn't know what was coming.

But there was one thing I did know: This man's marital history didn't mean squat to me.

I sat down, wrote the story and didn't mention one word about his questionable fidelity.

And nobody said a word about it.

In 2009, I made the move permanently from Features to Metro. And I struggled, trying to fit my sensibilities into their hard-news frame. One of my community connections had tipped me off to a great story about a quadriplegic woman who was opening her own nonprofit, Compassions, to train home health care workers. She had somehow found the will to establish a 501c3 organization after tiring of being repeatedly victimized by home health attendants who'd stolen from her and left her lying in bed all day. I breathlessly pitched the story to my editor in Metro.

Editor: "Use her story as an anecdote and go get the stats to flesh it out. Is any state agency even overseeing these workers? This is great! It's an expose of rampant abuse of seniors and disabled people by their caregivers."

Me: "No it's not! It's a profile of an inspiring woman who can't walk, bathe or dress herself alone and was repeatedly victimized by her caregivers but managed to successfully start her own nonprofit and now has a stable of young devoted health care aides who say their hallmark will be compassionate care."

We actually had to go get mediation from a higher editor to resolve our dispute. I was told to do it the editor's way.

I tried. I really did! But I couldn't even force my fingers to type it in such a hard-boiled way.

In the end, I came up with a hybrid approach that was equal parts news and feature. And my cranky editor gave in and glumly published it. OK, it was Rutti.

In 2010, reporter Stan Donaldson and I collaborated to research and write profiles of each of the 11 women who had been murdered by the Imperial Avenue serial killer. I had felt compelled to do it. Concerned that our coverage had concentrated only on the victims' deaths and not their lives, I'd actually been clipping out from our paper what little biographical material we'd written about them in the months since the bodies were discovered in 2009. And for several of them, we'd published less than five paragraphs.

I felt like we owed it to those women to tell their stories.

So, Stan and I tracked down every family. We knocked on doors and introduced ourselves, often encountering hostile relatives who laid into us when we explained what we wanted to do. Stoically we let them complain to our faces about the news media. They had a point. We met family after family who had tried to publicize their missing daughters and moms but couldn't get coverage in the paper or on TV.

I vividly remember victim Michelle Mason's mom giving me the business. This woman had put up missing person fliers all over Mount Pleasant and had tried unsuccessfully to get the media to cover it. One day, she told me, she had been watching TV and happened to see a news story about a missing dog.

"A damn dog!" she fumed to me. "And I couldn't get anyone to write about my daughter."

Stan and I worked really hard to win her trust, and the trust of the other 10 families too. It took weeks of going back and meeting with them. Eventually, one of Michelle's sons took me to her gravesite in a nearby cemetery via his personal shortcut, showing me how he would slip through a hole in the fencing to see his mom.

All that good intention and hard work is why it broke my heart when nearly every family I interviewed lashed out angrily at me when the stories were published. Michelle Mason's family was livid that I mentioned she had been addicted to crack and heroin, although her convictions were public record and I had taken pains to make her successful recovery the focal point of the story. Victim Crystal Dozier's mother – who had gotten used to sympathetic news coverage when the bodies were first discovered – was deeply hurt that I wrote that Mom herself had two drug convictions.

These were facts that I included because I had committed to shedding light on the circumstances that led each woman to Anthony Sowell's doorway. Where they perished.

There were shards of hopelessness in each of the women's stories, but we'd also uncovered moments of triumph. I saw the value of telling the unvarnished truth, but these families didn't. And why should they? They hadn't gone to journalism school, they already felt burned by the news; they were the ones who had actually lost a loved one, however flawed. If this was the only time their daughters' stories were going to make it into print, they didn't want the moment sullied with a litany of convictions and family failings.

I didn't agree but I understood.

I had peered into a truly dark part of Cleveland. It was a cycle of helplessness, and I wasn't feeling particularly like my articles had helped the situation.

That was a turning point for me.

I started challenging myself to do more, as a journalist. In 2012 I went to Managing Editor

Thom Fladung and told him I was ready to write a "solution-oriented column," identifying people and programs that were finding ways to move people out of poverty and improve the Cleveland landscape.

After I got the go-ahead, I started bombarding readers with ways they could take action: Support re-entry programs for ex-prisoners. Become a Big Brother or Big Sister. Adopt a vacant lot.

I wrote about programs such as the Baldwin-Wallace Scholars which established pipelines to college and careers for Cleveland schools' students and urged more universities and companies to do something similar.

I wanted to spur activism. But it was still as painful as pulling teeth. Only a few columns generated much response, most notably something I wrote about College Now's mentoring program for first-generation college students. It recruited so many volunteers that the organization had to create a waiting list.

The more columns I wrote, the more convinced I became that illiteracy was one of the main culprits dooming Cleveland's children and adults to remain stuck in the poverty cycle. And Ohio's soon-to-become-law Third Grade Reading Guarantee was scaring my socks off.

Everything changed when I spied my first Little Free Library. I saw my first one in October 2012, and wrote a Sunday column about how this little book box had sparked excitement for reading among Miles Park School students.

This time, something was very different.

With every subsequent column, I heard from dozens of readers wanting to help. They donated enough money to install 13 more Little Free Libraries across Cleveland.

I had white suburbanites offering to drive books into the inner-city, to put them into the hands of low-income black kids.

Eureka! I had finally tapped into that vein of compassion that I'd been seeking, the one that could unleash a flood of activism across racial and socioeconomic lines.

I could see a new pathway emerging for me, at the exact same time that The Plain Dealer announced it would be downsizing again.

And that's how I ended my career at The PD. I volunteered for the Great Layoff of 2013, acutely aware that if literacy was to be my mission, then writing in the pages of The Plain Dealer was not going to help me reach my target audience.

I had outgrown my newspaper career, and was ready for the next chapter, as a literacy advocate.

A daughter remembers Cleveland's real best-kept secret

SUSAN CONDON LOVE

George E. Condon was truly born to write. It was his passion, his talent, his main amusement in a life that he found endlessly bemusing. Being his daughter – and someone equally fascinated by the art of telling a story and drawn to the pursuit of journalism – I was intimidated. At the same time, however, I grew up in a house where storytelling and the beauty of the English language were celebrated and part of everyday conversation.

One of the earliest stories about my Dad's talent was a tale he told from his high school days at West Tech High School. There was a writing contest and the prize for the best essay was a trip to Columbus and back … in a plane! The teenage George Condon of course won it. And a trip on an airplane in the mid 1930s – when the newly opened and then-called Municipal Airport was a dirt field in the middle of nowhere – was beyond exciting for the youngest of eight children of poor Irish immigrants.

His telling of the experience made you feel as if you were standing next to him for the whole trip. Why? Because he talked exactly as he wrote – with vivid words that evoked the emotions and visuals of whatever experience or person he was talking about. I could picture his cocky grin as his teenage self boarded the plane and waved jauntily to his probably very worried parents standing by a fence on the outskirts of the fields.

His tales from more than 40 years working at The Plain Dealer are no less colorful and vivid. While many may have been colored by the passage of time and a fondness for Irish blarney, he was a journalist at heart who honored accuracy and fairness above all. So, we can safely assume a kernel of truth to all the stories.

My favorites revolved around the early days of television in Cleveland. As the first TV editor in 1948 – a side beat to his radio column – he was there when the first stations went on air. He loved talking about how early station officials didn't really know what to do with the new medium. They would book a few performers, usually old vaudevillians and radio stars, and put them in front of the camera, and expect black-and-white miracles in between the test patterns.

His most frequently repeated party story involved the night of Dec. 19, 1949. He and my mother, Marjorie, went to the opening of the Dumont Network's newest station and Cleveland's third TV station, WXEL, Channel 9, which is now WJW, Channel 8. Family lore is that after everybody had had a drink or two, he decided he had to do some reporting. He wanted to know what show would be broadcast first on WXEL that night. He went to the station director and was told – presumably because the station director didn't know he was supposed to plan something – to ask the advertising manager. The advertising manager had no clue either and directed my Dad to the

Cornell University professor who had been overseeing the construction. He also didn't know the plans for the first broadcast.

It was about this time, my Dad said, that they ALL realized that there was no plan for that first broadcast.

Panic set in and the station officials had to throw a show together on the spot. Morey Amsterdam was in town. A veteran of vaudeville and radio, he was now 41 years old and had had a show on Dumont since the previous December. They asked him to emcee a discussion with the three TV critics who were there for the opening. It was Dad for The Plain Dealer, and reporters from the Press (Warren Anderson) and somebody for the News. The problem was that all three critics were pretty tipsy. And Amsterdam could not get the names correct. He kept calling Dad Warren and Warren George and the third guy by another name. One of them, according to Dad, threatened on air to punch Amsterdam if he didn't get the names right.

When the show ended, Dad filed his story by phone and went to the Statler Hotel for a dance/reception celebrating the opening. He was dancing with Mom, he said, when he noticed out the window that the sky was red. He called the City Desk and was told there was a fire at the Central Market. The editor told him they couldn't get another reporter there in time for the first edition and asked him to go over and write the first story. He sent Mom home and took a streetcar to the fire. As he recalled, when he stepped off the curb, his foot sank in a big hole and he got soaked thoroughly, nearly getting electrocuted by downed power lines in the water.

After filing the story, he went to an after-hours place frequented by city councilmen and ne'er-do-wells. While drinking there, there was a police raid and they were all swept off to jail. We don't know why – perhaps there was gambling?

A note of research for that story. According to records, the opening of WXEL was on Dec. 19, 1949, and the Central Market explosion was Dec. 20, 1949. But according to Dad, both happened on one night and I trust his memory above academic notes.

In today's world of special previews, DVRing and thick layers of media relations flacks, critics should be jealous of the access of those early days of TV. Once he got a phone number from New York or Hollywood agents, Dad had whenever-he-wanted access to all the early stars, including Jimmy Durante (we found a note from him among Dad's papers after he passed away) and, my favorite as I look at old clips, Ernie Kovacs, a huge star in the late 1950s and early 1960s. Kovacs hosted the "General Electric Theater," "Goodyear Theater" and the hysterical ... even now... "The Ernie Kovacs Show." Dad once said to me that one of his biggest regrets was turning down an invitation during one of his trips to Hollywood for a night-on-the-town with the inveterate gambling, cigar-chewing star. Dad said he turned it down because he was tired after a day of press junkets.

Not too much later, Kovacs died in a car crash. It was an opportunity lost to tragedy, but I have to think that Kovacs must have seen something fun in the Cleveland Irish journalist that made him want to spend some time with him. Cool.

One of Dad's oft-repeated TV/Hollywood stories involved Desi Arnaz and Lucille Ball. On one of his L.A. junkets, he interviewed Desi and then Lucy – separately for some reason. Desi rhapsodized about working on the groundbreaking "I Love Lucy" TV show because it allowed him to be home every night with his wife. As Dad told the story, when he went to interview Lucy, he mentioned how nice it must be to have her husband home every night. She blew up at him (to his confusion) and started screaming at him to leave. He didn't know that the Hollywood gossip at the time was that Desi was out womanizing every night. The PR person was nowhere in sight, so Dad left the interview.

Late that night, asleep in the hotel room, he got a call. His story:

"Hello George. This is Lucille."

"Lucille who?" my Dad asked in confusion.

"Lucille Ball. I want to apologize for today. I didn't mean to blow up."

Apparently, when she calmed down, Lucille Ball heard from Desi and her publicist that my Dad hadn't been baiting her, but simply following up on a Desi statement.

What a hardship it was to be a newspaper critic in those days. He would sit at home with our one TV, flipping channels manually trying to watch as many shows as possible. Then he would take his notes to the phone and dictate reviews for the next day's paper. Notes on paper and diction skills honed on the police beat. Unheard of now.

Some of his best stories – and these are related to me by my siblings, since I don't remember him talking about them – were about the early live commercials on Cleveland TV stations. "He always told one about a shampoo commercial with a live duck happily swimming in a tank. Then they shampooed the duck and he sank to the bottom because of what it did to his feathers/down/whatever," according to my brother George. "He also told one about a local fire marshal who was supposed to close the broadcasting day with a fire safety message. But when the camera came on, he froze. He started lighting the papers in front of him. And Dad always ended with them getting him off the air 'when he started looking at the American flag' and they feared he would set that on fire."

My all-time favorite Dad characters story revolved around the infamous-among-PDers reporter and copy editor Roy Adams. Roy was quirky and unique – the type of person who made newsrooms interesting.

One day Roy asked Dad to give him a ride home. Roy lived in an apartment on the Gold Coast in Lakewood and, since Dad also lived in Lakewood (having moved there from Fairview Park in 1976), he said sure. Roy invited him into the apartment for a drink. When Dad looked for an ice cube in the freezer, he found instead a frozen (presumably dead) cat, right next to the ice cube tray. Calmly, Roy told him that he couldn't bear to part with his beloved pet, who had passed away. And looked at Dad like he was crazy for finding that odd.

Another time, according to Dad, reporters told Roy that publisher Tom Vail's son was named Mot (Tom backward). Roy believed it because Vail's daughter was Siri (Iris backward. Iris was her mother.) Roy went up to Vail and told him what a good job "Mot" was doing. Vail, according to Dad, was perplexed.

Famous names were dropped in our household like they were next-door neighbors, which I didn't realize until years later. Bob Evans? He wasn't just a restaurant name. He was one of my Dad's friends. He and my mother were frequent guests at Evans' sprawling farm down in Rio Grande, Ohio.

Before he was Ohio governor, Jim Rhodes came to our house to fix dinner. He was still State Auditor. Apparently, Dad challenged Rhodes' claim that he could cook the best soup in the state. Rhodes was not going to let his honor remain besmirched – and he wanted to suck up to the PD before he launched his 1962 gubernatorial campaign. So, he arrived at our Fairview Park small colonial loaded with vegetables and beef and who knows what other ingredients, as well as a large cookpot. I was too young to remember, but my brother said the soup was not very good at all and there was a lot left over.

"We put it in the pot in the garage (it was winter)," said George.

Being a journalist was never an easy financial path, especially for a man who had six children in 15 years. We were – completely unbeknownst to me – "word" rich and cash poor. This I learned from, you guessed it, reading one of my Dad's columns. Back in the days when there were gas station attendants who pumped the gas for you, Dad drove his car sputtering on fumes into a station and tried to casually ask for only $1 worth of gas like it wasn't because he was broke.

Here's how he related the ordeal:

> "Fill-'er up?" asks the man with the pump.
>
> "No-o-o," I say thoughtfully, as if torn by indecision. "A dollar's worth ought to do it, I think."
>
> "A dollar's worth?" says the attendant incredulously, stooping to peer into the car for a closer look at the cheapskate.
>
> "Yes, sir," I say, hearty as you please, "make it a dollar's worth. The old tank is pretty full, but she might take that much."

He continues with the story, reprinted in his compilation of columns "Laughter from the Rafters," noting that he and the attendant both know that the parsimony is because of a lack of funds, not a feisty gauge.

He ends with the tale with the final words of the exchange, using his wit to put the reader right in the gas station bay with him, to the point you can almost smell the pungent tang of gasoline pervading the air.

> "Too much mass production these days," I said, bringing my voice down a bit. "They make gas gauges by the millions. By the billions, if truth be known. They pour off the production

> *line like sausages and nobody cares if they work or not. That's the real trouble, if you ask me!"*
>
> *"I wouldn't be surprised," said the man with the pump. "Did you say a dollar's worth?"*
>
> *"If you can squeeze that much in," I said in a soft, low voice.*

Gas stations were, apparently, his nemesis. Another story famous at our dinner table that made it into the same book involved his convincing another gas station attendant that he was involved in a secret experiment involving putting only 38 cents worth of gas – precisely – in a tank. The attendant really got into the experiment, even offering to assist by checking the car's tires, batteries and oil. My Dad got flustered (a rare occurrence), assured him everything was fine and got into the car for a quick escape.

> *"I looked out at the man and he was stooping again, staring in at me. He had the same look you see on people as they stare into the cages at Brookside Zoo."*
>
> *"In fairness to the attendant, I had to conclude that he was entitled to this particular stare because, somehow, I had wrenched open the wrong door in entering my car and there I was, comfortably settled in the back seat."*

With as much dignity as he could muster, he opened the back door, he said, stood up, straightened his jacket (I am adding that because I can picture him doing it) and got into the driver's seat.

> *"I remember the attendant sort of stepped backward as if not too sure what my next move would be. We didn't exactly bow to each other from the hips, but we did bob our heads a bit in passing, the way foes who respect each other on the field of combat often will."*

For years, I wondered about the Baltic Avenue street sign – an official, made-by-the-city sign – holding a place of pride in the finished basement of our Fairview Park home. If I thought about it at all, I figured it was something my Dad picked up at work. Or garbage-picking (OK, I just made that last part up. But I like the imagery.) It turns out that my Dad was inherently and frequently annoyed by Baltic because it was hit or miss – sometimes literally – which one-way direction Baltic would be at that particular moment for commuters heading to or leaving the Shoreway. He wrote about it. A lot. As a joke, someone from the city gave him the old sign when they redid them.

The life of a journalist. You pick up a lot of odd souvenirs – and friends – along the way. One of Dad's closest friends in his later years was Linn Sheldon, famous for being Barnaby, a beloved children's show host in Cleveland. Barnaby was an elf who lived in an enchanted forest and happened to show a lot of cartoons. The show ran from 1968 to 1990. I remember coming home for a visit from Savannah, where I worked as the features editor at the Savannah News-Press, unaware of the renewed friendship. Dad asked me to pick up a friend of his at the friend's apartment on the Gold Coast and bring him to my parents' Lakewood home. This friend was Linn Sheldon. When he got into the car, I just stared. I hadn't made the connection between Barnaby and the name Linn Sheldon. I stuttered like a toddler awarded a bag full of lollipops for the entire drive. I'm pretty sure my face was redder than all the stop signs I probably ran from inattention. And yes, I checked to see if he had pointy ears. He didn't.

When I started at the PD, my Dad had been retired for nearly 10 years. But he was still a vibrant force on the Cleveland scene, involved in the city's bicentennial celebration in 1996, writing books about near West Side characters, and writing, writing, writing – did I mention writing? He never stopped. Well into his 90s, he was intrigued by the city he had loved since moving here as a young boy in the 1920s. He was proud that two of his children (my brother George and I) followed in his footsteps at the PD. He tried to embrace computers, but he probably would have preferred his old Smith-Corona typewriter, used for decades in his basement office in Fairview Park. My husband Brian got nearly daily calls to help him out of computer dilemmas, including the time he somehow managed to switch the computer to typing only Asian characters (not sure if it was Japanese or Chinese now) – going from right to left, of course. That fix nearly stumped us.

The old newsroom at 1801 Superior Ave. was familiar to me when I walked in as an employee in 1995. Why? Because almost every Sunday when I was young, Dad would bring me with him to work as he banged out a column or two. I would wander around, playing with typewriters (I'm sure that was appreciated on Monday morning by the reporters) and absorbing the inky smells and lingering vibe of a classic newsroom.

Walking as an adult through the maze of fake walls, dropped ceilings and raised floors to accommodate electrical cords, I managed to ferret out the spot that was Dad's old office. It was the editorial cartoonist's office. It was much smaller than I remembered. And not drab green.

The era in which my Dad was in journalism and at The Plain Dealer was, in retrospect, the golden era of smoky rooms, irreverent reporters and a love of a profession worthy of such movies as "The Front Page."

At this writing, there have been Condons employed by The Plain Dealer in every decade since the 1940s. When we hit 2020, the streak will end. But it was all started by George E. Condon. He was such a movie-image character – one with such talent and wit that he will long be remembered. Want to hear him speak? Just read any of his old columns. It's like listening to him in person. What a gift.

A three newspaper family

ROBERT MCAULEY

I'm blessed to this day. I was fortunate enough to be born into a newspaper family.

My Dad, Regis, was a sports writer and sports editor at The Cleveland News and later the baseball beat writer and executive sports editor for The Cleveland Press. He and my Uncle Ed are members of the Press Club of Cleveland Journalism Hall of Fame. Ed was a gifted writer – a general columnist and sports writer for The News and briefly a syndicated columnist after The News folded. He died very young at 58. Uncle Logan was circulation director of The Plain Dealer. Brother Tom was a district manager at The PD and Cousin Ray Daull was single-copy sales manager at The PD. All held multiple positions at the paper over the years.

It was a great way to grow up. I remember going to The News sports department on Saturdays with my Dad and sitting on the lap of legendary Sports Editor Ed Bang as he opened his desk to retrieve chocolates. Bang, also a Hall of Fame member, was everyone's grandpa. Our house, first on E. 147th Street, just off Lake Shore Boulevard, in Cleveland and later on Lincoln Boulevard in Cleveland Heights, was always an unannounced drop-in spot for sports writers, entertainment editors, drama critics, photographers, broadcasters and ballplayers.

Whenever they showed up, the Stroh's and stories would flow. There was lots of laughter, and the kids were able to sit in and listen.

Christmas gatherings would sometimes include Tribe owner Bill Veeck and in the summer, there would be calls to my Dad from future Hall of Fame Indians pitcher Early Wynn, who would dictate columns he had agreed with my dad to write for The News. The first time he called I answered the phone. "Who is this really," I asked.

It broke my heart in 1957 when Wynn was traded to the Chicago White Sox. In 1959, when I was just a little guy, he dropped by our Lincoln house with Chicago's first baseman Earl Torgeson. They asked to see my baseball glove. Embarrassed, I showed them a mitt with the web torn out. Torgeson asked if I was going to the game that night and when I replied yes, he told me to drop by the dugout before the game. When I did, Torgeson came out holding a long leather cord and offered me a choice. I could repair my mitt with the cord, or I could accept a replacement glove that turned out to be Luis Aparicio's mitt.

I was the hit of the neighborhood that summer as we passed the glove around to play catch. Both Wynn and Aparicio made the All-Star roster that year and went on to play in, but not win, the World Series. Years later, Wynn surprised my new bride and me by picking us up at airport in Tucson, Arizona, on our honeymoon. He, former Tribe play-by-play broadcaster Jimmy Dudley, their wives, my parents and three sisters all crowded into Wynn's Winnebago and went back to my folks' home for a party.

In early December 1969, at 22, I had to make another decision.

I had left the circulation department and newsroom jobs that I had held at The Plain Dealer and The Press since my high school days in 1963. I began to sell real estate but had run face first into an economic slump. I had special training and a new real estate sales license from the state, but there were few buyers. No money was coming in. I prayed to the Blessed Mother that I would land a good job and went back to The PD and applied for a Teamster job – driving a delivery truck and managing a district and its paper carriers. Brother Tom gave me a crash course on driving a stick shift truck. It had a long gear shift cut into the floor and I had a high perch on an elevated single front seat. Trial, error, a bumpy ride, and finally I got it down. I passed the driving test.

But the next call didn't come from HR. It came from the newsroom. It was a day or two from the Feast of the Immaculate Conception. Could I hold off accepting the Teamster job and accept a copy boy learner assignment to The Plain Dealer police beat? Johnny Rees, the day city editor and a longtime friend of my Dad, told me that if I worked out reporting on police matters I could become a full-time reporter after a six-month probation. I would make far less money at first. But, if it worked out, I would be better off financially later.

I got that opportunity because a number of reporters had been lost to the Vietnam draft. The police beat was shorthanded. Police reporting was so different then. We had one mobile phone attached to a car equipped also with a police scanner. We had a small room in the Central Police Station. It had a couple of dated typewriters and police and fire scanners attached to the walls.

Reporters didn't write stories. They called information into a rewrite desk where two writers put everything into a news story. It wasn't uncommon for one reporter to work on two unrelated homicides and a fatal car crash, plus a major fire in a single shift. I loved the work, especially not having to write my own stories. But I learned a great deal about simple declarative sentences and tight writing from the rewrite folks, especially on lunch breaks when we got together to drink beer in a bar across the street from Central Station.

Bob Daniels was perhaps the best on the rewrite desk. When I was just a copy boy running page proofs to the editors I used to marvel at Daniels laughing and repeating aloud every word the police reporters were calling in. He would type without looking and spout off a list of questions that the police reporter needed to find out. By the time the reporter called back, Daniels had finished the story, leaving blanks where the answers would be inserted. He was so good that it intimidated me.

Chief Police Reporter Donald L. Bean was my first boss and perhaps the most widely known character in the business. Seemingly, every cop in Greater Cleveland knew him. Bean had wild stories about everyone. Some were even true. Recounting some of his antics and stories came from his own hand in writing his own obituary. An excellent obituary writer, Alana Baranick, posted Bean's obit on a blog: Ohio Obits Life and Death, Lives and Deaths in Ohio http://obitsohio.blogspot.com/

In the obit about himself, he wrote:

> *Bean had a stormy shouting confrontation with George Steinbrenner, best known as owner of the New York Yankees, after three employees of his American Ship Building Co. died in*

> *an explosion aboard one of his ships being built at the Lorain shipyards. Marsh Samuel, Steinbrenner's public relations man, told the media the victims' names would not be released although the families had already been notified.*
>
> *"Let me talk to George," Bean requested. Ushered into the owner's spacious office, Bean pounded on the huge desk and told Steinbrenner, "You, sir, are suppressing free flow of information." The names were released...*

Can you imagine that happening today?

And then there were the Bean pranks, like his Soldiers and Sailors monument spoofs, which Bean also recounted in his obit, saying:

> *One April Fool's Day, after waiting for one hour at the monument, a male reporter called the city desk and told the then-city editor, Ted Princiotto, "Ted, she didn't show up."*
>
> *"Who didn't show up?" Princiotto asked.*
>
> *"The mother of the unknown soldier," the reporter replied.*
>
> *"Who sent you down there?" asked Princiotto.*
>
> *'Bean did," said the reporter.*
>
> *Incredulously, Princiotto replied, "You damn fool! Don't you know what day this is?"*
>
> *Another time, Bean sent a beautiful, blonde woman reporter on the same absurd assignment. After she had waited more than an hour on a hot, muggy August night, she called Bean to ask, "Bean, how long must I wait for the mother?" Sarcastically, Bean told her, "Until she is identified." With that, the reporter gasped and shouted, "Bean, you bastard!" Maybe I was, but it was fun.*

I was working that August night and had to leave the room when the reporter returned to continue her protestations. It was just too much not to laugh.

One prank almost got my boss fired. As he said in the obit he wrote about himself:

> *It was newspaper tradition to pull the leg (hoax) of the reporter who was taking his first stint as obituary writer, a job nearly all reporters had to do at one time or another.*
>
> *One night in the late '70s, Bob Holmes, a talented, athletic, broad-shouldered Englishman who had emigrated to Cleveland from Liverpool, was on the obit desk. Bean couldn't wait to get to work to pull a hoax on him.... He called Holmes about 7:30 p.m., some hours before*

deadline, and said, "This is the Donald B. Johnson Funeral Home in Northfield, and we might have an obit for the paper."

Before Bean could say anything further, Holmes said, "I can't talk to you now. I'm too busy." He then hung up.

Bean bided his time and called back at 10:30 p.m. – right on deadline. He told Holmes again that he was the mortician from the Northfield funeral home. "I tried to talk to you earlier but you were too busy. We do have the body of Cyrus Eaton in here."

Eaton was a great Cleveland industrialist, millionaire and railroad owner, and his death would be front page news any time it happened.

Holmes, between a snit and a sweat, panicked. Bean could hear him as he shouted to the night city editor, Vern Havener, a pipe-smoking, no-nonsense WWII veteran, "Vern, oh. Vern!"

In his excitement, Holmes hung up the phone before Bean could tell him it was a joke. Within minutes, the entire city staff sprang into action and just about everyone in the newsroom was busy on the fake obit. All the phone lines were tied up as the staff called notables for comment, worked to update the standing Eaton obituary on deadline and contact the funeral home for confirmation of the death.

Failing to get a line into the city room, Bean knew he had to rush to the city room from the Central Police Station (a block away) to stop the story from seeing the light of print. And also to try to save his job and to at least prove he was sober.

Bean liked to recount that as he approached the city desk with his hat in his hand – and he didn't even wear a hat – dense clouds of smoke rose from the pipe of a very angry night city editor.

"What do you know about a Cyrus Eaton obit?" Havener asked in the coldest, iciest voice Bean ever had heard.

Bean said, "I know everything about it. I was trying to pull Bob Holmes' leg."

Havener replied, "You'll be pulling your leg on the street."

To his everlasting credit Vern never filed a complaint against Bean.

Listening to Bean's telephone interviews of police and the families of victims was my best education. Empathetic yet direct, Bean could apologize for calling at such a terrible time and then grill a widow about her husband's life and career. Many of his and my calls would end moments after they started, but just as often, we were surprised that the survivors wanted to talk and wanted to portray their loved one in the best light.

Violence dominated the news then as now. Cleveland had more than 300 homicides one year when I was on the beat. We went to the scene of most of the killings. We competed with Press reporters on most, but sometimes we just shared our notes because we knew the story would only be a few paragraphs long.

There had been riots in 1966 and again in 1968, a year before I went on the beat. Black Nationalist groups, according to cops, were fighting one another for power. Police relations with the community were horrible.

Reporters got heat from all sides. The Plain Dealer issued police type helmets to reporters and photographers at one point in the early 1970s, but no one really wanted to stick out like a cop, so we put them in the car and didn't use them. They were available to us but went unused on May 4, 1970, when four students at Kent State were killed by Ohio National Guardsmen and Case Western Reserve students blocked Euclid Avenue, threw rocks and other debris at police and dug four graves in protest.

In 1973, The PD hit on a new theme. We were going to do more "people" stories. In March, I was loaned from my rewrite position to team with Investigative Reporter John Depke and general assignment reporter Tom Andrzejewski to cover the disappearance of 9-year-old Roxie Ann Keathley from her Sheffield Township apartment.

Our first story was a Sunday workup, but we had frustratingly little to write about. Roxie Ann was an aggressive youngster who knocked on apartment doors, sometimes bothering residents, to collect empty pop bottles for spending money. Police thought she might have been kidnapped or run away. Our story noted police believed she was still alive. She had cashed in $1.70 in bottles at a nearby Lawson's store.

Unknown to the three reporters who were piecing the story together on deadline that Saturday at a local restaurant was a key missing element. At the next table sat Timothy Papp, the 300-pound man later charged and convicted in the child's death. No doubt he could hear our loud banter as we chatted about each paragraph and quote. Later, by canvassing her apartment complex after her body had been found in the woods, I learned from the man who loaned it to him that Papp had borrowed a footlocker – the one he used to remove the body without others seeing what he was doing. But it was a short Page 1 story about mourners coming to the funeral home that drew so much attention from editors and changed my career path. Really, it was just a few paragraphs on the jump:

> *At one end of a large room lined with wooden chairs, was a small white coffin.*
>
> *Many of the family's friends cried as they stopped and offered prayers.*
>
> *Roxie Ann's body was dressed in a new light blue dress and had a pink hair ribbon. White*

lace gloves covered her hands. Beside the coffin was a folded newspaper with a picture of Roxie Ann on Page One.

Above the picture, a headline read: Police Say Roxie Ran Away; Mother Doesn't Believe It.

Absent from the funeral home for most of the afternoon were Roxie Ann's parents.

Clarence Carter, the funeral home operator, said: "They just couldn't take it anymore."

Two months later, I was a general assignment reporter doing investigative pieces.

I moved to a desk in what was called "The Swamp," a collection of desks held by some of the most talented reporters at The PD, among them political writer Robert McGruder, who would later become managing editor; John Depke, a great investigative reporter; medical writer Paula Slimak.

Don Bean told me it was too much, too soon for a youngster like me. My second week in the Swamp, Slimak chastised me for smelling like vodka in the morning. "You're way too young to start drinking like that," she angrily snapped one morning about 9 as I arrived for work with a slight buzz.

What she didn't know was that I had been trailing a municipal judge to Tasse's Lounge in Lakewood that morning to watch him down four shots of Dewar's White Label Scotch. He then left to drive to work. I had to drink, too, so as not to be noticed. We never talked, but we sat a couple of stools apart for days at a time.

The issue wasn't so much his drinking as his behavior on the bench afterward. In the previous 60 days he had dismissed charges against 19 defendants who later were indicted by a county grand jury. The crimes included rape, burglary and robbery. In one case, the judge granted personal bond to a mother and son charged with the murder of an off-duty Cleveland policeman. After police complaints and our questioning, the judge reversed himself and ordered a $50,000 bond for each. Fortunately, they turned themselves in.

Two bar association panels cleared the judge, Richard Matia, of wrongdoing in the 19 cases and criticized The Plain Dealer for its stories. Matia died from a cerebral hemorrhage in 1977 at the age of 62.

In January 1974, amid the Watergate investigation by a pair of Washington Post reporters and others, The PD formed a three-person Investigative Team headed by Depke. It included me. We had a great year starting that same month with a series about a half-dozen physicians selling huge amounts of prescriptions or actually dispensing the drugs for cash.

Reporters Christine Jindra and George Condon Jr., working undercover, purchased prescriptions from one Beachwood doctor, but we had to prove that the doctor actually wrote the scripts.

I had a cold sore, so I went in, handed the receptionist my old real estate card, and said I needed a script to clear up the mess on my face. Instead, the doctor came out and told me to roll up my sleeve. I thought our surveillance of his office might have been detected, but I rolled up my sleeve.

He gave me a shot. But then I asked if he knew of a prescription that might work. He pulled out his pad and wrote one. An expensive handwriting analysis later and we proved he was doing the scripts himself. Other doctors in Rocky River and Brooklyn also supplied us with scripts.

The medical board took action against all the doctors and one went to prison for a short stint.

In March we began a month-long series into police corruption starting with a story about how police with automatic weapons stood guard while their partners conducted a bank burglary. You couldn't make these stories up: Policemen involved in robberies and burglaries; cops who ransacked homes looking for money in full view of supervisors; policemen stealing car parts and accessories; policemen bribed to protect prostitution or cheat spots where gambling and drinking went on unhampered; on-duty cops drinking afterhours in bars and ignoring radio calls; and a policeman paying the rent for and hanging out with a prostitute.

Unbelievably, Mayor Ralph J. Perk appointed five members of the clergy to investigate the police department. It was dubbed the "God Squad" and the federal government sent $100,000 to help pay for the effort. Some police were sentenced to prison based on the FBI's and straight police investigations. They were already under investigation when our series started. Some police reform and reorganization resulted.

That August, Depke threw a pool party at a club near his West Side home to celebrate our successes.

About 2 a.m. I gathered a collection of box lunches left over from the party and headed to the St. Alexis Hospital emergency room where my wife was working the all-night shift. She was the only RN on duty.

Trudy was seven months pregnant with our first child. Everyone there was grateful for the food. I had some coffee with them and left. A short time later I was back, my face and arms covered in blood and glass shards. I was hit by a bullet in my neck. A rifleman had shot me through the driver side window as I pulled onto Interstate 77.

The bullet lodged near the carotid artery. A secretary went back to warn Trudy. When they got me on the gurney, Trudy inserted an IV into the back of my hand; the staff summoned a priest. Doctors began working on me. I made a quick, foggy confession when the priest arrived, received what was then called the last rites and headed to the intensive care unit while doctors pondered surgery.

Depke and Managing Editor Bob Burdock showed up in the ICU and grilled me about what I might have done to cause the shooting. Their questions agitated me so much that it set off the heart monitor, which summoned nurses who threw them out.

The shooting remains unsolved. I feared surgery might damage the artery so when doctors game me a choice, I decided to keep the bullet where it was.

My little incident soon disappeared from the news. As I sat in my hospital bed awaiting an Indians telecast, the game was pre-empted. President Richard Nixon resigned Aug. 8 at 9:04 p.m. to a nationally televised audience.

Trudy delivered a healthy baby boy, David, that November during a protracted, ugly newspaper strike, which began Halloween night and ended around Christmas. He was the first strike baby so he got his mug on TV. I was a picket captain on the midnight to 3 a.m. shift and freelanced police stories to the Sun Newspapers, which added publishing days to their once a week operations.

Today, I'm Chair of the Board at Rose-Mary, a Catholic Charities nonprofit that cares 24/7 for more than 90 children and adults with physical and developmental disabilities in 17 group homes in Cuyahoga County. Rose-Mary also runs an adult day care program for 30 men and women with disabilities. I'm happily retired from 43 years at The Plain Dealer. The first six were in circulation sales and in the newsroom as a copy boy; the last 25 as an executive in the newsroom, starting with city editor in 1981 and ending in 2006 when I was editor over the Washington bureau and the medical reporters.

It was a great run.

Shooting from the heart

WILLIAM WYNNE

"I saw him on an ash limb by morning's golden yellow light
Among shimmering green leaves after winter's flight"
~*"Morning Song," photograph and poem by William "Bill" Wynne*

Once in a while, a peaceful and mundane scene springs to life. That's the case with "Morning Song," the picture and couplet above. Our cottage on Charles Mill Lake in Mansfield, Ohio, was the scene of peaceful messages. In the early morning, while photographing daisies from the patio deck, the air was interrupted with the melody of a Song Sparrow. He continued his song so beautifully that I called the family out to hear it. The land drops off the back sharply toward the lake, adding another 10 feet of elevation to the deck height, so I had a 20-foot high vantage point – a bird's point of view.

The first photo I published was in YANK Magazine during World War II and was taken only two weeks after I got my destined-to-be-famous dog, Smoky, in Nadzab, New Guinea. We were just transferred into the 26th Photo Reconnaissance Squadron of the Fifth Air Force. I borrowed a

Speed Graphic camera from supply and placed her in a helmet inside my tent. (It was important to have a known object in the photo to show the true size of this four-pound dog. What better scale than a GI's helmet?)

There was no way of knowing at the time that her expression would reflect the epitome of happy anticipation involving what our lives would become during war and peace. Sixty years later, the photo became the model of three bronze memorials of Smoky, two in the United States and one in Australia, created by sculptor Susan Bahary.

Each phase of my photography is based upon what I learned while running the streets and fields in Cleveland, and from my companions before I turned 18.

What makes us who we are?

My wife Margie had two sayings: "Bill describes his photos, get out the violins" and "Bill is going to begin when he was 6 years old." And that's where I'll begin because in life, and in the arts in particular, your view of the world is the summation of life's experiences that start at a very early age. Those early experiences reflect in many ways your life as a whole. For some, early negative experiences can result in defeatism. For others, such experiences springboard into inspiration.

There are advantages and disadvantages to everything.

There can be influencing factors. For example, whether someone is part of a large or small family, or a family with no children. Each has its advantages and disadvantages. Further, the difference between growing up in a nuclear family or broken family adds to the mix that can affect one's life. A wealthy or a deprived upbringing, and having siblings or not can make a difference. How you make life choices may be influenced by the kids you played with, which may be absorbed negatively or positively.

I was from a broken family.

Dad took off when I was 3 years old. I spent two years in the Parmadale Children's Village of St. Vincent de Paul in Parma, from 1928 to 1930, with 400 other children. There were 40 kids to a cottage each run by one nun.

Coming home to my mother at age eight, I was a poor student who had flunked two years in grammar school as I ran the streets and fields of the West Park neighborhood of Cleveland. This is where I gained my most valuable education; I have drawn upon this my entire life. I cannot emphasize enough the value and sheer pleasure involved in the freedom of running the streets. However, this was not conducive to traditional homework and study (the disadvantage), and thus the failures. The streets were the foundation of who Billy Wynne was and is: the dog trainer, the inventor at the National Advisory Committee for Aeronautics (later, in 1958, theNational Aeronautics and Space Administration), and the photojournalist with unusual views.

At age 20, I graduated from West Technical High School, where I specialized in horticulture, a Cornell University three-year program, along with one year in elective photography. During this period, my high school grades moved from Ds to Cs. Mr. Howard, an accountant neighbor, would say, "Bill is going to amount to something someday," giving me an unforgettable upward lift in spirits. Meanwhile, my family would ask, "I wonder what will become of Billy?"

Following high school, I was fortunate to be associated with highly educated professionals. The Air Force in WWII required at least a 100 IQ score. My 26th Photo Reconnaissance Squadron had college professors working in photography, not to mention the bright and young "just out of high school" pilots. As top scientist and friend Irving Pinkel said, "Bill learns by osmosis." (Pinkel worked for the National Aeronautics and Space Administration). My work at NASA Lewis Flight Propulsion Laboratory followed Air Force schooling in laboratory and aerial photography and having served two years overseas in the Pacific Theater with the 26th Photo Reconnaissance Squadron (New Guinea to Okinawa), to the war's end. I also did a three-month stint in Hollywood as a motion picture dog handler, another continuing story.

I was hired for NASA's Flight Icing Research Program as an aerial photographer. I learned so much over the seven-year period I was there. At end of the first three years, I became a "photo engineer," and I invented a camera timer and other photo technology for the Full-Scale Aircraft Crash Fire Program. The timer illustrated the *true speed* of any motion picture camera within 1/10th of a second.

With my large family and low pay, and with much regret on my part (and my supervisors), I had two weeks to decide whether to take a job at the Cleveland Plain Dealer in the photo department. By switching jobs I went from working 25 years into the future to working 25 years into the past. The PD was getting racetrack results in the sports department via Morse Code, using dots and dashes – 19th century technology. I was hired to replace Ed Solotko, a fine photographer, working on The Sunday Magazine.

So what is a SPEAKING photograph that has a message?

Today, most photos are images that are captured by millions of people everyday by smartphones. They are, by and large, merely "let me show you something." Then, there is photojournalism, a form of communication involving photography*and*journalism that, unfortunately, often just "shows something" as well. Few news photos really *say* something. Digital cameras can shoot multiple frames per second, and the photographer can select the best frames. In my early days, cameras were cumbersome, and required several steps of preparation for each shot, going through the routine again and again. Timing by the photographer in action photos was critical.

So, what can photographs SAY? Oh, so many things. A photograph can record a sacred scene that can generate tears, or deliver an instant smile.

It can be a symbol so profound it says it all.

Photography is so often like music rather than art; often an event building to a crescendo.

On a slow day for hard news, "weather art," stand-alone photos or people or nature, would more than likely make Page 1. Photographers were asked to look out for "weather art."

Readers are overwhelmed by gloom every day, and always hunger for some good news.

My good friend Bill McVey, a great artist, teacher and the sculptor of the Winston Churchill Statue in Washington, D.C., was a great admirer of photographers. He demonstrated for me how a photographer is similar to a javelin thrower. Leaning in a low backward stance of a javelin thrower and pointing with his arm along an imaginary javelin line up toward the sky, he proclaimed, "You point to an imaginary sky spot, get ready – and then thrust yourself with all your might." Then he followed through by standing on his left leg with his arm and forefinger still pointing at the spot that followed the imaginary release of the javelin – frozen in midair.

"This is a photographer" exclaimed Bill. He gathers all of his worldly knowledge into a compressed self and suddenly, with his timing, presses the shutter with the forefinger and the mental power of everything he is – and it all comes out in a tiny 'click.' That is a photographer."

Thank you Bill. I never thought of it that way.

As my wife Margie said, "Now you see why Bill explains his photos."

So there you have it – shots from the heart, from a sometimes funny guy.

~

Photographer William "Bill" Wynne was interviewed by Dave Davis and Bill Barrow on Jan. 27, 2018. The following Q&A was edited for space and clarity.

Davis: So, for an image, what are you looking for? What's a Bill Wynne picture?

Editor's note: Wynne opens a scrap book of photographs, newspaper clippings and note's about his life and work. He points out a picture from the day President John F. Kennedy was shot.

Wynne: What had happened- Gordon Cobbledick was the sports editor. And Cobby came into the photo lab about noon and he says, "Hey Bill, any photographers here?" I said, "No, what's up?" He said, "Well, the president's been shot down in Texas and an AP photographer saw blood." So, the story (was) still coming over the wire at this point. And he says to me, "Will you go out and tell the people in the city room and I'll go to the brass' offices and I'll tell them."

So, I'm looking around for a picture and there was no picture there. I went out on the street and nobody knew about it yet. I look at St. Peter's across the street. It's diagonal from The Plain Dealer. St. Peter's was a high school. I'm waiting and waiting, and I thought someone's going to have to know something about this and sure enough, all of a sudden, I hear a lot of sobbing and I look and the kids are filing out through the corridor to go to the church to pray.

There were two white girls and a black girl (who) came out and I got the pictures of the teachers sobbing and the kids sobbing. And so, these two came along and the black girl is crying so much that the white girl turns around and puts her arms around her.

Davis: Wow.

Wynne: And so I took a picture of that. So that became "Summation, Nov. 22, 1963." It was a summation of the way the nation felt. Trying to get it published in The Plain Dealer was something else because no paper would ever publish any of these interracial photos.

Davis: Did they publish it?

Wynne: They had to, finally.

Davis: It sounds like such a powerful image.

Wynne: I had to go to Ted Vorpe and get Bill Ashbolt to put it in the paper. Ted Princiotto came to me and he had the four pictures. He wanted the sobbing kids and the teachers, and that picture and Bill says, "No we haven't any room in the paper. There's too much stuff coming from Texas." So, OK, then I said to Ted Vorpe, he was the head of photography at the

St. Peters High School students comfort each other after hearing of the death of President John F. Kennedy. Special Collections, Cleveland State University Library.

time, "I think this picture is an important picture. It ought to be published." He said, "I agree with you Bill."

So, he went over and talked to Bill Ashbolt and they put it in a first edition and killed it after that.

Davis: Really, are you kidding me?

Editor's note: The Catholic Universe Bulletin published the picture.

Wynne: But the Catholic Universe Bulletin wire service wouldn't pick it up.

It was only in- Well, it's in the (Plain Dealer) first city edition. Only the city edition had it, which goes down state. We had 84,000 circulation down (state) at that time.

And so that's the story of "Summation." (In the print), the girls even accidentally came out where their uniforms looked like one jacket they're both in and one dress that they're in, (with) their four legs – black legs and white legs – sticking out the bottom.

And so, I have another couple pictures that- This was an accidental picture here. I got up on a diving board at CSU. The NCAA diving championships were played that year, 1975 or '76, I can't remember. But anyhow after they had their competition they start practicing. So, I got up on the highest diving board. And I take the picture of this guy doing a swan dive. See it? But it was taken on Holy Thursday and here look at the cross in the water.

So (sports editor) Hal Lebovitz, being an Orthodox Jew, ran this on Good Friday in the sports page. Honest to gosh.

Davis: Did he get any-

Wynne: I don't think so. He didn't have any flack at all.

Davis: Did anybody ever complain about the picture of the school girls hugging after the assassination? Did any readers ever call anybody?

Wynne: No, nobody ever did. If they did, I didn't hear about it.

Davis: So, it was just journalists being anxious about what their audiences might think.

Wynne: That's right. So, this is the Lima State Hospital story.

There was abuse at the Lima State Hospital, which was (for) the people who didn't get the death sentence because they were mentally ill. So, they threw them in the Lima State Hospital. And they had these guards there, they used to beat the people up every day. They killed some. There's unmarked graves there. So, we found out about it through the governor's office.

Editor's note: After receiving a complaint, Ohio Gov. John Gilligan asked a lawyer to investigate the claims.

Wynne: So, he calls us. And Ned Whelan, Dick Widman and I go out. Ned and Widman were changing motel rooms every day because these guards will kill you.

Barrow: Really?

Davis: This looks like it was in May of 1971, Bill.

Wynne: Does it? OK.

So anyhow. We ran a series. We ran a Page 1 story on this for 30 days straight and this was a big exposé. And one day one of these guys (at the Lima State Hospital) comes up to me, and I got the camera dangling around my neck and I've been taking pictures. And he said, "Who are you with?" And I pointed to (the lawyer) and I says, "I'm with him." I didn't tell him I was with The Plain Dealer.

I was a state roving photographer/reporter for four years.

Davis: You did some reporting too?

Wynne: Oh, yeah.

Anyhow, this woman here was kept like this in a stupor, under a shower. When she'd go to the bathroom, they'd just flush the shower down on top of her.

Editor's note: News that the governor was sending people to Lima reached the hospital, which cleaned up its act when The PD team first got there.

Wynne: They got word up there, so they let her get up. You see she's sober (alert) here. So, they (the governor's representatives) look, and they couldn't see anything wrong.

Editor's note: But Wynne returned the next day, when he wasn't expected.

Wynne: Here she is in a stupor.

Editor's note: Wynne flips through his scrapbook.

Wynne: These are Newspaper Guild (awards) – best picture, best photo of the year.

And this is called, "Three Touches of Freedom." Freedom of Expression. Freedom of Enterprise. Freedom of Religion. I just happened to get it all into one picture. And so, I was taking (pictures of) the kids... I was waiting outside. I saw the flag on the ground and I was going to see what they did with the flag. All of a sudden there's four of them together and this little boy jumps up and touches the flag and I snapped the picture.

When I develop it, I find I got the truck in there and I got the church. It was a natural.

This picture here- I saw this bird.

Editor's note: See picture "Morning Song" at the top of this page.

This picture of a woman in a stupor under a shower is one of many taken by William "Bill" Wynne, documenting abuse and deplorable conditions at the Lima State Hospital. Special Collections, Cleveland State University Library.

Wynne: What happened was. We're at my cottage and I'm shooting the daisies. And all of a sudden, I hear this songbird. It's May and (it's a) beautiful song because this is a song sparrow. So, I go over to see him, and I got a 500 mm lens on there and I thought I'd never get the picture because it's not particularly the sharpest lens. It's a mirror lens.

Anyhow, I hear the bird and I go out over there with this long lens and I take one shot. I don't think I'm going to get it. Two hundred fiftieth of a second because it's a 500 mm lens, you got to hold that really steady. So, I shot it and I forgot about it and it was in my camera for about three or four more days because I was shooting assignments. Later, and I came back I developed them. I said, "Gee, I'll try to print that."

I decided I'd give it to the picture desk. They're always looking for what they call weather art. They're gonna run it on Page 1. Something happened with the Pope. So, they bumped it inside to Page 6. And so, all of us got in that morning and the phones were jumping off the hook. Calls from all over the country. They were coming from everywhere.

(Publisher) Tom Vail's office was getting them. Everybody was getting them. We ended up getting over a thousand. Here are the letters to the editor that were written about it and they published it again. And one woman, a nurse, wrote that this older woman she was taking care of had this beat up clipping in her wallet and she was looking at it all the time. Could she get actually a print? So, we gave her a print.

And somebody else wrote and said, "Thank God that somebody sees some beauty in this world." It was a shocker. So, then I wrote a couplet for it. It didn't have the couplet when it went out.

Davis: They should have moved the Pope inside.

Wynne: The day when it was going out on the wire. I wrote a couplet and it was something like: "I saw him on an ash limb by morning's golden yellow light. Among shimmering green leaves after winter's flight." AP ran it under this picture. So, the couplet is in there under the picture.

Editor's note: The Plain Dealer hired Wynne because of his experience in color photography, which was new at the time.

Davis: And what year was this?

Wynne: 1953.

Davis: OK, so color was-

Wynne: Sunday Magazine was using color.

Davis: So, it was beginning to happen, but it was new.

Wynne: They were already- Vern Cady was working in it. But they needed a helper and they also needed a photographer.

Davis: Now how long were you at The Plain Dealer?

Wynne: Thirty-one years.

My comment is overall photography (is) not very well understood by journalism, journalists. And it became an arm of support (for) an article. They didn't really know how to hire people (and) so some of the heads of photographers are questionable. I don't want to name names.

The way you pick photographers- They were (the most) miscast bunch of guys I'd ever seen. Ray Matjasic was really good. He was a combat photographer in the Marines. He was a truck driver for The Plain Dealer and he fought his way into photography. He became chief photographer.

The brass on the upper level doesn't understand the photography at all. They leave that go the way it's been going for years and years. And what you end up with is a bunch of photographers that show something. They don't say something.

The mayor of Parma Heights said, "Bill makes his camera talk." And that was a good definition. I didn't realize it at the time. But the camera- it might have a purpose for having a picture. And we have so many pictures that don't really have a purpose.

You don't see pictures that say something, like the girls with their arms around each other.

The way they worked photography and photographers in most newspapers. (If) you happen to get somebody who's really interested in it at the higher level-

They had times where you had good people at the top and then you had better photography because they were more careful how they hired and more discriminating about what they ran in the paper. Most of it was to fill holes. It's a place to fill a hole so you don't have to have so much copy.

Davis: Do you remember what the circulation was at the high point?

Wynne: It was about 520,000 on Sundays.

Davis: OK, lots of readers. So, did it serve Cleveland well or not so well?

Wynne: Yeah, when I came to The Plain Dealer they used to say it was the "Grand Old Lady of the West." But it was very conservative. The Press did have some good reporters over there too. They were highly competitive and then the News had good people.

Davis: Well, it sounds like kind of a heyday in journalism in Cleveland because you had three dailies plus the Catholic Universe Bulletin.

Wynne: Really competitive. Even the Heights paper was pretty good, The Sun.

Davis: So, when all these people were going after things and you're competing-

Wynne: Oh, yeah, you're competing. You had competition.

Davis: And what did that fella say, the mayor- "Your camera tells a story."

Wynne: My camera talks. Yeah, but that's what it should be.

It's so easy now. Brrrrrrr and they can do it. We had to be very selective. When we took the picture, it was very selective, and you missed a lot of pictures. There was 17 ways to miss a picture. You gotta have film exposed, and the shutter has to work, and you have to have the right exposure.

Other than that, the curtain can be down in the back and blind out your picture. You could have no film in the camera, the film could fall out of the whole thing. There's so many ways to miss the picture, that there's hardly any ways to get it. And so, we were working with really clumsy equipment, but we made it work. And once in a while you come back to the office saying, "I missed it."

Barrow: And then you look at the paper, the rival paper and that guy caught it.

Wynne: That could happen to you. Now, they can send it back on telephone. They don't even come in the office.

I was not objective. I was subjective. And I'm editorializing because we're making a statement.

Why the Press used "all its editorial artillery" against Dr. Sam Sheppard

LOUIS B. SELTZER

On the morning of July 4, 1954, Mrs. Marilyn Reese Sheppard, a pretty Bay Village housewife, was found bludgeoned to death in her bedroom.

For mystery, for suspense, for painstaking putting together of fragmentary clues by the most scientific methods, the Sheppard murder, which was to become one of the country's most famous in modern times, had within it all of the elements of the classic criminal case.

It had one other element, which set it apart from most murder cases of this type. That was the deliberate effort to prevent the law enforcement authorities from finding the killer. The case became both a murder and, in a very real sense, a roadblock against the law.

At the time Marilyn Reese Sheppard was brutally killed, only two other persons were present in the quiet lakefront home, settled among big trees a comfortable distance away from the roadway. One of these was Dr. Samuel H. Sheppard, her husband, a young, handsome, athletic osteopath, and, the other, the Sheppards' sleeping son Chip, aged six.

Bay Village is a tightly knit community to the west of Cleveland. It is composed largely of young people who either have their own businesses, are fairly well established in the professions, or have a competence. It is a community of beautiful homes, peaceful and quiet, but socially vivacious. Families visit back and forth in the easy, relaxed, and buoyant way common to newly created small communities with a youthful flavor. They are very loyal to one another when any form of trouble occurs.

The family of Dr. Sam Sheppard owned a large osteopathic hospital in the village. His father and brothers operated it, with Sam Sheppard, of course, also on the staff.

It was to the Sheppard family's hospital that Dr. Sam was taken by his family immediately after the murder of his wife was reported. The reason given for hospitalizing him was that an intruder – a bushy-haired man, as Dr. Sam described him – had injured his neck in the struggle the doctor reported had taken place in the house. Thus, the Sheppard family surrounded Dr. Sam.

The investigating authorities were blocked off. The Mayor of Bay Village was J. Spencer Houk, who owned the local butcher shop and was a close friend of Dr. Sam. They visited back and forth; they went on vacations together; they owned a boat together. Mayor Houk rejected the advice of Coroner Sam Gerber and the Cleveland Homicide Squad that Dr. Sam should be arrested.

Dr. Sam was fenced in by his family, his friends, and the public authorities in Bay Village. The protective wall had been put up quickly. It was almost impossible to penetrate it, and then only at the will of those who controlled the encirclement – and on their terms. The purpose seemed obvious — to hold the wall secure around Dr. Sam until public interest subsided, and the investigating authorities turned their attention elsewhere.

The newspapers began to lose interest — except one. The Press kept the Sheppard murder case in top position on Page 1. It kept steadily prying into the case, asking questions, trying to break through the wall around Dr. Sam.

On July 15, 11 days after Marilyn Reese Sheppard's badly beaten body had been found in the bedroom of their home, I addressed a list of 11 questions to Dr. Sam and his lawyers — one of whom was a prominent criminal lawyer hired by the Sheppard family the very morning Marilyn's body had been found.

Dr. Sam's reply was published on July 17. The answers were noninformative and inconclusive. The situation was just as tight, just as completely roadblocked, just as walled in as before.

On July 20, with the investigation lagging, with the Coroner still fended off by the family and Bay Village friends and officials, The Press published on Page 1 an editorial. It took the upper quarter of the page, and the eight-column heading said: "Somebody Is Getting Away With Murder."

It was a calculated risk — a hazard of the kind which I believed a newspaper sometimes in the interest of law and order and the community's ultimate safety must take. I was convinced that a conspiracy existed to defeat the ends of justice, and that it would affect adversely the whole law-enforcement machinery of the County if it were permitted to succeed. It could establish a precedent that would destroy even-handed administration of justice.

Because I did not want anyone else on The Press staff to take the risk, I wrote the editorial myself. It may not have been a good editorial, but it was a hard-hitting editorial. It was intended to be. It read in part:

> What's the matter with the law enforcement authorities of Cuyahoga County?
>
> Have they lost their sense of reason? — or, at least inexcusably, set aside the realization of what they are hired to do, and for whom they work?
>
> If ever a murder case was studded with fumbling, halting, stupid, incooperative bungling — politeness to people whose place in this situation completely justified vigorous searching, prompt and effective police work — the Sheppard case has them all.
>
> Was the murder of Mrs. Sheppard a polite matter?
>
> Did the killer make a dutiful bow to the authorities and, then, proceed brutally to destroy the young childbearing wife?
>
> Why all of this sham, hypocrisy, politeness, crisscrossing of pomp and protocol in this case?
>
> Who is trying to deceive whom?

From the very beginning – from the first hour that the murder became known to the authorities by a telephone call from the husband to the Town Mayor – from that moment on, and including this, the case has been one of the worst in local crime history.

Of course, the trail is cold. Of course, the clues have been virtually erased by the killer. Of course, the whole thing is botched-up so badly that head or tail cannot be made of it.

In the background of this case are friendships, relationships, hired lawyers, a husband who ought to have been subjected instantly, to the same third-degree to which any other person, under similar circumstances is subjected, and a whole string of special and bewildering extra-privileged courtesies that should never be extended by authorities investigating a murder – the most serious and sickening crime of all.

The spectacle of a whole community watching a batch of law enforcement officials fumbling around, stumbling over one another, bowing and scraping in the presence of people they ought to be dealing with just as firmly as any other persons in any other crime – that spectacle is not only becoming a stench, but a serious threat to the dignity of law enforcement itself.

Coroner Sam Gerber was never more right than when yesterday he said that the killer must be laughing secretly at the whole spectacle – the spectacle of a community of a million and a half people brought to indignant frustration by Mrs. Sheppard's killer in that white house out in Bay Village.

Why shouldn't he chuckle? Why shouldn't he cover up, shut up, conceal himself behind the circle of protecting people?

What's the matter with us in Cuyahoga County? Who are we afraid of? Why do we have to kow-tow to a set of circumstances and people where a murder has been committed?

It's time that somebody smashed into this situation and tore aside this restraining curtain of sham, politeness, and hypocrisy, and went at the business of solving a murder – and quit this nonsense of artificial politeness that has not been extended to any other murder case in generations.

The evening this editorial was published in The Press on Page 1, the Bay Village City Council met and voted to take the investigation away from their own police force and hand it over to the Cleveland Police Department's Homicide Squad.

The next day, also on Page 1, The Press published an editorial headed: "Why No Inquest? Do It Now, Dr. Gerber."

> Why hasn't County Coroner Sam Gerber called an inquest into the Sheppard murder case?
>
> What restrains him?
>
> Is the Sheppard case any different from the countless other murder mysteries where the Coroner has turned to this traditional method of investigation?
>
> An inquest empowers use of subpoena.
>
> It puts witnesses under oath.
>
> It makes possible the examination of every possible witness, suspect, relative, record and papers available anywhere.
>
> It puts the investigation itself into the record.
>
> And – what's most important of all – sometimes solves crimes.
>
> What good reason is there now for Dr. Gerber to delay any longer the use of the inquest?
>
> The murder of Marilyn Sheppard is a baffling crime.
>
> Thus far, it appears to have stumped everybody.
>
> It may never be solved.
>
> But this community can never have a clear conscience, until every possible method is applied to its solution.
>
> What, Coroner Gerber, is the answer to the question –
>
> Why don't you call an inquest into this murder?

A few hours after this editorial appeared on Page 1 of The Cleveland Press, Coroner Gerber ordered an inquest.

At the inquest, Dr. Sam insisted his married life had been a happy one. He denied an "affair" with a former Bay Village Hospital technician now living in California. The Press flew a reporter to Los Angeles with the police. The technician was brought back to Cleveland. She admitted her affair with Dr. Sam, and related talks she had with Dr. Sam about a possible marriage.

The wall still surrounded Dr. Sam. He had gone back to the family-operated hospital.

On July 30, The Cleveland Press published, again spread across the top of its first page, another editorial. This one was headed: "Quit Stalling – Bring Him In." Once more I wrote it myself. It was my neck I was sticking out.

Maybe somebody in this town can remember a parallel for it. The Press can't.

And not even the oldest police veterans can, either.

Everybody's agreed that Sam Sheppard is the most unusual murder suspect ever seen around these parts.

Except for some superficial questioning during Coroner Sam Gerber's inquest, he has been scot-free of any official grilling into the circumstances of his wife's murder.

From the morning of July 4, when he reported his wife's killing, to this moment, 26 days later, Sam Sheppard has not set foot in a police station.

He has been surrounded by an Iron Curtain of protection that makes Malenkov's Russian concealment amateurish.

His family, his Bay Village friends — which include its officials — his lawyers, his hospital staff, have combined to make law enforcement in this County look silly.

The longer they can stall bringing Sam Sheppard to the police station the more surer it is he'll never get there.

The longer they can string this whole affair out the surer it is that the public's attention sooner, or later, will be diverted to something else, and then the heat will be off, the public interest gone, and the goose will hang high.

This man is a suspect in his wife's murder. Nobody yet has found a solitary trace of the presence of anybody else in the Lake Road house the night or morning his wife was brutally beaten to death in her bedroom.

And yet, no murder suspect in the history of this County has been treated so tenderly, with such infinite solicitude for his emotions, with such fear of upsetting the young man.

Gentlemen of Bay Village, Cuyahoga County, and Cleveland, charged jointly with law enforcement –

This is murder. This is no parlor game. This is no time to permit anybody — no matter who he is — to outwit, stall, fake, or improvise devices to keep away from the police or from the questioning anybody in his right mind knows a murder suspect should be subjected to — at a police station.

The officials throw up their hands in horror at the thought of bringing Sam Sheppard to a police questioning for grilling. Why? Why is he any different than anybody else in any other murder case?

> *Why should the police officials be afraid of Bill Corrigan, his lawyer? Or anybody else, for that matter, when they are at their sworn business of solving a murder?*
>
> *Certainly, Corrigan will act to protect Sam Sheppard's rights. He should.*
>
> *But the people of Cuyahoga County expect you, the law enforcement officials, to protect the people's rights.*
>
> *A murder has been committed. You know who the chief suspect is.*
>
> *You have the obligation to question him – question him thoroughly and searchingly – from beginning to end, and not at his hospital, not at his home, not in some secluded spot out in the country.*
>
> *But at Police Headquarters – just as you do every other person suspected in a murder case.*
>
> *What the people of Cuyahoga County cannot understand, and The Press cannot understand, is why you are showing Sam Sheppard so much more consideration as a murder suspect than any other person who has ever before been suspected in a murder case.*
>
> *Why?*

That night Dr. Sam was arrested on a murder charge and taken to Police Headquarters.

The rest of the Sam Sheppard case is familiar. He was indicted by the grand jury, tried in a courtroom crowded with newspaper, radio, and television representatives from all over America, convicted of second degree murder, and sentenced to the Ohio Penitentiary, where he is now a prisoner.

The Cleveland Press was both applauded and criticized. It was criticized on the ground that The Press inflamed public opinion by its persistent and vigorous pounding away at the case. It was criticized by some who expressed the belief that the Sheppard case had been "tried" in the newspapers before it reached the courtroom.

The question confronting The Press, as a newspaper properly concerned about the whole structure of law enforcement in the community, was – Shall we permit a protective wall to shield a solution to this murder, by saying and doing nothing, or –

Shall we move in with all of our editorial artillery in an effort to bring the wall down, and make it possible for law enforcement authorities to act in their normal and accustomed way?

There were risks both ways. One represented a risk to the community. The other was a risk to The Press. We chose the risk to ourselves.

As Editor of The Press I would do the same thing over again under the same circumstances.

~This piece was originally published in "The Years Were Good: The Autobiography of Louis B. Seltzer." It is used with permission. See https://tinyurl.com/CSULouisSeltzer.

Editor's note: On Dec. 21, 1954, Sam Sheppard was found guilty of second degree murder in the death of his wife, Marilyn, and sentenced to life in prison, beginning a series of appeals that ended when the U.S. Supreme Court in 1966 overturned the verdict. Sheppard was retried and found not guilty on Nov. 16, 1966. The aggressive coverage by the media in the investigation and trail of Sheppard prompted a heated debate over the public's right to know versus the right of a defendant to a fair trail unprejudiced by excessive publicity. In 1991, the City Club of Cleveland held a forum on the issue with reporter Doris O'Donnell and lawyer J. Michael Murry. (See: https://tinyurl.com/CityClubSheppard).

A backstage pass to momentous events

CARRIE BUCHANAN

How a Cleveland journalist wound up onstage with Jane Fonda, when the actress came to this city in 1979 to promote the movie "9 to 5," is a somewhat circuitous story, much like the careers of many female journalists of her generation. Gail Stuehr's onstage presence arose from an article she'd written on women in the workplace for Cleveland Magazine's special issue on women in December 1978. A scene from the article, featuring female employees meeting in the ladies' room at a Cleveland savings and loan association, examining pay stubs of men doing the same job as theirs for higher pay, ended up in the movie. It was one of many stories of challenges, unfair practices and harassment in Stuehr's article, which explored the lives of women entering the workforce in large numbers in a new era of supposed liberation. An italicized biographical note beneath the article says, "*Gail Stuehr is a Cleveland-area freelance writer who knows firsthand the stresses of balancing a job, home and a family of four.*"

No kidding. It's the story of her life.

Stuehr's career has had its ups, downs and sidetracks, but journalism, she says, has always been her calling. She discovered it during college in the 1950s and is still practicing it today at age 80. In the intervening decades, she balanced a freelance career during the tumultuous 1970s in Cleveland's inner-ring suburbs with raising four children – duties her then-husband, like many of his generation, did not share – covering evening meetings as a stringer for The Plain Dealer and the Southeast Sun, a member of the Sun chain of community newspapers. When it came time for a full-time job in 1978, she opted for the somewhat more regular hours of public relations, working for many years at Case Western Reserve University, then the Cleveland Heights-University Heights School District and later, the United Way. This work kept her involved with journalists, facilitating their stories while doing her own interviews, writing, editing and production of magazines, brochures and annual reports – and winning many awards along the way. Now, in her supposed retirement, she writes regularly for the Lake County Tribune.

"I can't even keep up with her and she's 80," says her youngest daughter Andrea Stuehr, 45. Andrea and her siblings recently put on a party for their mom's 80th birthday at which their mother's friends told stories even her children didn't know about their "unassuming" parent. That's a term several people, including her children, used to describe Stuehr. She's modest, doesn't brag about her accomplishments, but if you ask she's got lots of stories to share.

The world of journalism opened up for Stuehr in her late teens at the University of Michigan, where she spent one glorious year in a top journalism school, transferring there after two years in liberal arts at Muskingum University. But it was not to last. Her senior year, she had to transfer back to Ohio as her family in Parma found the out-of-state tuition prohibitive. She finished up her degree at Kent State University, where she combined an education major with a few courses in journalism — Kent State didn't yet have its large journalism school — graduating with a teaching certificate that she never actually used. It prepared her for a career in which women were readily accepted. She ended up, instead, in one where the path was far less smooth. But, as she repeats many times in an interview, "It was interesting."

At Kent State, Stuehr had her first encounter with Theta Sigma Phi, the journalism fraternity for women (and no, they didn't call it a sorority), who were not welcome in Sigma Delta Chi, the all-male journalism honor society that later became the Society of Professional Journalists. SPJ did not admit women until 1969. What Stuehr discovered later was that having an all-female professional organization supporting your career was a blessing rather than a problem.

"It was one of the best things that could have happened to me," she says. That group of female colleagues, now called the Association for Women in Communication, was a godsend when she returned to work after a decade as a full-time wife and mother to four children, part of it living in Germany, where her scientist then-husband, John E. Stuehr, spent a postdoctoral year in 1963 and a later term as a visiting scholar at the Max Planck Institute, after becoming a chemistry professor at Case Western Reserve.

By the time her oldest child was 6, in 1970, Stuehr was ready to return to journalism, which she had practiced as a student but had not been able to develop right afterward as a career. She got her start in freelancing thanks to a Theta Sigma Phi contact, Jean McCann, who went on to become an award-winning medical writer. McCann recommended that Stuehr apply for the freelance gig McCann was vacating as a stringer for The Plain Dealer, covering Maple Heights. Soon afterward, Stuehr took on the Maple Heights beat for the weekly Southeast Sun as well.

Banish any image you might have of sleepy suburban coverage! The early 1970s were days of racial and civil unrest, as African-Americans moved out of Cleveland's inner city and into inner-ring suburbs like Maple Heights, the Vietnam War and anti-war protests were raging, and the environmental movement was picking up steam. And then there was Stuehr's relentlessly energetic approach to journalism. Her children, particularly the two older ones, have vivid memories of that time.

"There was always a Minolta camera in the car," recalls David Stuehr, 51, now an attorney in Massachusetts. "We would see fire trucks and (she would say), 'Wonder where they're going?'" Then, his mother would "whip the car around, reaching for the camera" and head for the scene.

"Half the time, I remember not making it to where we were supposed to be going," says Laura Gruszczynski, 53, whose career in video production, animation and motion graphics carries on her mother's focus on communications. Life with her mom was "never boring," she recalls. "It was unpredictable."

One day, Gruszczynski remembers being at a medical appointment on Green Road when a bomb scare led to the evacuation of the building. "My mom takes me to the funeral home across the street and says, 'Stay here,' and runs off to go talk to the bomb squad."

David Stuehr recalls being at Cedar Point for the first day of the Gemini roller coaster. "That was a big deal," he says. "We were having a great time and she was taking notes."

Another time, also at Cedar Point, a balcony collapsed during a well-attended Christian youth festival, causing serious injuries. The Stuehr children were clamoring to go on the amusement park's rides, "and Mom's on the damned pay phone," calling in the story. "Sometimes it was a colossal pain in the ass" being a news reporter's kid, he quips.

Another vivid memory was of a school board meeting that Stuehr had to take her children to because a baby sitter wasn't available. "There had been some pretty brutal racial fights going on in the schools. We were sitting there with our coloring books ... people were screaming, people were crying" as they addressed the school board about the situation, David Stuehr recalls. "And we're in the middle of this."

For Andrea Stuehr, the youngest of the four, whose career is working with show jumping horses, the memories are mostly of her mother's later years in public relations, when she would sometimes accompany her on cross-country trips to interview famous Case Western alumni for the medical school's alumni bulletin. "She traveled the country doing this, and I came with her." She remembers being in an elevator in Washington D.C. and suddenly saying to her mom, "Get me out of this elevator!" Turned out the interviewee, who was with them, was a psychiatrist with Veterans Affairs whose specialty was post-traumatic stress. He was very understanding of the child's need to get out of the enclosed elevator.

While she didn't fully appreciate it at the time, Andrea Stuehr said she later realized that her mom was "kind of a big deal" who knew important people all over the country and even abroad. While at Case Western Reserve, Stuehr helped to arrange visits by international speakers whom she squired around the city. She often talks about one such visit, when Stuehr had to pick up a then-Soviet minister of health, Dr. Yevgeny Chazov, and his interpreter in her tiny car during a blizzard. Chazov was recalled to Russia earlier than expected because Konstantin Chernenko, then president of the Union of Soviet Socialist Republics, was on his deathbed. Chazov's early departure touched off a flurry of international media calls and speculation about Chernenko's failing health.

Stuehr's work colleagues also recall her aptitude for hard work, nose for news, writing ability and the kind of vision that can take a publication from piles of paper on the dining room table, as daughter Andrea recalls, to a printed publication fit for national distribution.

Paula Slimak, who hired Gail Stuehr twice to work with her in public relations – first at Case Western Reserve and, 20 years later, at the United Way – said her journalism skills meant she worked well with the media and was able to anticipate and meet their needs. "She always stayed in the background. She was a facilitator," Slimak said.

When producing publications of their own, Slimak said, "I could count on Gail – like when we did the Guitar Mania project." Stuehr wrote descriptions of all the giant-sized guitars featured around the city in a campaign that has, since its first appearance in 2002, raised more than $2 million for the United Way and the Rock & Roll Hall of Fame's educational programs, according to United Way.

"She and I have been on deadline together many times," says Slimak, who also has a journalism background and worked for The Plain Dealer before moving into public relations.

Their first campaign together was for the 1980 centennial of the former Case Institute of

Technology, which had joined with Western Reserve University in 1967 to form Case Western Reserve. "We did a tabloid. She and I did the entire thing," as one of many initiatives the public relations team at Case Western Reserve produced for the centennial. A speaker series, including several Nobel prizewinners, was another major initiative.

Perhaps most important, says Slimak, "She's someone you can count on – professionally and personally." This sentiment was echoed by retired University Heights Councilwoman Adele Zucker, another woman who started out in journalism, who worked for years with Stuehr as a volunteer with Theta Sigma Phi and later, Women in Communications, including organizing major conferences and speakers.

"She will do anything, if you need something. She's right there, Johnny on the spot, to help you if you need something," says Zucker. "She will find a way or say she can't do it. You could always discuss things with Gail."

Stuehr herself points to three major skills she learned in journalism and brought to her public relations work later: first, her understanding of what makes a good story; second, her ability to conceive, write and edit a publication; and third, her gift at "schmoozing" – another word for networking.

"My mother can hang with anybody," says daughter Andrea Stuehr. "She does ask questions, and that's unusual. Most people don't ask questions."

For David and Laura, the two older Stuehr children, the dinner-table conversations and behind-the-scenes knowledge of how things work were a major benefit of their upbringing.

"Growing up, we had some strange insights because of the journalism background. We knew things," David says. "It's like a world view that other people didn't have. An attitude, an understanding that there was stuff in the world and there was stuff behind the stuff – a layer that most people don't know exists.

"We kind-of-like had a backstage pass."

How I became a newspaper woman against all odds

JANET BEIGHLE FRENCH

I was born into a family of teachers – grandmother, parents, aunts, an uncle, and, eventually, sister, brother-in-law, cousin and her daughter. I understood that I was expected to follow suit, specifically to become a home economics teacher, "so you can get a job," said my mother.

But in junior high school, in Bellingham, Washington, a friend suggested we both try out for the school newspaper staff. We were accepted. I was named sports editor, then editor. I discovered that writing was a LOT of fun. In high school, I joined the staffs of the newspaper, the annual, and poetry magazine.

College was a given in our family and I mentioned majoring in journalism, perhaps at the University of Washington. "That school is too big," said my mother, and besides prospects for a journalism job would likely be much dimmer than for teaching. And I should spend my first year at the local teacher's college to save money. So that's where I went, and I began to major in textiles, with no clear goal in mind. I did love making artificial textile fiber in chemistry class.

I must have been on the college newspaper staff, but what I remember is writing an alumni newsletter and printing it with a mimeograph machine, in a dim, under-equipped basement office. Then hand-addressing envelopes. The summer after my freshman year, the local Bellingham Herald let me write college news. The always-hatted society editor warned me that journalism was a hungry beast and if I chose it, I would have to "marry" it, and that I should not hope to have a family. Looking back, this all seems immensely improbable.

I was next sent to Washington State College on the frigid border of Washington and Idaho. (The University of Washington, with an excellent journalism department, was deemed "too big" and anyway, I was supposed to study home ec.) I was the only textiles major in the department and spent hours weaving fine placemats with breakable thread (I finished hemming them recently) and pulling threads to create perfect one-inch squares for a staff member's comparative tests of sheet material. I struggled with pharmaceutical chemistry experiments in place of a required textiles chem course that did not exist. Again, I joined the newspaper staff, walked at night to and from the town newspaper office, which printed the college paper, and learned to proofread lead type upside down and backward.

The next fall, my mother decided I should join a sorority because hers had helped her make the leap from a small-town girlhood. Every sorority deemed me too old. I didn't care, but mother did. My favorite cousin was attending Oregon State University and would I like to go there? I thought the timing a little late, but I wasn't busy just then, so I packed the trunk mother and I both took to college and sent it home, though I'm not sure why. I packed a suitcase for immediate needs, called my cousin to reserve me a room, hopped on a train, and headed for Oregon State in Corvallis. Looking back, I can't believe I did that. I took entrance tests and passed, went through rush and pledged mother's sorority. I quickly joined the newspaper staff and offered to write a code of conduct and whatever else came along.

Being a slow learner in some ways, I continued majoring in textiles. I remember that a fellow student cut through my underwear during creation of my personal dress form (which, like Mother, I never used), that I made endless bound buttonholes and a wool suit I never wore. Just before graduation, the dean of home economics called me in and asked what kind of job I had in mind. She sighed and said, "You better go talk to the journalism department. Maybe someone there has an idea."

Someone did. The University of Wisconsin offered four fully-paid assistantships (two for home economists) in "agricultural journalism." They were to learn to use the new medium of television, teach extension agents in turn, and write home economics newsletters for state-wide distribution. I also wrote an idiotic thesis about most readable font type for television use. I loved a class taught by a real foreign correspondent and overheard him say it was too bad I had majored in home ec.

In Wisconsin, I got to live in an old governor's mansion with women from around the world, bats in the attic, and a bookcase that moved toward me one night while I typed up an account of the meeting of the combative Madison city council (which had to be turned in before the local paper was distributed in the morning.) My fellow resident scared me silly when she stepped out from behind that bookcase, and said she thought I knew there was a hidden staircase.

A black housemate, getting a doctorate so she could head a home economics department in a black college, invited me to her sister's home in Washington D.C. for Thanksgiving. Her brother-in-law was a medical doctor, yet her sister-in-law could not shop in department stores and the family and their friends lived in a community of their own making. I was treated warmly and learned a lot. As my friend did very well, I saw her at professional meetings for a few years. When I last tried to locate her, I found her name listed on a governor's special commission.

Degree in hand, I had a choice between an extension job in Oklahoma (too hot) or churning out small cook books at (under-air-conditioned) Better Homes and Gardens in Des Moines, Iowa. At Better Homes, I learned a lot about test kitchens, food styling and photography. (I would choose possible props and haul them to Chicago on the cheap night train, then run around Chicago to borrow others if need be.)

I was dispatched to Texas in a sick colleague's place to pick up tips on home decorating for the very rich (one homeowner claimed her chandelier once belonged to Marie Antoinette and she had gold plated bathroom fixtures and a spotlight on the toilet). I was asked to create patterns for Christmas decorations photographed in California, designed some impractical Christmas packages using dyed egg shells, and protested that an already-printed cook book cover of a place setting was backward.

In Des Moines, I was under-paid, had two roommates at a time in a one-bedroom apartment walking distance from work, was active at a Methodist church and the YMCA, created – for free

– a cook book for a foreign students group, which taught me the need for in-home observation of cooks. After five years, I could afford either a car down payment or a six-week tour of Europe. I never regretted that trip. One memory: Charles DeGaulle, preceded by uniformed men on prancing horses, helped his wife out of the car at the Opera in Paris; other diplomats did not bother. I returned ready to move on.

I picked up the mantle of Plain Dealer food editor in 1963. I succeeded Helen Robertson, a rather towering figure among newspaper food editors. She retired in the middle of a strike. She left behind a test kitchen, very unusual for newspapers then, and a cook and two pregnant food writers wishing to retire. During the strike, The Plain Dealer cast about for replacements, because supermarkets were a new phenomenon. The three largest were locally owned – Pick N Pay, Stop and Shop and Heinen's Grocery Store. The PD ad department was clamoring for their full-page ads and promised they would be surrounded by "women's interest material" (food, fashion, furnishing, gardening and society).

The latter four subjects were each served by one reporter, with society editor Mary Strassmeyer being best known. Society matrons had "arrived" when their parties and events were covered by either Mary or Marge Alge of The Press. But the food staff was unusually large – with a food editor, two additional food writers and a test kitchen cook.

Pre-Plain Dealer, while creating small single-subject cookbooks at Meredith Publishing Company (Better Homes & Gardens), I learned the value of a test kitchen and how to prop food photos. I yearned for a real journalism job, a craving kindled from my days as sports editor and then editor of my junior high school newspaper. When the PD contacted area colleges about its newly empty post, I was recommended.

The PD food staff would be rounded out with home economists and newly minted food writers, Pat Weitzel and Jeanne Bishop, one from the Illuminating Company, one from East Ohio Gas Company. (Pat would eventually marry PD reporter Mike Roberts. Jeanne would marry, move to Detroit, join the food staff of the Detroit Free Press – and be murdered by a psychopath while walking home on a Halloween night.) With the strike over, we joined the rest of the "women's interest" staff, walled off from the real editorial staff with bookcases. Among female reporters to have desks in the city room were noted reporter Doris O'Donnell and medical writer Josephine Robertson.

The PD food section was greatly assisted by having a test kitchen, rare in newspapers. After the pre-strike part-time test kitchen cook quickly retired, she was replaced by Latvian refugee Irma Lewis, and later by Vera Beck, an alumnus of the PD cafeteria. Vera grew up in the south, on her father's farm, the only girl with many brothers. She helped her mother feed the large brood and became an expert in southern cooking. Vera once said that her friends loved seeing her picture in PD food photos "because it's a colored face associated with something good."

With big food sections, staff and kitchen, we could cover a lot more than recipes – nutrition, food safety and technology, local farming, appliances, consumer issues, restaurant reviews.

Clevelanders and Ohioans COOKED. An Ohio cook was a Pillsbury Bake-Off contestant almost every year. I was a judge one year for a contest in Hawaii sponsored by an aluminum foil manufacturer. A Cleveland guy won. I was a Pillsbury Bake-Off judge once, too, and plumped for a recipe that used flour instead of a (more profitable) mix. That winner turned out to be a rural married student too poor to afford a telephone. Company reps were sent by car to tell her husband she won.

Supermarkets hadn't quite gotten the hang of their new status and tended to close at 6 p.m., unmindful that many women were now working and very annoyed, full-page ads or no. An early Sunday series featured meat cuts, because each chain created its own cuts with their own names. The new frozen foods, many from Stouffers – which used new rapid freezing plate technology – were often dumped on docks and left there for some time, then stocked in freezers with erratic temperatures. Home canning was very big early on, but gradually declined. One year a shortage of canning lids caused panic.

Early advocates of nutrition labeling were sneered at "because customers will never be able to figure that out" and "what will you consider standard intake?"

Food (and laundry product) safety flared into headlines now and then.

Over the next 25 years, we would note the disappearance of local greenhouse tomatoes and cucumbers and the rise of local specialty farms and farm markets, the explosion of prepared foods in supermarkets, the acceptance of wine from "dare we call for real wine in recipes" to wine columns, the passing popularity of fondue pots (highlighted by Wisconsin cheese promoters serving fondue from a giant pot on Public Square) and the introduction of blenders and smooth-top ranges, the development of nutrition labeling and artificial sweeteners, food recalls, laundry detergent issues (some fatal to infants). Fred Waring demonstrated his blender after shows. One celebrity's personal chef peeled her grapes.

Ralph Nader objected to a lot. Baby food was a pet peeve. Why weren't mothers making their own healthy food? We sent a staffer into stores to ask mothers. We printed the printable parts of their replies.

The Johnson White House chef released recipes for the wedding cakes of both Johnson daughters. He failed to downsize either recipe correctly. (Slow learner.) Food sections all over the country gleefully ran photos of batter over-running pans and of fallen layers. We made note and revised before printing.

Hough Catering was the notable Cleveland caterer. One of its annual jobs was catering for attendees when the Metropolitan Opera came to town. My first year on the job, I asked for one of that year's recipes. Hough was sorry, but it had promised the Press' formidable Florence LaGanke sole coverage. I pointed out that the PD had a larger circulation – perhaps particularly among its more likely clients. We got a recipe. (Florence continued in her role even as her sight faded, and she had to taxi to work. We became friends and I respected her greatly. Her staff writers were Barbara Bratel and Helen Moise.)

Restaurant reviews began to note whether restrooms were handicapped-accessible. (I once asked a restaurant inspector to take me step-by-step through a restaurant inspection. We went to the PD cafeteria. He cited on the spot an open hole in the pantry floor through which rodents could enter and nibble food – and leaving a scoop with a germy handle on top of the loose ice. Esquire printed a really REALLY over-the-top "gourmet" dinner each year and offered it through selected restaurants. I was invited to attend a local trial run, in hopes of free advertising. Once. Noting that it was probably a clue to what started the Russian Revolution did not get me invited again. Looking back, I should probably have been a little more charitable, at least for the sake of the restaurant.

We got a LOT of reader calls, which eventually led to part-time hires, including Jane Moulton, who became one of the first Ohio wine judges, and Blodwen Fleurdelis, a retired home ec teacher. Phone calls about diet caused us to start Dial A Dietitian columns, eventually written by dietitians, because it made more sense for them to take calls directly rather than relaying their answers. We learned recently, during the centennial of the founding of the American Dietetic Association – in Cleveland – that such columns spread across the country from our first ones.

Our call volume always peaked the day before Thanksgiving. One year, an editor forbade us to take any calls. Not our job. I suggested that was unwise. He insisted. I told the women who took all general calls what to expect – and, if overwhelming, to direct said calls to the editor. Calls went not just to him, but to food advertising and all over the building. He stomped over and reversed himself, rather crankily.

Our ethnic communities were a rich source of recipes and tradition. Eventually. Shortly after I arrived, our publisher declared that ethnic cooks would participate in a PD-sponsored booth at a big Coliseum show. He handed us a batch of hand-written recipes, many skimpy in detail. One cook told us a recipe was "printed in a cook book" and she provided that version, but "that's not what I do." We hurriedly collected, tested and printed workable recipes. At zero hour, we learned actual cooking was forbidden and running water was confined to bathrooms. With the first demos, it was evident that samples, if not exactly promised, were expected. Cooks promptly hid finished dishes. We survived somehow and were later able to publish our first PD cookbook, of those "what I do" ethnic recipes.

An orthodox rabbi went above and beyond to further ethnic education. After I printed a Jewish holiday recipe from a non-orthodox friend, he called to tell me gently that it would not be acceptable for an orthodox cook. Then he asked if I would like to spend every Jewish holiday for a year with his family. It was a warm, wonderful, very Cleveland experience.

"Oriental" food stores evolved into Japanese, Chinese and Korean as new waves of refugees arrived. Annual church celebrations then and now highlight traditional fare and our restaurants allow you to eat around the world at will. Or you can shop the West Side Market and cook just about anything from anywhere. Cleveland is very special, food-wise.

Space food development led to new innovations; kitchen appliances became more sophisticated, though a kitchen with floor plug-ins that allowed moving appliances on a whim never caught on.

During strikes, a strike kitchen was a nice service, especially in winter. I ran one for several weeks, funded by coins mostly. I found all the food outlets in town. A Cleveland-bred New York cooking school owner (and friend) promoted her new cook book one day on local TV, using a cooked turkey as a prop. She contributed it to the strike kitchen at day's end. One reporter insisted on food prepared for his special diet. One of the food staff prepared a huge pot of soup and hauled it from her distant suburb.

Along the way it soured. I can't remember its fate. One reporter worked part-time as a butcher and stocked the freezer with over-age hamburger.

Perhaps that experience led me to take a food-stamp user, armed with a week's balanced menus from the extension service, to a grocery store, to see how best to stretch a month's worth of food stamp dollars. Comparing national and store brands and sale items proved akin to taking a college economics course. When she had covered all the meals, she could buy whatever she pleased. She chose fresh produce, which she normally deemed a luxury.

Interestingly, of the food department's multiple small cook books and other publications, the most popular one ever was on substitutions – for times when you don't have quite the right ingredient on hand. We measured constantly for recipes and collected substitutions along the way. Finally, we published all that information in a small booklet. I think we originally gave it to folks who finished a "course" co-sponsored with the county extension service. We gave the booklets away for some years, on request. A national magazine asked for a copy, because it considered publishing something similar, but decided not to. Years after I retired, a librarian in central Ohio said a library customer had worn out her copy and wanted another. I had one extra. I sent it.

Newspaper food editors attended annual meetings around the country, hosted by their advertising departments and food companies. We were expected to sample products in often-odd recipes in rows of hotel suites during limited hours or in meals with the same product in several dishes. That did not have the intended effect. I also learned, on-site, about cattle ranching in the west, cheeses in Denmark, olives in Spain (where male hosts brought their mistresses and bellied up to the buffet tables before guests), bananas in Guatemala.

After 25 years as food editor, I moved to general features with additional columns on new products and consumer concerns. And new learning. Meyers snowplows are manufactured in Cleveland and require trucks of a certain weight. Rosalynn Carter advised to never co-write a book with one's husband. Creativity for Kids craft kits were started by two Cleveland mothers who realized that they were concocting such kits for gifts and maybe similar commercial kits would sell. They do.

Cleveland had exactly one person to handle all consumer complaints. The worst one I covered was perpetrated on a poor, ill woman who needed repair of a second-floor balcony on the back of her house. She paid the purported repairer and went upstairs the next day to inspect her new balcony. Luckily, she only opened the door, because she would have stepped into thin air.

I was privileged to be in the right places, at the right time. That newspaper era seems unlikely to come again. Having taken home that quarter century's worth of food department scrapbooks, I am indexing them – remembering readers who requested copies of articles about relatives, dates unknown. Once indexed, the scrapbooks are to be housed in the archival library at Cleveland State University – souvenirs of a time that is past.

At my retirement party, I said that my job had been like being in college all your life, constantly meeting new, interesting people and recording their experiences. Once in a while I think back to that little mimeographed junior high school paper and all that it triggered.

~ You can visit Janet Beighle French's archive on The Cleveland Memory Project at https://tinyurl.com/JanetFrench).

A muckraker comes to Cleveland and founds Point of View

ROLDO BARTIMOLE

So many years have passed since I made my way to Cleveland in 1965 to work for the Cleveland Plain Dealer. I now wonder why I didn't seek work at one of the many New York City newspapers since I had started reporting in Bridgeport, Connecticut, in the shadow of the New York City media market.

I'm happy that I didn't think of our biggest city as a job possibility, though in 1965 I also applied to the Philadelphia Inquirer and the Washington Post. The Post showed enough interest by writing to an unhappy former editor at the then Bridgeport Sunday Post (now Connecticut Post). I had left the Bridgeport Sunday Post for the Sunday Herald, considered racier and leftish, because I had been barred from writing any more articles about the city's dangerous housing situations. I had been hitting hard. The editor ignored the Washington Post's inquiry, I was told by a former colleague.

As I walked up Euclid Avenue headed to the Superior Avenue offices of the Plain Dealer that spring day to be interviewed, Cleveland appeared to me to be a big city. The census data of 1960 reported a city of 750,000. It was somewhat intimidating. Euclid Avenue was busy with pedestrians.

At the time I also feared I was making a step into a situation where I would have a tough time keeping up with big city reporters. I'd be outclassed.

Now, however, I don't believe I could have made a better choice. Cleveland has always been a good news town as far as I'm concerned. Can you beat electing Carl Stokes, the first black mayor of a large American city, or electing a young Dennis Kucinich, a progressive with an urban outlook who flamed out, or Ralph Perk, who set his hair afire with a blow torch for the cameras, or George Forbes, who kicked half the city's population with words of abuse, then wanted the same voters to make him mayor. His run was a strange strategy. I described his campaign bluntly in 1989 as "fuck you, vote for me!" It didn't work.

And then there has been the historic establishment of corporate and civic leaders, very well-funded by the institutionalized riches of the city's great past of wealth and power. Cleveland had been almost perfectly located for the industrial age by long-ago glaciers with a lake at the doorstep, available iron ore and coal in close shipping proximity, all used to produce the steel for an industrial era. The city birthed many corporate behemoths including John D. Rockefeller's Standard Oil. And banks and law firms to go with the businesses.

And it had worthy leadership.

Lincoln Steffens wrote in his early 1900 book "The Struggle for Self-Government," that "It seems to me that Tom Johnson is the best Mayor of the best-governed city in the United States." That was Cleveland.

That hereditary wealth made for a dominate power structure. It ruled the city and its agenda to fit its needs. Really still does. It fit my purposes as a journalist and as a critic of the power structure operating for its own benefit at a time when major movements of change were about to burst forth as I arrived and began to understand. The major media would not tell the brutal truth.

I left the PD to join the Wall Street Journal before events forced me to start my own newsletter, Point of View. It doesn't mean the Cleveland Plain Dealer, as it was once known, was a bad newspaper. (It dropped "Cleveland" from its name during the tough times when Cleveland was known as the "Mistake on the Lake").

However, in 1965, there was a lot of talent here. There was also an exodus. James Naughton and Gene Maeroff went on to careers at the New York Times. Don Barlett passed through on his way to the Philadelphia Inquirer to scoop a number of Pulitzer Prizes as did Walter Bogdanich, and his wife Stephanie Saul, one, at The New York Times and the other at Newsday. Jim Neff was lead writer at the Seattle Times for the 18-part series, "The Terrorist Within," a finalist for the Pulitzer Prize for investigative reporting in 2003.

Others peeled off in other directions. Joe Eszterhas escaped to Rolling Stone magazine and then movies, Bob McGruder to editorship of the Detroit Free Press, Jim Cox to Channel 8 TV, Terence Sheridan became a private investigator, and Mike Roberts to Cleveland Magazine and then Boston Magazine editorships.

The Plain Dealer, which Sir Winston Churchill said, "By all odds the best newspaper name in the world," became a pass through for many talented reporters. The plain truth suffered too often.

So, there was no shortage of high-quality reporters at the Plain Dealer. Time magazine labeled the PD reporters as "Tigers," maybe at that time more the work of the paper's publicist rather than its journalistic production.

More realistically, the Plain Dealer revealed a weakness as the city became an object of national scrutiny. This troubled Publisher Thomas Vail. His photograph and bragging had accompanied the Time magazine article. Now the city was facing criticism. Vail ordered a response to the critical material about his city. All beat reporters in 1967 were ordered to write a positive article about their area of coverage. The truth apparently didn't matter. Thirty-four articles, under the banner "What's Right with Cleveland," were published in the newspaper. A promotional booklet was produced for further distribution. I was covering the welfare beat and refused to write anything positive about Cleveland's poverty. I felt the times were more reflected by a bumper sticker of that time: "Pray for Cleveland."

The nature of thinking by Vail and other editors was reflected in coverage of a mine disaster. Seventy-eight miners were killed in the Mannington Mine in West Virginia in 1968. The PD used the occasion once again to try to burnish its reputation.

A tear-jerking series proclaimed the paper's interest in the disaster:

"Now that Hartzel Mayle is buried in the mine," began one article in a series asking for public donations, "his wife, Juanita makes sandwiches with one slice of meat instead of three."

Another noted, "The Plain Dealer Christmas Express stirred the people yesterday. Trucks carting food and clothing roared onto Main Street, and a helicopter carrying $75,000 landed in the middle of everything."

Vail said, as I reported, "A great newspaper must not only be well-written and important in its community, but it must also have a big heart and do good things for good people."

What the PD didn't do, however, as it appealed for nickel, dime and dollar donations, was tell the public that the mine was owned by Consolidated Coal, a 100 percent owned subsidiary of Continental Oil, which had nearly $1 billion in profits in the preceding years. Nor did it mention the close corporate connections to Cleveland figures, including George Humphrey of Hanna Mining, a major establishment family in Cleveland. These facts were nowhere to be found in the PD. They did appear in Point of View, the newsletter I founded in 1968.

These kinds of corporate connections didn't make it into established media but a lone operation as Point of View could not only reveal such connections but make the issues known at least to segments of the community.

Point of View also allowed me to reveal what the PD actually censored at publication time.

For instance, in a fatal clash in the Christmas line at Higbee's department store, a big advertiser at the time for the Plain Dealer, an editor ordered the name "Higbee's" not appear on the front page of the paper. This tragic death of a black man in a line with children awaiting a visit with Santa Claus became less a tragedy than the need to safeguard an advertiser's name from Page 1.

Another example involved race. A PD reporter included in his article the fact that a leading businessman made racial jokes at a public meeting. The copy of the censored material was slipped to me.

The occasion was a formal dinner of Bluecoats, an organization primarily of corporate leaders. Its purpose was to provide charity funds of some $10,000 for police officers and their families when an officer was killed on duty.

New York Times editorial columnist James Reston was the guest speaker. He was introduced by Fred Crawford, a leading Cleveland businessman and the former chairman of TRW, Inc., a major US corporation.

These sentences from the article, later published in POV, were penciled out of the reporter's copy before publication:

"Crawford told two racial jokes to the all-white audience.

"In prefacing one joke, he commented upon someone being 'blackballed.'

"Crawford then added: 'I guess it takes two black balls to get elected in this city.'

"The remark elicited a mixture of laughs and agitation."

Crawford was referring to Mayor Carl B. Stokes, first black mayor of Cleveland.

Apparently, editors consider this too revealing of the racism of a corporate leader and by eliminating the references protected Crawford.

It wasn't the only time editors bowed to corporate leaders.

The hard-hitting and tiger image would be unrealized at a newspaper that a leading attorney, Jack Reavis, managing partner of Cleveland's largest law firm, Jones, Day, Reavis & Pogue (now Jones-Day, one of the world's largest) told the U. S. Civil Rights Commission in 1966 that he had received "a pledge from the editors of the newspapers that they would give us no publicity except as we asked for it." A year later, Ralph Besse, former chairman of the Cleveland Electric Illuminating Co., claimed the same arrangement about a $40,000 secret fund to pay black militants to keep peace. The story was grist for the second issue of Point of View, which made no such arrangements.

Bowing to power wasn't unusual.

There was a dearth, however, of what I felt was the kind of journalism I saw as necessary, especially for the times. A lot of essential hard-edge reporting went unattended.

Yet I had worried when I arrived that Cleveland was a major city with sharp-witted talent. I would be hard-pressed to compete.

But signs appeared early that made me realize maybe I was mistaken.

Before I left Bridgeport, I had the opportunity to interview Robert Penn Warren. He had just published "Who Speaks for the Negro." He had traveled America interviewing young black activists. When I told him I was soon headed to Cleveland he advised me to look up Ruth Turner, a young black woman who just graduated Oberlin College. She was one of the people he singled out in a nationwide search for new African-American talent. When I mentioned my desire to meet Turner to other PD reporters they turned up their noses. She's a radical, not to be sought out. I did eventually get a meeting with her, but she wanted nothing to do with the Plain Dealer. She left the city soon after.

I also learned that Students for a Democratic Society (SDS) had left campuses at this time. They chose two cities to begin community organizing – Newark, N. J. and yes, Cleveland, Ohio. I wanted to meet them and write about them. They invited me to their West Side apartment on Jay Avenue for dinner but again wanted nothing to do with speaking to a Plain Dealer reporter for a story. The SDS activists also distrusted the newspaper's fairness.

These were newsmakers of the day, but they mistrusted and shunned the media.

Along with this rejection of the changing times, two other things should have given me pause about the new job. There was a tug among reporters as to where I would live – east or west. Strange to me as a newcomer. However, it revealed the bitter racial division of the city. West was white; east was black. Our family ended up renting in Cleveland Heights.

The next question I faced was "What was my nationality?" It indicated another significant characteristic of my new home. Nationality was a major feature in the dynamics of the city. It was another factor of division and problems.

There were more serious warning signs to indicate troubles and lack of recognition about what was going on in the city that the newspapers were supposed to cover and inform the public about. Dark days were ahead and those steering the newspapers didn't quite understand. The city and its civic leaders in particular needed a scrutiny the newspaper neither would nor could provide.

The 1960s, if anything, revealed the ignorance of the city's newspapers of their city. As we moved to the 1970s, 1980s (the Press was garroted in 1982), 1990s and onward the Plain Dealer became the mouthpiece of corporate & legal interests.

Let's look.

In the 1960s the mistakes of the Establishment (corporate, legal, foundations and their controlled instruments) decided urban renewal would be the savior of the once great city of Cleveland. They pushed for vast urban renewal projects east and west. However, almost all urban renewal took place on the east side, inhabited heavily by African-Americans.

Instead, it set in motion movements it couldn't control or direct.

In 1965, Hough, drained of its middle class and overcrowded by the population movement of the central area, inhabited mostly by African-Americans, exploded. Nightly conflagrations climaxed with the 1966 Hough riots.

It was clear Cleveland's newspapers were searching for an answer to what had been brewing for years, if not decades. It was no surprise then that a grand jury, headed by the celebrated Press former editor, Louis B. Seltzer, came up with the laughable conclusion that the riots in the city it covered for decades had been caused by "Communists." It was testimony to the serious lack of newspaper reading of the city it covered. Indeed, the Ohio National Guard Adjutant General concluded that the assessment by the Seltzer led grand jury had "absolutely nothing to substantiate his statement" of Communist action. The Plain Dealer credited the grand jury with having "guts" to so conclude.

You have to wonder what the city's two major newspapers were covering.

Seltzer had already seriously damaged the Press' reputation by his fixated desire to convict Dr. Sam Sheppard for the murder of his wife, Marilyn. In a front-page editorial the Press called out, "Why Isn't Sam Sheppard in Jail?" changed to "Quit Stalling, Bring Him In." Another headline: "Somebody is Getting Away With Murder." This trial by newspaper helped damage the Press' reputation. (https://en.wikipedia.org/wiki/Sam_Sheppard). The PD thereafter, I believe, became the "respectable" newspaper for suburban families to have delivered to their homes. It started the demise of the afternoon Press.

The Plain Dealer was stumbling through this period trying to placate black anger but not alienate its majority white population.

"Having fed racial passions with inaccurate reporting," I wrote in a 1973 special pamphlet, "the PD two months later called for an end to those tensions. This city must not be turned into a mutual aggravation society. It is time for all groups – for their own safety, for their own good, for their children's future – to work together, find peaceable, lawful, orderly community." The paper then condemned "anyone who tries to keep up the vendetta."

It couldn't obey its own admonitions. The paper ran a series of articles, based on interviews with Cleveland police officers, entitled, "What's on Their Mind." The series simply opened old wounds day after day with assaults on the black community. It gave police the opportunity to dirty Mayor Stokes.

I countered with the findings of the Civil Violence Center of Case-Western Reserve University in its report to the National Commission on the Causes and Prevention of Violence. It charged the PD with "opening old wounds" and "effectively keeping the vendetta going."

The report added that other reports in the PD "fed suspicion that the newspaper was carrying on a vendetta of its own."

It cited in particular a PD "expose" of a six-month-old issue.

It involved dismissal of concealed gun charges by Mayor Stokes of two bodyguards arrested outside the home of a black stockbroker. They had been guarding CORE national director Floyd McKissick the night the Rev. Martin Luther King, Jr. was assassinated. Stokes and other prominent blacks were engaged in keeping peace in Cleveland as other U. S. cities erupted in violence

They did not trust white Cleveland police to guard McKissick. Stokes said at the time, "We were trying hold the city together."

The PD knew of the situation. Indeed, didn't publish its "expose" until months later. The Center zeroed in on the article as an example of PD provocation.

In its report, the Center noted the delay in the PD's reporting of the dropped gun charges. It wrote, "Reporters interviewed for this study indicated that the editors of the Plain Dealer had knowledge of the dropped charges months before they decided to publish their expose."

It was just another example of Cleveland newspapers ignoring responsibility.

The times, however, were changing as the Vietnam War and the Civil Rights movement took over media attention.

When I came to the Plain Dealer in 1965, the PD had one black reporter and he, McGruder, was in the Army. I was at first a general assignment reporter, but they soon teamed me up with a young black college student, Bill Davis.

The editors realized that something was changing. Events were forcing them to attend to the half of the community – blacks – that they had long ignored.

The paper began on the back of the Metro pages a series of examinations of the city that they had so long neglected – impoverished areas. The sporadic series was labeled "The Changing City," and each article took the entire back page of the section.

Between May and July of 1965, I did five Changing Cities, always with a young intern, Bill Davis, who was still a student at Hiram College. I complained that if Davis was never expected to write any of the pieces, how was he to learn the job? The question went unanswered.

The paper's management, however, was using Davis as a social link to blacks rather than training him to be a writer. They needed a black face in the black community.

In l973, I produced a booklet called "Mediaocrity," that touched on my media coverage during the first five years of Point of View.

It foretold the troubles that would plague the business as change hit hard.

I started the booklet with the Plain Dealer and its motto as "The Starter."

The Plain Dealer used Davis, who was 19 years old and had no other newspaper experience, in its desperation to have a black face. The paper sensed its lack of diversity and the void it had to fill.

I began the booklet, "The weekend – much discussed in the Cleveland Plain Dealer city room for months before – started a bit peculiarly. Some 30 PD editorial workers and their companions had been invited to join in the anniversary celebration of a small African nation. The host was a 19-year-old black reporter who said his uncle was Ambassador to the United States and had asked him to invite his newspaper colleagues to the festivities."

The trip took reporters to New York City, a stay at the Americana hotel and a special visit to the United Nations as part of the anniversary fete. However, the visit to the U.N. seemed to reporters suspiciously like a normal U.N. tour, not a special event.

From NYC there was a shuttle flight to Washington, D. C., and what was supposed to be a celebratory ball that might also include a visit by then President Lyndon B. Johnson. It didn't turn out that way.

Instead formally dressed participants were taken for taxi rides (expected limos didn't show up) to the home supposedly of the Ambassador. As I described it, "Upon arrival, instead of the President and other notables, they found a sleepy-eyed man and his abundantly pregnant wife. After a hushed conversation with the host-reporter (Davis), the unexpected guests were invited in for sandwiches and coffee by the couple."

The young man chosen to be the "PD social secretary to some segments of the Cleveland black community" was really being misused to allow the uncomfortable editors to escape dealing with blacks. They had put so much investment in what seemed a solution to them that editors had co-signed for his furniture in an apartment, which they had also wrangled for him.

The commitment turned out to be more than the editors had bargained for. Bills for the New York and Washington trips, air flights and hotels began arriving at 1801 Superior Avenue, the PD offices. Davis disappeared and was never located by the newspaper. However, one day some time later a photograph came over the wire depicting someone accepting a check from some other men. City editor Ted Princiotto called me over, "Is that Bill Davis?" It sure looked like him.

The Plain Dealer was tripping its way through the turbulent Sixties.

Some of the miscues made for journalistic fodder for me.

I wasn't taking the entire trip with them.

My pieces in the PD were noticed by a Wall Street Journal reporter who recommended me to Clayton Sutton, the Journal bureau chief here. I made a trip to New York for an interview and was hired.

My stay at the Journal didn't last long and was hardly auspicious. The main piece of work was a profile of Dr. Benjamin Spock, an anti-war doctor then at Case-Western Reserve University. I shared a byline in a front-page examination of riots in Cincinnati and a piece on Mayor Carl B. Stokes.

What ended my stay there was a happenstance invitation to a conference of Ohio University professors at the Aurora Inn in Aurora, Ohio, on April 5th, 1968.

I had no idea it would have a lasting impact on my life.

It was my 35th birthday. It was also the day following the assassination of the Rev. Martin Luther King, Jr., in Memphis, Tennessee.

The speaker that day was George Wiley, a black man and head of the National Welfare Rights Organization, fighting poverty especially among welfare clients.

Wiley, a graduate of Cornell University and a formidable advocate for poor people spoke to the all-white group.

I remember him saying he would no longer "plead" with white people for understanding. But that's essentially what he was doing.

I was shocked by the reaction to his obvious plea.

The reaction of the educated audience more than his words moved me. They were asking questions about "when would blacks stop rioting" as riots had broken out in many U. S. cities. And when will they stop burning our cities.

At the time, though working at the Journal I had been surreptitiously writing for a small newsletter called, I believe, Common Sense, put out by some people associated with the Council of Churches. I don't remember how many nor have I unfortunately saved any of the issues. Common Sense was ending its tenure. So, I essentially created Point of View, a similarly small (usually 4-page) newsletter. The size was dictated by use of a small printing press that was least expensive.

I published it for 32-1/2 years – May-June 1968 to December 2000. More than 700 issues were published, with a few by others during down times when I had a heart attack in 1974 and a first bypass surgery three years later. During the latter years I also wrote weekly columns for the Edition, published by Bill Gunlocke and the Free Times, started by labor lawyer Richard Siegel. There were other alternative papers during those years with the Great Swamp Erie da da Boom, a classic alternative newspaper name.

It's difficult to cover my 50 years of boss-less writing and adding my three years of conventional journalism at the Plain Dealer and later at the Wall Street Journal Cleveland bureau. I wrote for a short time a column in the Call & Post. It ended when W. O. Walker refused my column critical of United Way. My deal with Walker was I'd write a weekly column and he'd print Point of View in exchange.

However, anyone who has been observing Cleveland journalism knows that my reporting continued into 2018 with several websites, ending exclusively with Jeff Hess and his Have Coffee Will Write site.

It's also clear to anyone who has been reading POV or other work that the main subject has been how Power Works and primarily an attempt to determine one question: Who Rules.

The answer to the question Who Rules? (and how) remains one task that is rarely touched by the local media. It was always essential, whether achieved, in my mind as I tried to cover what was important – and within my ability to grasp – here in Cleveland.

In the 16-page POV issue I wrote marking the 30th year of publication, I included randomly in the issue headlined: 30 YEARS OF SHAMING DEVILS a short clip from previous issues of POV. The brief notes indicate the breadth of subject matter covered over the years. They included some of the following with a time note:

"It's like a giant whale, beached in shallow water. Too embarrassing not to look at, too big to give it much help, and too obvious to ignore... the very Plain Dealer." Vol.16, No 7 1983."

"George Voinovich isn't the candidate of the Fat Cats. He's the candidate of the Bloated Cats, as we shall see." Vol. 12, #5 1979."

"It's almost inconceivable that two seemingly politically wise operators – Bob Weissman and Dennis Kucinich – could toil for a decade to takeover City Hall, do just that, then in five months have the whole thing fall in on them..." Vol. 10 #20, 1978.

"The proposed purchase of a radio station for $1-million by a corporation controlled by Council President George Forbes' wife has the financial support of one of the Cleveland banks involved in the city's default." Vol. 12, #18. 1980.

"They buy dead horses don't they...For some reason, generous Ralph Perk has taken quite a fancy to the tax delinquent ($49,000), 40-year old, empty Euclid Ave. eyesore (arena). He wants very badly to purchase Nick Mileti's obsolete building with $1-million of neighborhood renewal money..." Vol. 9, No. 2, 1976"

"They ain't heavy, they're our Civic Leaders. Dick Jacobs strolled into city council's finance committee hearing with a model of proposed building covered by a black plastic garbage bag and by the time he walked out city council had filled the bag with potential subsidies of more than $125-million." Vol. 20, No. 14, 1988."

"Convicted conspirator George M. Steinbrenner, III, who channeled illegal campaign contributions to former President Richard Nixon, recently arranged with Supt. of Schools Paul Briggs to funnel $10,000 to pay 10 striking Cleveland reporters and editors to speak about journalism to high school English classes for up to two weeks at $500 a week." Vol. 7, No 13, 1975.

"Council President George Forbes has once again steered legal business to members of the Climaco, Climaco, Seminatore, Leftkowitz & Garofoli law firm. Forbes personally picked Tony Garofoli as council's legal representative in dealing with Figgie International... for massive Warrensville Township (Chagrin Highlands) development." Vol. 21, No. 7 1988."

> "The Frightened Men at the Plain Dealer have struck again. This time it was a favorite of theirs who fell. Joe Eszterhas was fired last Friday because he wrote an article in Evergreen that said nasty things about the Plain Dealer and its editor-publisher Tom Vail." Vol. 4, No. 5, 1971.

> "Cleveland business leaders last summer 'bought peace' in the ghetto by paying some black activists about $40,000 in a 10-week period to do what they had decided to do already – keep it cool." Vol. 1 No. 2, 1968.

> "Some tactics get grotesque. For example, a (Council President Jim) Stanton aide was discovered at 1 a.m. in the office of Dick Green, urban renewal director. (Another) was found rummaging the wastebasket in the Law Dept. in the dark. He explained he was looking for a copy of the morning Plain Dealer and 'hope no one thought he was a spy." Vol. 2, No. 24. 1971.

It was difficult for me both in gathering, writing and publishing, then mailing by ZIP code packages, and keeping records of subscriptions and sending reminders for renewals. A small business, in this instance a tiny almost microscopic sized business, was also a financial struggle.

I never had more than about 1,700 subscribers at a peak. My likely high number came during the Dennis Kucinich mayoral term. POV was likely the most supportive of many of Kucinich's aims. He also came at a time when Council President George Forbes likely had as much or more power than any single politician in Cleveland. He helped sales too. And in one incident gave me a boost likely desired by most journalists.

Forbes made me better known by tossing me – literally – out the door of a hotel meeting he wanted to keep closed to media. His misfortune was that the rest of the news people obeyed and left. However, they were at the open door – news photographers and TV cameras at the ready. (Some years later, invited to address a class by Forbes, teaching at Baldwin-Wallace, I showed up with a blow up of that photo. Before my talk, I said, I want the class to view another aspect of their professor. I produced the photo. Forbes merely laughed and said, "Pass it around."

What about the future of journalism in Cleveland? My guess is it will be as bleak as or worse than the past. Again, the Plain Dealer has some excellent young reporters, many of them young women who write with passion.

But the same old story of hands off those who make the big community decisions rules.

In 2013, I wrote a very long piece in which I talked about toting up the hundreds of millions, certainly more than $1 billion, of public money that has poured into downtown, mostly for sports facilities that pay no property taxes on their structures. It was the result of hard work over the years to keep track of the money. It can be found here: http://havecoffeewillwrite.com/?p=34684

I had followed the sports facilities issue closely while the Plain Dealer gave little attention to how public money was being poured into Jacobs Field (now Progressive Field) and Gund Arena (now Quicken Loans Arena.) While the main stream media ignored expenditures, POV watched carefully.

I reported that the Gateway Economic Development Corp., nonprofit vehicle created to operate the two sports facilities, built into them lavish, upscale restaurants, fully equipped down to wineglasses and dinner knives, spoons and forks. Gateway spent $5,155,893 for the baseball field's Terrace Club with a clear view of the playing field. It became the largest downtown restaurant requiring paid membership ($800 a year) for game day access. The Club is a double-decker with 450 seats on each level. Kitchen equipment alone cost $1,054,320. The costs for tile and stone for the kitchen and bar totaled $146,600 and carpeting $343,450. All property taxes exempted. Major media ignored these details.

In the arena, it provided a smaller restaurant named Sammy's after an exclusive downtown restaurant operated by an original member of Gateway Board. She resigned to operate arena Sammy's. This restaurant's cost with equipment was $2,370,134.

Gateway also built the Cleveland Indians a building not in original design plans at a cost of $5.1 million. I was told it was necessary to hide an unsightly ramp into the stadium. I noted that shrubbery would be less costly. The offices included a table affixed with a metal emblem of Chief Wahoo, the team's racist mascot. It also had metal tabs embedded to resemble the stitching on a baseball.

Unreported elsewhere POV revealed a debacle over coffee tables for Jacobs Field loges. Jacobs demanded they be a certain marble despite the company handling the purchase warning Gateway that the marble quarried at Lucca, Italy, was not suitable. Indeed, cracks soon appeared and Jacobs wanted replacements at a cost of some $260,000.

Stephen Lau, president of Industrial First, the marble supplier, told me, "They asked for the marble, we provided it."

In a recent example revealing that the subsidy party will continue the Cleveland Cavaliers, owned by a billionaire, forced the city and county to again donate public money in the millions to revamping Quicken Loans Arena.

What made this most disturbing is that various citizen organizations in a short time collected more than 20,000 signatures from Cleveland residents to force a vote on plans for the city and county to pay tens of millions of dollars for Quicken Loans Arena expansion.

Yet high-level corporate interests, along with Plain Dealer support, worked to derail the verified petition. No vote was ever conducted. Public money is now dedicated to the project despite the fact that original bonds on the arena from the early 1990s remain payable annually until 2023.

There is no way major Cleveland media – newspaper, television news or radio – will forthrightly examine these public expenditures for private interests. Privilege demands obedience.

Ironically, these same civic/corporate interests have now broached the need for a new football stadium to replace the 73,000-seat First Energy (Browns) football stadium owned by the City of Cleveland. The pitch is too familiar – it will be combined with other economic ventures with a monetary payoff to the larger community.

Will Cleveland and Cuyahoga County taxpayers really allow its representatives to once again ignore the serious problems of Clevelanders for ANOTHER fancy, highly publicly subsidized sports stadium to replace one built less than 25 years ago?

These are perilous times for newspapers and thus reporters.

Newspapers must change to survive. They must better represent those who need champions.

"There is an instrument of devastating effectiveness which we have only superficially, often hypocritically, employed. It is called the power of the press.

"Let's face it. We in the trade use this power more frequently (for self-interests) … than to keep the doors of an open society open and swinging, by encouraging honest controversy, or, if you'll pardon the term, crusading for truth and justice."

The quote is from Edward P. Morgan of ABC News, from Robert Cirino's "Don't Blame the People," a book every reporter should study.

The newspaper of the future must work for the underdog and against privilege. Will it?

~You can read Roldo's work on The Cleveland Memory Project, where his archive holds every issue of "Point Of View," more than 700 of them in 32 years. (See http://www.clevelandmemory.org/roldo.)

Confessions of a wayward reporter

TERENCE SHERIDAN

I was a relative short-timer at The Plain Dealer, from the end of 1963 to the beginning of 1970, and when I left, editors celebrated. So did most of my coworkers. The truth of the matter: I was an insufferable pain in the ass.

The days of typewriters, pencils and paste pots.

Take, for example, 1968, the year The Plain Dealer hired five women in a group, the renowned "Class of '68," all of whom went on to be excellent reporters and editors.

One of the young women, straight out of The College of Wooster and lovely in tartan skirt, sweater and Peter Pan collar, was doing rookie grunt work, writing obits a few desks from mine. The desk chairs were on rollers so I rolled over and asked – 50 years before "Me Too" and "Time's Up" – "Are you a virgin?"

She should have stabbed me in the eye with a pencil. Instead, she blushed and typed even faster, sympathetic words about the recently deceased. She was the daughter of a Pennsylvania judge and a Christian. She forgave me, and subsequently did monumental typing at her breakfast table in Gates Mills.

I had written a long piece in pencil on legal pads about a precocious politician, Dennis Kucinich, and she typed it as fast as I could read it – the cover story for the inaugural issue of Cleveland Magazine, April 1972.

The 60s. What a decade. What a time to be in the newspaper business. John Kennedy, Robert Kennedy, Martin Luther King, and Malcolm X assassinated; John Glenn in orbit, Cuban missile crisis, civil rights and voting rights, U.S. cities on fire, Vietnam on fire, Neil Armstrong on the moon – a decade ending with Woodstock, anti-Vietnam War demonstrations and news of the My Lai massacre.

On Oct. 6, 1968, The Plain Dealer officially became Ohio's largest newspaper and readers were greeted with: "You meet the nicest people when you're Number One!" and some stats: 409,414 daily, 545,032 Sunday.

The PD could have been, should have been, the best paper between the coasts. The newsroom was loaded with young talent. Unfortunately it didn't bewitch the editors, far too many of them semiliterate archivists promoted for loyal time served and given an impressive title and a paltry raise.

Even with honorable old gents who had paid their dues and earned their stripes there was time warp in a wild decade.

Here's dialogue with one of them in the paper's elevator. He was running the show in 1965, the year before he retired, and 30 years before the Rock and Roll Hall of Fame opened in Cleveland:

"What do you think of these ridiculous names rock and rollers give themselves? The Animals, Lovin' Spoonful?"

"I like it," I said. "What do you like?"

"I think 'Four Freshmen' has dash."

The city was beginning to decay from the inside out but high-ranking editors were curiously indifferent.

Four days before Armstrong walked on the moon, July 20, 1969, I walked around a Hough neighborhood that had been ripped by riots, fire and fury in July 1966, chatting with residents who believed that Hough, ravaged real estate controlled by absentee landlords, needed a whole lot of fixing before we messed with the moon.

One of them was a mother of four who lived in a top-floor apartment with a leaky roof and rats in the hallway. The moon shot? "I don't know nothin' about that," she said. "But I have plenty of mices and I can't keep flour for the roaches in it."

"I don't know why we're running this," an editor said, shaking his head. "It's like insulting the moon story."

This was a man who fervently endorsed a grand jury report defining social and racial unrest in Cleveland as being "Communist inspired," five days of looting and arson and confrontation between armed black militants and Cleveland police that left seven dead (three policemen, three "suspects," one "civilian") and 15 wounded. The "Glenville Shootout" in July 1968.

Still, I was fond of my battered steel desk in the big, sprawling, loud, smoke-filled city room. There were ashtrays, and cigarettes in the ashtrays.

To my left was Roldo Bartimole, before he departed to do his own thing as the muckraking publisher of an annoying newsletter, Point of View. In time, I'd refer to him as "the poor man's Tom Paine" and "the conscience of Cleveland."

To my right was Joe Eszterhas, a onetime Hungarian refugee. He was just a kid but a bear for work, and it wasn't all fiction. Fame and fortune in Hollywood were in his writing future, 19 movies, or thereabouts, and eight books. Who can forget "Basic Instinct"?

On Nov. 20, 1969, the Plain Dealer published pictures that shocked the world, gruesome images of Vietnamese civilians massacred in March 1968 by American soldiers in a 50-man unit armed with automatic rifles, machine guns and grenade launchers – "clumps of bodies." (Eventually the Army set the number at 347, although the Vietnamese claim 504.)

The pictures were taken by former Army photographer Ron Haeberle and buttressed by an exclusive eyewitness account written by Eszterhas. A Fairview High School graduate, Haeberle called the Plain Dealer because he recognized Eszterhas's byline. They had attended Ohio University at the same time and Joe was a writer and editor at the school paper.

Straight ahead was the rewrite desk where the laidback aces, Bob Daniels and Al Wiggins, were always laughing about something as they banged away, making the unreadable lyrical, or at least readable.

But they didn't screw around when rewriting. Perhaps you were calling in a story and you had a word like "Courvoisier." You'd start to spell it and one or the other would snap, "Go on with the fucking story."

Another way of saying, "I know how to spell, genius." They believed in short sentences, active verbs, and getting to the tavern on time.

Try to sneak jargon or cliché by them – junk like today's iconic, surreal, on the ground, end of the day, begs the question, first and foremost, at this moment in time, impacted, or "literally" this and "literally" that – and they might hang up on you.

It was said that each time Daniels was sent out of town, he came back with a wife. I didn't believe it. Maybe two spouses. Three at most.

Wiggins had only one wife, but he was a poet. At first glance, no big deal, since nearly everyone in the city room except editors was a poet. Even the copy boys (no copy girls) were poets.

Speedy Kucinich, for one, would zip by, deftly depositing his latest work on your desk. The difference was that Wiggins was published with actual poets. When I had something in a coffeehouse rag, he had something in a book.

Nonetheless, many think one of his finest lines was his resignation on a postcard after leaving town in hurry, deeply in debt to two bookmakers and one very angry restaurant owner: "By the time you receive this comma I will have resigned period."

Me, I argued incessantly with editors about items large and small. I thought it great that Muhammad Ali changed his "slave name" and turned his back on war ("No Viet Cong ever called me nigger"), and that for sure a family newspaper should have room for a feature story on a stripper who read Walt Whitman and used a boa constrictor in her act.

One editor was confused but sincere when he blurted, "Negroes are now blacks?" "Seems so, sport," I said. "Ask McGruder, the tall Negro who works for us."

Under the circumstances, I should have been given a pass for doing mad things.

For instance, the day I cut Bob McGruder's phone line with my penknife because I was tired of waiting for him to go to lunch. At the time, McGruder, the Plain Dealer's first black reporter, was talking to Carl Stokes, Cleveland's first black mayor. But I didn't know that.

Rev. King had a dream; writer James Baldwin had a prophetic spiritual ("God gave Noah the rainbow sign/ No more water, the fire next time"), and McGruder, who would go on to be executive editor of the Detroit Free Press, had a lunchtime story: stopped again by police while driving through a white neighborhood at night – another DWB, Driving While Black.

But no one dreamed that the 44th President would be black man, or that a birther-crazed real estate mogul who spent years claiming 44 was illegal (not born in the United States) would be the 45th President.

McGruder was one of two friends I had at the PD. The other was Don Barlett. The three of us had lunch daily. Later, McGruder would become the PD's managing editor. Later, Barlett would win two Pulitzer Prizes working for the Philadelphia Inquirer. Later, the PD would ask me to go to its bureau in Lake County and work for an editor who thought "penultimate" meant beyond "ultimate."

The paper made it clear that it didn't want Barlett working with me. I think they were afraid I might corrupt him. A box-like figure who wore button-down J.C. Penney shirts, a beige raincoat, and a dark beret atop a bald dome, he neither drank nor smoked and spoke barely above a whisper.

We fooled them just once, together writing a series about the city's business elite bankrolling a reactionary ploy to get "anti-Communist" tripe into Cleveland's public schools. When the PD killed the series, we sold it to Nation magazine.

It became kind of a joke when we got an award for investigative reporting from the Cleveland Press Club, for the first part of the series, the weakest part.

Admittedly, I had a bad attitude. It began at the Alliance Review and continued at the Akron Beacon Journal, where Barlett and I were assigned to the sticks – Barlett in Portage County, me in Wayne County.

They gave you a Rollei twin-lens reflex camera, paid for your gas, and you filled an entire page: pictures, news, features and a column. You learned to write swiftly but day became night mighty fast.

John S. Knight, legendary editor and publisher of Knight Newspapers, had an office in the newsroom. I'd go in and drink his whiskey and smoke his cigars. He was never there at night.

I certainly didn't expect him the winter night I was sitting in his chair, my feet on his desk, a glass of aged scotch in one hand and a Cuban cigar in the other, when, suddenly, there he was, the great man himself, hanging up his hat and coat and saying quietly, very quietly, "Mind if I use my office?"

That's all he said, and if he told anyone else, I never heard about it.

After a year glittering as a reporter in the PD's Akron bureau but failing as a collegial co-worker (I called the bureau chief an "asshole" because his idea of journalism was to clip Beacon stories and rewrite them), I was eager to star in the PD's windowless old hulk at E. 18th and Superior.

I was stunned when informed that they first wanted me to serve a tour in the suburbs. I sulked until I was assigned to Criminal Courts.

Now we were cooking. This was the place for me. Good guys and bad guys, though you sometimes needed a program to tell them apart. Every day was drama, with someone doomed to get it in the neck unless a crafty defense lawyer intervened.

The lawyers starred but others made it work, the people who didn't get their names in the paper – clerks, bailiffs, parole officers and court stenographers.

Need to check your courtroom notes? Run down to the basement and an affable stenographer would consult his or her machine and make you whole.

A grand jury clerk would tip you off to what was coming and you had a scoop. A parole officer would let you peek at a report disclosing hilarious dialogue between members of an incompetent gang drilling a safe in a jewelry store, and you would get a laudatory note from the PD publisher, dapper Tom Vail, the prince of Hunting Valley. (Vail's notes were commonly known as "Snowflakes" and nearly everyone got at least one.)

After the hardnosed Newhouse family acquired the 125-year-old PD in 1967, it kept the well-bred Vail, born rich, in place.

He was a bright shining bauble with the right high-society business and social connections. But they sent in one of their own men to keep an eye on the bottom line.

In 1965, Newsweek described Vail as appearing "more like an F. Scott Fitzgerald hero than a publisher," which, I guess, made him our Gatsby, while we were his "young tigers," according to Newsweek.

You were sadly out of luck, however, if you were an old tiger, such as Bob Manry, a 46-year-old copy editor who was turned down when he asked the paper to sponsor his proposed voyage across the Atlantic in a tiny boat.

Bob said "bye" the day before his 47th birthday and pushed off in a 13-foot sailboat, Tinkerbelle – 78 days from Falmouth, Massachusetts to Falmouth, England, where he was greeted by massive crowds and a flotilla of large and small boats on Aug. 17, 1965.

Meanwhile, small scoops for me, days when there was a feisty rival, the Cleveland Press. One afternoon a court clerk nodded toward a stack of books on the counter, journal entries made by judges. Just a nod.

But in one of the books was a judge's journal entry reducing Don King's sentence of second-degree murder to manslaughter, shortly after a jury convicted King, a hot-tempered numbers honcho, of second-degree murder for kicking to death a lightweight former employee in front of Art's Seafood House at Cedar and E. 100th.

I had covered the trial and it took the jury only four hours, counting lunch, to find the burly defendant guilty of murder. Sam Garrett, stomped and pistol-whipped, owed King $600.

Years earlier, in 1954, 23-year-old "Donald the Kid," as he was known, killed a man who was trying to rob one of his gambling joints, shot him in the back, which was ruled "justifiable homicide" – a shootout involving three hoods from Detroit and King returning fire with a Russian pistol.

I got a Snowflake for the journal-entry story, the judge got re-elected, and after nearly four years in prison, Cleveland's Don King got New York City, where he grew his hair incredibly high and became the pre-eminent boxing promoter on the planet – "Rumble in the Jungle" (Ali-Foreman), "Thrilla in Manilla" (Ali-Frazier), plus promoting the fights of Larry Holmes, Mike Tyson, Roberto Duran, and Evander Holyfield, among many other champions, with enough energy left over to vigorously battle lawsuits filed by various boxers alleging he had stiffed them.

In 1992, he took the Fifth when questioned about alleged connections to Mafia boss John Gotti.

In any event, when the trial of the decade rolled around, the retrial of Sam Sheppard in 1966, I was ready. Sheppard, a former neurosurgeon, had spent 10 years in prison after being convicted of second-degree murder in the bludgeon death of his wife, Marilyn, in their Bay Village home in July 1954.

A federal judge granted Sheppard a retrial on the grounds that the "carnival atmosphere" of the first trial had made a "mockery of justice." Put that on the afternoon Press, which lasted until 1982 but was now being trampled by the morning Plain Dealer.

Sheppard's young attorney from Boston, F. Lee Bailey, dazzled with a mix-and-match defense that combined a left-handed mystery intruder with mathematically intriguing blood spatters. After 12 hours of deliberations, the jury returned a verdict of "not guilty."

The city was packed with out-of-town reporters but the PD did not embarrass itself. Its art, sidebars and main stories were on the money, as was the verdict story, written on deadline, in which I noted that minutes before the jury returned Sheppard removed his wallet and slipped it to Bailey under the table.

Right-handed Sam, who testified in the first trial but not the second, thought he was going back to the slammer.

I got a raise (five bucks), a Snowflake, and a happy new job, general assignment. The paper sent me everywhere. Montreal, New York, Los Angeles, New Orleans, Chicago, Miami. One month here, the next there.

Hey, Norman Mailer is running for mayor of New York. His buddy, Jimmy Breslin, is running for city council president. Why don't you take a look?

See where this is going? This a confession, a long epitaph for a guileless but arrogant loser. If the editors were idiots, how was I getting plum assignments, from homicidal maniacs to U.S. presidential candidates? The fact is, all the editors weren't idiots, and even the idiots were not idiotic all the time.

The fact is, I was not a nice person and, in many respects, quite dense.

A touch over 5-10 and 145 pounds, I had a history of shooting off my mouth, out of my weight class, and finding barroom floors. As someone said somewhere, I wasn't tough when I was tough.

All the same, in a matter of weeks I called an assistant desk editor a dope and asked another colleague to step outside. This was a mistake. No one told me he could fight and he kicked hell out of me. However, inside I caught him coming out of the men's room and punched him.

Regrettably, an editor witnessed it and didn't believe me when I said we were just fooling around.

In addition, editors didn't believe me when I denied carnal knowledge of a secretary or that she was giving me copies of management memos, several of them Tom Vail's omnipresent Snowflakes, including one to me. And yet they seemed ready to cut me even more slack.

A meeting was set with the executive editor. I prepared by drinking lunch. When he asked if I wanted a raise, I said yes. He asked how much and I said I wanted to make what he was making. He accused me of drinking and I said he would have made a terrific reporter.

That did it. The wee man, who had not distinguished himself as a reporter, told me I was going to Lake County and I resigned, with two weeks notice.

Say goodbye to Cleveland bars and hello to the bucolic delights of Lake County? Lake County when I was begging to go to Vietnam? Not a chance.

But the bosses knew that and I ended up muttering to myself something along the lines of: "Well played, motherfuckers."

Then something terrible happened. On Dec. 31, 1969, at about 1 a.m., three killers shot to death Joseph Albert "Jock" Yablonski, 59, his wife Margaret, 59, and his daughter Charlotte, 25, in the family's 200-year-old house in Clarksville, Pennsylvania. The bodies weren't discovered until five days later.

Yablonski, an official of the United Mine Workers of America, a dissident reformer, had been challenging William Anthony "Tough Tony" Boyle, president of UMWA, for the top job.

All roads, from D.C. to the hills and hollers of Tennessee, led to Cleveland, where three hillbilly hitmen were presently living.

One of them, an unemployed housepainter, was the son-in-law of the president of the 75-member UMWA local in LaFollette, Tennessee, a low but key link in the dippy Boyle scheme to murder Yablonski, financing the hit with $20,000 in embezzled union funds.

And I had most of it. Before the murder, during the murder, and after the murder. Who said what to whom, and where they tossed the guns (the Monongahela River); how they didn't have the heart to shoot the friendly family dog that didn't bark, Rascal, and how the plot soon went to pieces because Yablonski, the son of Polish immigrants, had noticed the dummies scouting his house and wrote down the license number of their car.

Moreover, before driving back to Cleveland, they left fingerprints behind. They were arrested three days after the bodies were discovered.

It was all sources. A federal agent, a bondsman, a federal prosecutor, a defense lawyer. They wrapped it up, put a bow on it and dropped it in my lap.

While out-of-town reporters hunkered down waiting for federal grand jury indictments, the PD was good to go, a copyrighted story below a banner headline and my byline.

Afterward, I went to Tennessee and paid a young guy $50 to drive me around. Home brew, biscuits, red-eye gravy, and Merle Haggard on the jukebox ("Okie from Muskogee"), genuinely tough people, some of them living on the edge in the natural beauty of LaFollette's Campbell County, coal and iron ore distant memories but high hopes for tourism.

They condemned the murders but didn't condone a Yankee sticking his nose in their business. They were courteous only because my driver was kin to most of them, and we traveled hospitably with a bottle of bourbon and a case of beer.

A week later I took a half-bottle of scotch out of my desk drawer and put it beside my typewriter. McGruder and Barlett had done all they could, knocked on doors, pleaded, promising I wouldn't do it again, but in their hearts knew I would.

And to the men at the top (no women), my resignation was treasure. When I left, I didn't say anything to anyone and no one said anything to me.

I didn't leave crying but I wasn't laughing either. It's too late, not to mention absurd, to say "sorry" to the dead. But I will admit to the living that my years at the Plain Dealer were the time of my life.

The cop shop

MICHAEL D. ROBERTS

Years later mature men, and some women, would talk about the police beat with the fondness of special matriculation, a rite of passage through the thickets of journalism. A ritual in the golden days of journalism, they would say at Nighttown over wine or at Press Club Journalism Hall of Fame Dinners where the past was painted with such romance.

As for me, I wanted to get the hell off the police beat before I got there. There were few bylines to be had out of that shabby carbuncle of an office in Central Station on Payne Avenue where it smelled of urine, disinfectant and stale tobacco. You were afraid to touch anything for fear of contracting a disease. In those days the police liked to show rookie reporters the black homosexuals they jailed for the mere fact they were gay.

The police beat was where you learned that journalism was an unnatural act. You were called upon to abuse any civility you possessed, thrust yourself into uncomfortable if not dangerous situations, work ungodly hours and all this for modest wages. Here you learned to argue with the front office over cleaning bills for a smoke-smelling suit worn when covering a fire. You learned to be insensitive and brash. You also learned a distaste for editors. Most importantly, you learned whether this was what you wanted to do with your life.

And aside from the decor, you found a grinning bulldog of a man with a bald head and a lascivious laugh that almost always made you uneasy. This was the legendary Bob Tidyman, a combat veteran of the fierce battles waged to recapture France in World War II, and the most jaded man I ever met. He was also the chief police reporter. His father, Ben, had held the same job for nearly a quarter of a century and had trained Bob and his brother, Ernest, in the vagaries of the beat when they were in their teens.

All those years on the beat can do things to a man, and Bob Tidyman was the recipient of every lesson the street could teach, maybe each a dozen times. The environment of the beat was enough to erode even the most virtuous soul. Tidyman had overseen the basic training of a generation of Plain Dealer reporters, making some and breaking others.

He liked to tell the story of when he and his brother witnessed a prisoner escaping from a window in the Cuyahoga County Jail on knotted sheets, which was visible from the police beat office.

When they excitedly called it to the attention of Ben Tidyman, their father smiled and said:

"Let him get away boys, and then call the desk. It's a better story if he escapes."

The key to getting along and understanding how the beat functioned was to know that Bob Tidyman did not work, he was an overseer. If you understood that, and accepted it the way you would the Gospel or the Constitution, things would be fine. If you did not, Tidyman would make your life so miserable you would pray for deliverance from the darkness of the place and become a librarian.

I received my draft notice the same day that I received a memo that I was to report to the police beat. I was able to skirt the draft because of childhood polio, but there was nothing I could do about Tidyman except show up at the appointed hour and accept my fate.

I spent the first few months on the paper on the rewrite desk, essentially writing shorts and taking notes from the police reporters and turning them into two paragraph stories. The day John F. Kennedy was assassinated I manned the phones taking calls from a mournful public seeking information. There was no cable news in those days.

The city room was all chaos as the bells on the Associated Press teletype machines announced bulletin after bulletin. Everyone labored in a strange slow motion, trying to contemplate the enormity of the event. There was so much discombobulation that the city desk had to hang a huge sign with the word A-S-S-A-S-S-I-N-A-T-I-O-N because so few of the staff could spell the word.

That night I asked the city desk for a byline in the paper for history's sake. I was embarrassed to do so, but I could not let the moment pass. An editor simply nodded yes.

Death was a strange, but vital part of the paper and I learned that from the obituary writer, G. David Vormelker, a thin man with wireless glasses, a string tie and a pleasant smile, who would softly express condolences to a bereaved family and then slam the phone down and mutter that death was secondary to his lunch hour. "People who die on my lunch hour get shorter obits," he told me one day. He had contempt for people who died on Cleveland Press time. He hated death on deadline, too. He advised me not to die on Thursday, when space was always short because of the food pages. For the record, he died on our time and the afternoon rival gave him a good obit just to stick it to us.

There was a lot of death on the police beat, too. Shootings, stabbings, house fires, drownings, car accidents, suicides, airplane crashes and any number of other bizarre exits from this life were in the beat's purview. One afternoon Hil Black, the chief police reporter of The Press and a man known for his dignity and skill, grabbed me and said that one of the respected federal judges just died.

Black was going to phone the widow and he wanted me there when he did so to spare the bereaved woman another call from the media. It was an uncommon and thoughtful gesture and I never forgot it.

There were plenty of those calls and visits to homes to collect pictures of the recently passed. If you got there before The Press you tried to get all of the pictures of the deceased, leaving the afternoon guys with nothing. They would do the same to us.

If you were truly unlucky, you would be the harbinger of death, announcing to a wife that she was a newly made widow because her husband had just been killed in some drunken accident on a nearby highway. Then there were calls to the coroner's office where an indifferent voice would yawn and give you the cause of death or tell you to call back because the body was still on the slab and they had not finished counting entry and exit wounds.

Often, we would go into the night and visit the scenes of the mayhem. I remember a shooting on the East Side where the victim lay dead on the tree lawn and a homicide detective bent over him dripping mustard from a bologna sandwich he was eating as he examined the body. These were great stories when the small talk on a date went for want, but the editors could care less about them.

In those days reporters could roam the emergency rooms like tourists, talking to police and doctors while patients were treated for their wounds. One night at Mt. Sinai an ambulance brought in a man, shot five times in the back of the head. Not one bullet penetrated the skull and the man lived. It was a good story, but a bad address, which was code for black, and it received scant attention deep in the paper.

I first set foot in the beat office early in February of 1964, at 6 p.m. I was wearing a blue blazer and a rep tie, pretty much standard dress for junior reporters. Tidyman was studying me and in a quiet but scary voice asked who the fuck I was.

I introduced myself and explained that I had been told by the city desk to report to the police beat.

"Those assholes never told me they were sending another college boy down here," Tidyman said. We already have a guy from Princeton who can't find his way to the crapper and washes his hands every time he picks up a phone. "He's worried about picking up some disease from all this filth. If this place is too sick for him he ought to go back to Princeton."

Oh, man, I thought, this was going to be joyful.

The beat was all about phones and we were on them constantly calling rounds of all the suburban police departments every hour before deadline. Sometimes one department would cover for another and mislead you about some episode taking place in the night. Other times when there were bad feelings between suburbs, they would rat the other department out.

The first thing Tidyman told new guys was never to answer a certain phone in the corner. This was the direct line from the city desk and Bob did not want anyone talking with editors on that phone. If the phone rang, you were to find Tidyman as fast as you could and tell him. He could generally be found in one of the many bars across the street on Payne Avenue. Tidyman would call the desk back, explaining he was up in homicide, where he never went because the detectives generally despised him for some decades old story he did on police brutality or some other injustice.

Where now exists Cleveland State's manicured soccer field, sat a row of shabby bars that served us late and often, and provided respite from our endless patrols of Central Station and telephone rounds.

Tidyman held court in Lubeck's Casino and other bars along the street. Cops drank there, homeless persons from the street would cage drinks, and some tired whores would take a nightcap at the joints. Tourists from the city room would stop by to catch some grit and a beer after deadline.

One night near closing, a cop shot the clock off of the wall when the bartender announced last call. The smell of cordite and the floating dust, back lit by the neon beer signs, along with the ringing in the ears from the shot, left a surreal memory . The police station was across the street and there wasn't the merest response to the shot. Another night someone fired a pistol into a phone book just for laughs and again the retort brought no response from Central Station.

At the beat you learned to assemble grisly facts as if it were some crossword puzzle. You phoned these facts to a rewrite person, sitting in the comfort of the office with the authority to question your very existence. If you missed a fact, they would tell you not to call back until you had them all.

Getting the facts often meant dealing with the homicide squad and being pin-balled back and forth between the cops and the city desk. It was usually the small things like a middle initial, caliber of the gun, model of the car, etc., but to be running back and forth up the stairs to homicide and back to the phone on deadline turned the perspiration running down your spine into a stream of tension that knotted every muscle in your back. This was how neophytes learned to ask the right questions quickly and effectively.

Whenever I'm asked about bloggers and what kind of experience they are missing, I think of those trips to homicide where Detective Carl Roberts would be cleaning his gun and looking at me through the barrel while I tried to pry some information from him on a two-paragraph murder that the city desk was obsessing over. Without these experiences, the essence of reporting is elusive.

But the relationship between the police and The Plain Dealer in those days was elusive, too, and tenuous at best. One summer afternoon Tidyman was drinking across the street with a detective who was on duty when a squirrel ran through the open door, leaped on the bar and bit the cop on the hand.

Fearing rabies, the detective went to the emergency room at St. Vincent Charity Hospital and reported the incident as a dog bite obtained while investigating a break in. The only problem was Tidyman turned in the story about the squirrel which appeared the next morning.

The policeman, who was not supposed to be drinking on duty, was reprimanded and as an act of reciprocity all the police reporters had their cars ticketed.

There were other reasons for the police animosity toward Tidyman. One night, a brand-new police car was stolen. The car had been parked beneath the window of our police beat-room. We often exited the building through the window, down onto a parking lot where a Plain Dealer car was parked. The atmosphere on the beat that night was strange, kind of electric with anticipation. And then Tidyman walked in and announced he just got a tip on the stolen vehicle.

Several of us began to make calls as the police began a frantic search for the vehicle. They could see tomorrow's headline. To make matters even more tense, Tidyman received an anonymous tip of where the car was abandoned. The police were furious and embarrassed by our potential story.

The number two man on the beat was Donald Leander Bean, a rumpled reporter who squinted through thick glasses and, if the truth were told, was really the mentor of many aspiring journalists. He loved practical jokes and was infamous for sending young reporters to the war memorial on the Mall in the event that the mother of the unknown soldier appeared.

He would go to great lengths to create a hoax that would draw a Press reporter to the scene of crime that never took place. A veteran of the defunct INS news service, Bean was the one reporter that you would want on deadline in a late breaking story. He was respected by the police and had a certain tenacity that endeared him to editors. Bean complained from time to time that he was not promoted, but the desk dared not elevate him for without his presence the beat would be naked.

Bean came up with a suspect in the case of the stolen police car. The suspect was Tidyman himself and Bean swore us to secrecy. I suppose the police suspected too, but there was always that lingering doubt. Years later when I learned that Tidyman had once stolen a jeep for a joy ride during the war, and was later punished for it, I couldn't help but remember that night.

One Christmas Eve, the town a silent night and the police beat slow in celebration, we got a call from a suburban police department on the West Side with a tip. A widow, with four children, had reported that the utility company had shut off the gas in their home and the kids were freezing.

It so happened Tidyman was just passing through on his way home from a quick stop at Lubeck's when I got the call. Standard practice was to call the utility company's public relations man and get a comment. Instead, Tidyman ordered me to call the company president at his home and disturb the family dinner.

"Wish him a Merry Christmas," Tidyman said.

I made the call and, of course, the president was angered, referring the call to his PR person. The day after Christmas all hell broke loose as Executive Editor Phil Porter demanded a memo on why the call had gone to the company president. He knew that the idea was to embarrass the company for going Scrooge on Christmas. Tidyman just shrugged as I sweated over the memo.

In those days we spent a lot of time on the city's East Side. We saw a city that was never mentioned in the newspapers other than in shorts that told of some crime or tragedy. The overcrowded apartment buildings were hard to conceive for those of us who drove home to the suburbs. Sorrow and despair filled the night air along with the smell of smoke and garbage.

Glass broke underfoot in trash-filled alleys where wild cats darted across your path as you struck a tin can. Dark shadows foretold of danger and abandoned cars dotted the roadways, stripped of tires and chrome. I saw my first colored telephone, a pink princess style, in the apartment of a woman whose boyfriend had been shot and killed earlier in the day. I didn't know they made colored phones and wondered why the phone company would sell them to people in such need.

The city was yet to be overwhelmed by drugs and you could navigate those neighborhoods fairly at will. In 1964 narcotics detectives told me there were a half dozen heroin addicts in the city. In a matter of only four years the streets became considerably meaner as the drug dealers began to prey on the despairing.

Those of us who would witness this side of the city would often tell editors how bad things appeared. Perhaps the most concerned among us was Roldo Bartimole, a veteran reporter from Connecticut who had an abiding sympathy for the impoverished of the urban core. Bartimole would quit the newspaper twice in frustration and then go on to publish his own pamphlet, Point of View, addressing the city's ills for the next 32 years. He savaged the established institutions of the city and was uncompromising with his former colleagues in the media.

There was no middle ground with Bartimole. Supporters viewed him as the city's conscience and critics despised his attacks on the establishment. Bartimole criticized The Plain Dealer for decades with withering and unrelenting force.

To understand where the city was in the early 1960s was to examine the mass migration of blacks to Cleveland which began in the years around the beginning of the century. Cleveland was prospering and there were jobs available for those who would leave the poverty and racial climate of the South. By the time of World War I, the city's population counted some 10,000 blacks mostly living on the near East Side.

The industrial boom caused by the war, and the lack of immigration from Europe during that period, made more jobs available for blacks and by 1930 there were some 72,000 residing in the city creating ghetto-like conditions in the Central Avenue area.

The best jobs were not available to blacks because of discrimination on the part of businesses and labor unions. Blacks were forced to work in low paying service jobs. The nation's first public housing projects were built here in the late 1930s, but they were largely occupied by whites. The construction of these projects displaced many blacks and further exacerbated the crowded living conditions.

At the start of World War II, there were some 80,000 blacks in Cleveland. As before, the war industry attracted thousands of new workers from the south. By 1960 there were 251,000 blacks squeezed into an urban area that lacked services and schools.

It was this combustible atmosphere that young reporters found themselves confronting while their editors went about their work as if these gathering ills were a normal part of the city's life.

Naive, our world filled with daily discoveries of eye-opening events and angry people, we reported our findings to a city desk inured to the race problem with its numbers rackets and street beggars.

After all, the ghetto was a "bad address" and the papers did not bother to write much about such places not because they were not deemed newsworthy, but because the news that emanated from it was universally common and bad. Hence, the reigning editorial policy was not to pay much attention to that area because the environment had become an established norm.

As late as 1959, The Press would quote a real estate agent and prominent civic figure, in a page one story, that he did not rent to blacks because they were too messy.

This myopia would come back to haunt not only the newspapers, but the entire city itself. The town, enraptured with its ethnic politics, dealing more with the past than the future, launched into the largest urban renewal project in the country and managed to make housing conditions even worse for the minorities.

Compounding this was the fact that Louis B. Seltzer, the editor of The Cleveland Press had discovered it was to the benefit of his newspaper to play to the ethnics and in doing so managed to cripple the two-party political system and replace it with the power of his newspaper. He did this over 30 years while The Plain Dealer watched haplessly, having neither the appetite nor the ability to engage Seltzer in the trenches. Now, as the city entered the 1960s, Cleveland was on a precipice and its bewildered establishment clung to the tired marketing slogan coined by the Illuminating Company: "Cleveland, the best location in the nation."

If you were an aspiring reporter in 1964, answers to all of this were beyond reach, yet the experience of being out in those streets left you with an uneasy feeling that something was wrong, and that something was going to happen.

We all dreaded the Saturday overnight. This was the shift where only one reporter was responsible for the city between the hours of midnight and 8 a. m. No other news organizations were on duty and even The Press relaxed its relentless vigil since it did not publish on Sunday. The trick to handling this lonely assignment was to get an early edition of the Sunday paper and offer it to police radio like some groveling supplicant, begging that if something happens in the city to call me at the beat. Being overwhelmed at having responsibility for a whole city, I then returned to our shabby office and went to sleep.

About 3 a.m., the harsh ring of one of the phones woke me. It was police radio and there were shots being fired on an East Side Street. Multiple shots, the officer said.

The best thing for me was to stay where I was and try to put the story together by phone. I had an address and went to the crisscross directory, the virtual bible of the beat since it listed by address all the occupants on the street and their phone numbers. A skillful reporter could deputize an entire street and ask what neighbors had heard or seen and assemble a fair idea of what was taking place without leaving the police station.

The shooting awakened nearly everyone on the street and they reported that dozens of shots had been exchanged, blowing out windows of parked cars, shattering picture windows in houses and bursting streetlights. Stop signs were riddled with bullet holes. The police estimated 40 shots had been fired and reported that no one saw a thing which was not unusual because there was little rapport in those neighborhoods with the authorities.

It took six hours to get what facts I could, and I stayed over on my shift working the story thinking that it would be worth something for the slow news hole for Monday's newspaper. I was chagrined when the desk asked me to boil it down to a paragraph which did not even make the paper. The frustration of seeing stories like this night after night made you question yourself, the city, the system and the future of all the aforementioned.

One of the worst things a journalist could experience was appearing in the middle of a breaking story on deadline. It probably is not as bad today because of improved communications, especially cell phones. Then, it was paramount when you got to the scene of a breaking story to locate a phone as soon as possible. There were plenty of pay phones available across the city, but not nearly enough when a murder, fire, or some other macabre event took place and you had to report it. Thus, you always had to have a pocket full of change to feed the phone to talk to a panicked city desk which was freaking out for facts which would not be available for hours.

(One day a public relations man from the telephone company, a former reporter, stopped at my desk and gave me a sticker that said: PHONE IS OUT OF ORDER. "Use this to reserve a pay phone in a moment of need," he instructed.)

When faced with the confusion surrounding a story, you need some luck. Actually, all the luck you could amass. The timing of your arrival was the first bit of fortune you needed. When an accident or catastrophe takes place there is a sense of shock that descends on witnesses and victims that makes them particularly vulnerable to questioning. They talk easily and often provide the most dramatic accounts while still feeling the effects of the incident. Once the authorities arrive on the scene the mood changes and gathering information becomes more difficult and in some cases almost impossible.

And then comes the part where you sort out the information you have gathered and judge the worthiness of those you have interviewed and seek the best account of what occurred while keeping an eye on the opposition and an ear to the phone where the editors are in a state of conniption. By now, elements of the story are no longer at the scene, and the focus shifts to families, hospitals or the morgue.

All these factors came to play on the windy night of April 24, 1964. It was early on a Saturday evening when we got a call that a Northwest Airlines plane had crash landed at Cleveland-Hopkins Airport. It was a flight from Washington with 77 passengers. I was told to get to the airport immediately. That was all the information available at the moment. The drive to the airport seemed interminable.

The luggage area of the airport was a mass of humanity that was milling about in a kind of animal anxiety. I checked the phone banks, and each seemed to be occupied. I then checked the crowd and saw a tall man in a gray suit with a brief case. There was something about him that attracted my attention.

"Excuse me, sir," I interrupted. "By any chance were you on that Northwest plane?"

"I was," he said. Great. A break, I thought.

He went on to explain that the nose landing gear on the turbo prop plane had collapsed ten seconds after touchdown and the aircraft veered sharply to the right, the propeller blade on the right side snapped off and ripped into the fuselage.

"I expected that to happen," he said as I looked at him quizzically. The blade had punctured the aircraft in the midsection where the cloakroom was located. There were no seats in the space.

"The woman sitting across the aisle from me did not have her seat belt fastened for the landing," he said. "She was eating, and her tray flew from her lap and she began to slide down the aisle. I figured the other prop would break and she was heading toward the spot where the blade would rip into the fuselage.

"That is when I grabbed her by the shoulder and held her until the plane came to a halt."

The man saved the woman's life, and he was acting like he did this routinely. I was writing all of this down as fast as I could. The TV crews were beginning to arrive and, as always, we were on deadline. The adrenaline was reaching rock and roll frenzy. I could see a phone open up nearby and I asked the man if he could wait for me.

When I finally got the desk, the editors were in their usual restlessness. I related my story while a rewrite man typed it to paper as an editor assaulted me with question after question.

"And young man, who are we going to attribute all of this to? We can't let you make all of this up you know."

I told him I'd be right back, and hung up before the whole exchange became personal. I called back a few minutes later in an exultant mood, almost dreamy.

"OK who is the guy giving you all this information?" The editor asked with the usual city desk skepticism.

"His name is I. Irving Pinkel."

"Who the hell is I. Irving Pinkel?

I paused at this moment to savor what I was about to say next.

"Well, he happens to be NASA's leading expert on air crashes."

(Pinkel had studied more than 50 crashes that he created by remote control making him a leading expert in the world on aircraft accidents.)

There was a pause, a brief moment of silence and then the grudging admission that the desk was offering the story for page one. We beat The Press. I was jubilant.

A few days later I received a memo ordering me to report to the city room for assignment.

He never knew it, but I. Irving Pinkel had plucked me from adversity the way he had done that woman. I was free of Tidyman's purgatory.

~This piece is from an upcoming book by Michael D. Roberts, "Hot Type, Cold Beer and Bad News," scheduled to be published later this year by Gray & Company. (See https://www.grayco.com). We thank Roberts and David Gray for allowing us to use it.

Precision journalism and uncovering disparities in the courts

TOM ANDRZEJEWSKI AND LESLIE KAY

Tom Andrzejewski and Leslie Kay each worked for The Plain Dealer for more than 20 years. Their eight-day series, "Justice in the Seventies: The System on Trial," was one of journalism's first – and to this day best – computer-assisted reporting projects. The husband-and-wife team worked on it for 19 months, analyzing more than 6 million pieces of data for more than 28,000 Cuyahoga County court cases in the early and mid-1970s. They found that sentences for the same kinds of crimes varied widely among judges, that the poor faced higher bonds and stiffer sentences and much more. The series won local, state and national awards, including the Silver Gavel Award of the American Bar Association.

They were interviewed by Dave Davis on April 24, 2018. The following Q&A was edited for space and clarity. See the Resources section in the Back Matter of this book to read the series.

Kay: The main accomplishment of the court series was that our marriage survived working together for 19 months.

Davis: Yeah, I imagine there were long hours and frustrations.

Andrzejewski: A lot of frustrations because of some of the flaws in the idea that we first had about the series. For instance, we did not know how deficient the data were that we were buying from the courts. And for many of the stories, we had to gather samples (manually). True random samples. For instance, we did a parole sample. We wanted to find out when a judge sentences somebody, how long that person actually spends in prison.

So that took some manual work. Because when we first started doing it and we ran some things, we went back to the court to double-check them and we discovered that there were dates missing, names missing, etc. So, patching up the (court's) data was big.

Davis: How did you come upon this idea to do this is as a computer project?

Kay: I think it was your idea.

Andrzejewski: Yeah. I had started working on some neighborhood stories, including population and crime statistics. And I discovered that- Well, there was a wealth of information out there that could be diced and sliced. And you can make stories out of it. Numbers are facts just as statements from politicians or business people, whatever, are. And the idea of using numbers as the facts for our stories intrigued me.

Davis: Well, I mean I think this is such a great example of precision journalism because, going through it, you really take apart every aspect of it. I think about what we would typically do and that would be that we would cover something, so we would be aware that there was a problem. And then we would come up with anecdotal evidence. And then try to find people who could talk about that. This really has a lot of authority in that it's everything. It's the whole world.

So this was published, Dec. 24, 1978- the first story. But I thought I read someplace in here that it said, Tom, that you had this idea going back to 1973 or earlier.

Andrzejewski: Well, yeah. I had covered criminal court. When I got off military leave and came back to The Plain Dealer, my first assignment was- I got on the criminal court beat.

Davis: So this wasn't just like a recent "Let's do something on courts," right?

Andrzejewski: Well, you know, I had some familiarity with criminal courts and-

Kay: Well, we had both covered the courts.

Davis: You probably knew there was something there.

Kay: A lot of questions.

Davis: So the series, from what I could tell, was an eight-day series where you were looking at basically every aspect of the county court system. What did you find? What were the big things, the big takeaways?

Andrzejewski: Well, No. 1 was an affirmation of many of the things that appeared to be true were based in fact. That the indigents didn't get as fair a shake as (other) people.

Davis: Yeah, you wrote pretty clearly that poor people were sort of screwed.

Andrzejewski: Yeah. And there were racial disparities. There weren't that many women involved in the justice system from the end of offenders at that time. But it was growing. One of the things that did occur in comparison to prior years is the explosion of criminal cases that had besieged the county.

Davis: Right. Well, one of the big takeaways that I got from it, too, which was that sentencing varied pretty greatly among judges for the same (kinds of) crimes.

Andrzejewski: Yes. Yes.

Davis: Which is a very big deal.

Andrzejewski: Yeah, and everybody sort of- The defense lawyers and the prosecutors pretty much knew that. They knew which judges would give the toughest sentences. Although we did find, surprisingly, that one judge who was perceived as not a heavy sentencer ended up being one of the toughest sentencers.

So that was sort of revealing. We did find little nuggets like that as great exceptions to the conventional wisdoms.

Davis: Yeah, I noticed- Well, the big things that stuck out to me were that the poor tended to get higher bonds and stiffer sentences. And that the sentences varied greatly among judges for pretty much the same (kinds of) crimes. And then there were a lot of plea bargains. I think you found that about half of (all dispositions were plea bargains).

Andrzejewski: And I thought that was important because nobody really had ever looked into plea bargaining at all. We knew it existed. And we knew that in some cases, if somebody came in with multiple cases, pleaded guilty to one, the others are dropped and stuff like that. That was occurring all the time. But nobody really knew the extent of it and what the result of it was.

Davis: Yeah and then I happened to notice that it looked to me from like one of the graphics that people sentenced to prison went from 23 percent in (1971) to like 40 percent in 1975 and '76.

Andrzejewski: Yes, yes.

Davis: Leslie, was this the biggest project you worked on? I know you (previously) mentioned another one that was quite big.

Kay: Well, timewise for sure. I don't think we came even close to 19 months on anything else. The other one I mentioned was one that I worked on – well, there were a couple – but (one) had to do with a family that ran nursing homes. And it had other sort of affiliated business. And I worked on that with Walt Bogdanich and Stephanie Saul.

Actually, they finished it because I went on maternity leave in the midst of it. There were (other) projects that took a while. But nothing like this.

Davis: You joined The Plain Dealer, I think, in 1968 as an assistant travel editor, which surprised me from what I've heard about you.

Kay: Right. I started right out of college. I had some other offers but, you know, I had grown up in a Plain Dealer household. I looked at it like a foot-in-the-door kind of deal.

Davis: So you're from Cleveland?

Kay: Yeah.

Davis: OK. So when you say you grew up in a Plain Dealer household, did you have–

Kay: No, we got the Plain Dealer. Actually, I had a couple aunts who worked up in advertising. But that didn't have anything to do with it.

Davis: Do you mind if I ask you what high school you went to?

Kay: Mayfield. My mother was on the school board. My father was a councilman. And then I went to Penn State (University), majored in journalism. And got this offer at the Plain Dealer and it was assistant travel editor.

I wanted to break this town wide open and ferret out graft and corruption at city hall. But I figured it was a foot in the door, and so I suffered through being assistant travel editor for about a year and a half, I think.

Davis: And Tom, you started, as a copy boy in 1963.

Andrzejewski: Right. Can I back up for one second?

There's something I'm reminded of. When we first started this court project, we knew that the Plain Dealer had a computer. And in those days what is now in my pocket as a smartphone was a room this size with all sorts of stuff. Whirring big reels of tape and everything. As it turned out, I was pretty naïve about how this process was gonna go on. As a 30-something, here I was sitting in a room with The Plain Dealer marketing research director and a couple of other high-level Plain Dealer executives from the business side, 'cause it was their computer.

Davis: Right, it was their computer and it's expensive to–

Andrzejewski: And on our side (were) a couple of editors. And I remember we all sat down. I'd never been in a business meeting before; I was a reporter. And as a 30-something reporter I just sat down and started the meeting and started talking about why we needed this and how we can work this out and so on and so forth – not realizing we haven't even gotten permission yet to do this. And of course, there was the arrogance of the most important thing in the Plain Dealer is, of course, the news hole.

Davis: How did they respond?

Andrzejewski: They were very kind. And said, "Well, just hold on a second. We'll have to get this meeting in order," or something like that. But it was a little pat on the head. Don't feel so bad, kid. That sort of thing.

Davis: Now what year do you think that was? Do you remember?

Andrzejewski: Early '77, maybe '76.

And this thing then blossomed into this arrangement. Blossomed into other endeavors.

Davis: I couldn't help but notice that Donald Barlett was on the staff at the time. And I know he went on to do some of this in Philadelphia.

Andrzejewski: Yeah, he was gone already. (Barlett, who left Cleveland for the Philadelphia Inquirer, and his partner, James Steele, examined the criminal justice system in Philadelphia using survey techniques.) We did this afterward. We knew that this other one existed and had won awards and everything. But they just did a narrow piece using just social science research methods to determine sentencing disparities and such.

Davis: So I wanted to ask, you (previously) gave credit to the paper, to the editors, for support.

Kay: He did. Think about it. They had us on the payroll for 19 months. I don't think we wrote a single story the whole time until this came out.

Andrzejewski: I did. I had some weekend duty and stuff like that.

Kay: Well, maybe I did too. But we certainly weren't covering anything on a regular basis.

Davis: How was it? Did you feel like they supported you? Obviously, they let you do this. They gave you access to the mainframe.

Kay: Absolutely. But do you remember at the very end that they pushed us to publish before the end of the year?

Andrzejewski: They kept saying, "When are you going to be done? When are you going to be done?" I remember when we first started, we just laughed about, you know, "Oh we'll be doing this when the snow flies." Well, this was probably in June of '77 or something.

Kay: We had a head list that the staff came up with. A joke head list. Our 19-month investigation finds that the courthouse is on East 21st Street.

Davis: Yeah, because actually for some amount of this time there would be a question about whether you were actually going to produce something from it. Because you start out on a 19-month thing, and then how far along are you before you know you're gonna have something for sure? And then at some point, you reach the next level where you know it's gonna be good for sure. But that's not right away

Andrzejewski: Or with us, we started exploring parole, for example, and then discovered that we couldn't really do it unless we did further research beyond what the data was that we purchased from the county.

Davis: So how long had you been married when you started this? It couldn't have been too long, right?

Andrzejewski: Just a few years.

Kay: We were married in '73, so five years. Five years of wedded bliss.

Davis: Well, enough to know each other but past the honeymoon stage.

Kay: Right.

Davis: And then what was that like? Did you often work together?

Andrzejewski: No, no. We worked on a few things.

Davis: I didn't think so because from hearing stories separately about the two of you and the pieces you've done, except for this one.

So you'd been married a little while, about five years. I imagined there were a lot of late nights. Some stress. Was there ever a point where you felt like this wasn't gonna happen? That it wasn't gonna work out?

Andrzejewski: What, the marriage or the-? No.

Kay: Both. All of the above.

Andrzejewski: Yeah, sure. I mean we had doubts. And when we ran into all these problems with the data, said, "Oh my God, what have we wrought?" And that was a few months into the project, I think.

Kay: I mean I don't remember details of how- We probably disagreed on some things and had to reach some sort of compromise.

Andrzejewski: There (are) ups and downs, like anything else.

Davis: So one of the things I'm wondering about is, which was the better paper, in your opinion? The Press or the Plain Dealer?

Kay: Oh, Plain Dealer. Absolutely.

Andrzejewski: Journalistically, the Plain Dealer. As far as the issue of the people's paper, The Press had an edge. The Plain Dealer was always viewed, when I was growing up, as kind of a WASP-ish, upper-crust paper that really didn't pay attention to anybody- you know, the little guy. Where the Press was constantly doing stories about the little guy getting screwed.

They had that final edition. And they had that first edition. Both of which were newsstand sales. So the final would always have a big headline.

Davis: (The Press folded in June 1982.) So was it fun competing against them?

Kay: Well, when I was covering courts, for instance, they had a reporter there, too. We shared an office. Over at (East) 21st Street. And so we were constantly competing. And remember Bus Bergen over at Lakeside Courthouse? You know there was a big press office at Lakeside Courthouse for both reporters. And yeah. You were always looking out for what the other guy had. Always.

Andrzejewski: Yeah, the competition- I was the day city editor in 1982, for most of the year.

It was constant. There was a competitive spirit there. And we were constantly trying to ensure that we had the story and they didn't. And of course, they had some really good reporters who were out there. But we did too. And it used to be that if there were a big investigation- Like I remember something going on at the Western Reserve Historical Society. And somebody had a conflict of interest or something like that. Well, the Press ran a story, and the Plain Dealer immediately came back the next day with a bigger story. And it just kept going back and forth like that. And things would drag on for weeks sometimes.

City hall scandals. Some of them were minor and such. There was a real competitive spirit. So in 1982, the Press folds in the middle of the year. But all of a sudden, who were we competing against? And the thought was, well, there's TV. There's still substantial radio news departments at that time.

Kay: Nothing online. No Twitter. No Facebook. Nothing. Just television. I mean I don't think that there was anybody – in the city room, at least – who was happy about the Press folding.

Andrzejewski: No. Absolutely not.

Kay: And I think we were generally sad about it.

Davis: And why was that?

Kay: Well, because we appreciated the competition and we knew that more- I mean these people (the Plain Dealer staff) were honest journalists. They recognized the value of having different voices. And the value of competition.

Andrzejewski: We were colleagues. Competitors and colleagues.

Kay: We knew the people. We were members of The Newspaper Guild together.

Davis: It seemed like it probably served the community better to have-

Kay: Right.

Andrzejewski: Yeah, absolutely. Now, on the other hand, as I said earlier, some of the stories dragged on for weeks. That wouldn't happen now – you know, especially on some lower-level city hall official going golfing in the afternoon. That would be one story, maybe. But back then it would just drag on and on and on and on. Both papers would just hit everybody hard. That ceased. I shouldn't say "ceased." It abated tremendously.

Davis: So who were the most memorable people that you knew at the time, or that you respected or thought were interesting? What was the landscape like?

Kay: Well, I was thinking about that. It wasn't like "The Front Page" (a movie about tabloid newspaper reporters on the police beat), you know. We weren't fast-talking people running around grabbing whatever tidbits. We'd moved beyond that phase of journalism. But I think of a certain editor. I still have memos from him. He took a special interest in me when I was covering courts. That was a thing of his. And one time he wrote me a memo, typed it out on copy paper, and it said basically that he had tried to reach me over at the courthouse and couldn't reach me and asked the switchboard operators and the one he spoke to said she had no idea who I was. And that I should be (having coffee with the operators because they could be very helpful). Which was good advice that I had never thought of.

On the other hand, he once- I had covered something at court, I don't remember what it was, I remember the judge. And I was trying to understand what had happened and I said to the judge, "Does this mean such and such?" and the judge said quote, "Yes," unquote. So I wrote the judge said such and such, no quotes – right? Well, (the editor) made it a direct quote. And I said, "No, you can't. The judge didn't say that. All he said was 'Yes.' You can't make it a direct quote." And he bellowed out for the whole city room to hear, "This judge is an asshole. We can have him say anything we want."

Well, I went home in tears and called the editor from home and said, "Take my name off that." He was not beyond playing games like that.

One time I had a complaint against another judge, and he had a big civil case pending before him, and he (the editor, wrote in a memo) that the way to get back at that judge is when he makes that ruling, don't name him. Just say the court ruled. That was his advice. I was in my 20s and knew better than that.

Andrzejewski: There was a guy on the sports desk (Chuck Webster) who was also the Guild chair for the Plain Dealer unit. And there were a number of us who were in the city room and in through the back walks the general manager for the paper. Guy by the name of Leo Ring.

And he walked in and he saw all of us – you know, we're like from here to there – and he's with some people, and he said, "I'm showing these guys around here, and they can't believe the great conditions that you have here to work in." And Webster yells out, "What are they, coal miners?"

Davis: Would you change anything? Are you glad you did it?

Kay: I've always felt and still feel that journalism is a noble profession. And I think that out in the world people think that- I mean my experience is that there are a lot of people who think that the Plain Dealer has got a conspiracy against (them) or all you print is negative news. And honestly, I think that when I was there, there was a range of talent and some people were more hardworking than others. But I think everybody was really interested in putting out a professional publication and doing the right thing. Nobody had any of their own feelings spill over, in my memory, into their- You know, they were professionals.

And I still feel that way. I think it's a noble profession. I still identify with it all these years later.

Davis: In all the years, did you ever have a story killed or were you ever told you couldn't do something?

Kay: I was thinking of that. There's one thing that's a question mark in my mind that I think I might have been pulled off of (a story), but temporarily. But what about the (Jackie) Presser thing?

Andrzejewski: Yeah, there was a correction that the Plain Dealer- It ran on a Sunday on the front page about Presser being an informant for the (government) or not being an informant or something.

Kay: It was either a retraction or an apology.

We did a demonstration. We did a picket line.

Andrzejewski: Yeah, informational.

Davis: Yeah. You know what's funny, 'cause over the years, things would happen. There would be fights in the newsroom. There'd be disagreements and stuff. But I never had anybody tell me, "You can't go after this. You can't do that." I never had a story killed.

Andrzejewski: I have.

I had a couple of issues like that that occurred over the years. And one of them had to do with- I wrote a column about when the Galleria was built. The tax breaks that (developers Richard and David Jacobs) got for building it and so on. And the column was to run the same day that the grand opening VIP party was held. Well, that got killed.

Davis: Did anybody ever say why?

Andrzejewski: I think they just said that it wasn't suitable.

Kay: And didn't Roldo (Bartimole, publisher of Point of View) print it, though?

Andrzejewski: Roldo reprinted it, yeah. Well, Roldo got all the stories that were killed.

Davis: And he ran them.

Andrzejewski: And some of them- There were a few, I think, that were highly influenced by outsiders. Particularly (under one) executive editor. He just played golf with all the bigwigs in town and he loved that. He loved to be the "go to" guy for them. And, you know, he just did their bidding. And so there were some (stories) that were killed. But I don't think that discouraged anybody. I think the main point is, while there have been these incidents, it did not discourage anybody from going full go ahead. And the best example of that, I think, was with the Muny Light vote.

Bob Holden was working on a story about the election for selling Muny Light. And CEI demanded that he be taken off the (story). Well, The Plain Dealer (reassigned Holden). So they listened. But the editors then assigned Dave Abbott and Dan Biddle. And their stories are credited with having turned the vote around. So Muny Light was able to remain a public power (company). Anyway, and so that, I think, is a good example of the will that existed down on the second floor (in) the editorial department versus what might have been occurring in the front offices.

Davis: Can you talk in general terms about what you think about journalism today? What is the takeaway of all this?

Andrzejewski: There's some really good stuff being done at the Plain Dealer. There's no question about that. The stuff on the rape kits was excellent. And there were others, taking on bail and stuff like that. The only thing that I would worry about, and this comes from somebody who wrote something that ran eight days and was written over 19 months, I think some of the stories are a little too anecdotal.

Kay: It's so sad what's going on. I mean the loss of all these people. Not only on a personal level – what happens to them, although I'm glad that many of them have done well in the afterlife – but yeah, how many people are left there?

I mean I think there were 300 or something in the newsroom when we were there.

Andrzejewski: Yeah. And I remember when Bob McGruder, the late Bob McGruder, came to town and saw for the first time the new Plain Dealer building and was told that there were 350 people (in the newsroom). And he said that was bigger than his staff at the Detroit Free Press.

which, of course, was a bigger paper. But that was the Alex Machaskee buildup. (Machaskee was publisher of the Plain Dealer at the time.)

Kay: And, you know, because you started right when I left (in 1990), they were still growing at that time. They were still opening suburban bureaus.

They had hired Ted Diadiun, and I was on the metro desk. He was metro editor and I was assistant (metro editor). But he was gone all the time because he was out scouting properties for suburban bureaus.

They were just growing.

Davis: And they had that big buildup because they wanted to zone.

Kay: When I left I never in a million years thought this would happen. I just thought that we were doing so well.

Andrzejewski: You can only go so far, I think with the anecdotal stuff. At some point you gotta start tying it together, and I think that, on some of the longer stories, they're not looking at doing that. And especially in this day and age when everybody's on social media and reading stuff off of websites. Just three paragraphs, etc. I mean I would love to draw readers in and have them read 2,000 words or 3,000 words or whatever. But I don't think you can do that, and I think what you need to do is you gotta draw them in. At least so they read the first 10, 12 paragraphs. And maybe pique their interest all of a sudden.

I think you just take it overboard sometimes. And I think it's a good thing, too. I spent a whole career, except for these data projects, on columns talking about people walking the streets and boulevards in the city and stuff. And that's fine, but it's gotta have a point. It's gotta be drawn together. And it's gotta be more than just in the headline, I think.

Davis: Did either of you work with Bob McGruder?

Andrzejewski: Yeah.

Kay: Oh yeah.

Davis: What was he like?

Kay: He's another memorable- He was excellent. He was very good.

Davis: What was his job when-

Kay: He ended up managing editor.

I think when I started he was covering (Cleveland) city hall. He was covering city hall a while and moved up. Ended up managing editor before he went to Detroit.

Davis: Yeah, and he ended up having quite a career overall.

Andrzejewski: Yeah, but that was because he left. He was going nowhere at the Plain Dealer.

Kay: He was managing editor. That's somewhere.

Andrzejewski: I know, but the next step is executive editor, and he would have never been.

Davis: Do you have a story about him or about working with him?

Andrzejewski: His most memorable lede was when Ralph Perk, surprisingly, won the mayoral election. And it was still a partisan election at that point. And everybody thought that Perk was gonna lose. And McGruder was covering city hall, so they assigned him to cover Perk that election.

Maybe he was general assignment. In any event, he was covering Perk that election night and he (Perk) had a duck dinner at, I think it was St. John Nepomucene in his old neighborhood. And McGruder's lede was something like, "Ralph Perk last night dined on duck and flipped the Democrats the bird." And it went through. It made it all the way through.

Kay: How about Steve Hatch as a memorable-

His most memorable quote was during some sort of Guild issue. You know, he was executive secretary of the Guild.

And we're sitting around the Headliner (the bar frequented by journalists) and he's on TV and they're interviewing him about whatever this controversy was. And he said, "We will bend, but we won't bend over." And that made it. On television.

Davis: So he was a reporter originally before being executive secretary of the union local?

Andrzejewski: Right, right. And one of the most interesting stories that he ever worked on was the Santa line slaying at Higbee's, where two guys got in an argument and one stabbed the other to death.

And where it happened is an important part of the story – right? Journalism 101. Who, what, where – right? The editors decided to put the name Higbee's in the runover.

Davis: Oh.

Andrzejewski: And he wrote the story and put it in the lede as it should have (been). (But it wasn't published that way.) But, of course, he was powerless. He was on rewrite.

Catching a ride into the newsroom - and history

JACK HAGAN

My first visit to a newsroom was not unlike my first day working at the U.S. Steel McDonald's Works just outside of Youngstown, where I grew up. It was noisy in both places. Everyone seemed to be in motion and everyone seemed to know where they were going. No one walked; everyone was heading somewhere – fast. The roar of the presses in the basement was deafening in the newsroom, much like the rumble of the steel mill.

I was fortunate to enter the newspaper business when I was hired as a copy aide at The Plain Dealer in the mid-1970s. I had worked on my college newspaper – The Jambar – at Youngstown State University, but I had no professional experience in the trade. Still, my days as a college reporter and editor gave me a taste of the journalist's life, a profession populated by a smart, idealistic, caring, quirky, band of misfits who chronicled daily life and were the watchdogs of democracy. During the Vietnam War era and all the social and political upheaval that went with it, journalism gave me a front row seat to history. I wanted more.

When I arrived at The Plain Dealer, copy aides were basically gofers; we fetched coffee, sharpened pencils, and otherwise helped move copies of stories from reporters to editors and finally to the composing room where stories were pasted up on light tables. A few older editors and reporters still yelled out "Boy!" when they needed something copied or someone to perform some menial task. I ran across the street from The Plain Dealer to pick up dry cleaning for reporters and editors and was summoned a couple of times to run down the street to the nearest liquor store to purchase booze.

It took a while but with help from several editors I was offered a tryout to become a reporter.

It was the summer of 1975 when I entered that newsroom and I was there for nearly 30 years.

Newsrooms were being flooded with hard-driving reporters, fueled with high expectations after having witnessed how two Metro reporters for The Washington Post latched onto a second-rate burglary and stayed with it until their reporting set in motion the resignation of a U.S. president, Richard Nixon.

Reporters on staffs across the country realized that you could make a difference as a journalist. You could uncover graft and corruption and help put bad people in jail for doing bad things. We were out to comfort the afflicted and afflict the comfortable, as the saying goes. That guided many reporters as they went about covering their beats. I know it guided me.

In all my years at The Plain Dealer, there was no better craftsman in the newsroom than Lou Mio. He was one of the most humble guys in the business, a master storyteller and, to this day, one of the funniest guys I know.

Without him noticing, I tried my best to copy his demeanor and writing style. I thought it would be easy to write in a way that seem effortless, as he did. That was, until I tried it. I didn't realize how good he was. He could take a complicated story and shave off all the nonessential elements, introduce it with a great entry and end it with a zinger. His secret: stay the hell out of the story. He allowed the subjects of his story – many of them military veterans – to have a voice.

Mio was as close to Mark Twain as you could get. He wrote gracefully without mucking up the story. Too many journalists want to show their hand as the story unfolds. Lou let the story do the unfolding.

Others – too many to mention – guided me by carefully editing my copy, pointing out inconsistencies, eliminating clutter, checking for errors and otherwise challenging me to support the story with reliable attribution. Many were a pain in the ass, for sure, but they saved me too many times from making errors.

I was an active member and a leader of the Newspaper Guild, Local No. 1, the very first unit in the nation. It brought me great satisfaction and some frustration. The members were largely very supportive of the union and realized the challenge we had dealing with an old-style management. We once proposed job sharing and labor relations said that was a communist idea. We were a proud bunch and not afraid of throwing up an informational picket line if we believed management wasn't supportive of our reporters. The Guild will always stand for justice in the newsroom. I'll forever be grateful for having won the trust of the union which selected me to be part of the Guild leadership.

My favorite moment in negotiations was when during a break in talks one of our bargaining reps got sick and threw up in the wastebasket. When management came back to the table we told them what happened and that it was the answer to their latest proposal.

Those of us in the editorial end of newspaper operations had little understanding or appreciation for the business end. Advertising revenue flowed into newsrooms, which allowed the editorial division to expand staffs, open outlying bureaus and send reporters across the country and overseas to chase stories.

I used to tell newcomers, in my role as one of the union leaders that they had a job for life at the paper unless they shot an editor and even then they might still keep their job.

What I didn't see coming was that the gravy train that supplied the money would run out. It started about the time America was celebrating a new millennium, when I had about 25 years in the newsroom. And it has gotten worse with each passing year. These are among the toughest times for journalists. Newsrooms are shrinking and newspapers are on shaky economic ground. Each day seems to bring another story about newsroom layoffs, buy outs or both. This is not just sad for the journalists. Smaller staffs mean less news gets covered, despite what you might hear from newspaper owners and high-end editors who carry water for their bosses.

In my early years at The Plain Dealer, our newsroom and others across the country were filled with reporters and editors, all concentrating on providing accurate reporting. We had teams of reporters and stringers who kept a close eye on the suburbs checking in regularly with city halls, boards of education, municipal courtrooms and police and fire departments. Now the coverage appears to be happenstance. Today, reporters now take photos to go with their stories and photographers write stories to go with their photos.

Don't get me wrong: Reporters are working harder than ever and good journalism is happening. Reporters are unmasking years of haphazard handling of rape kits. Reporters are revealing a lackadaisical approach to lead poisoning.

Nationally, reporters are facing challenges from a White House that has cast them as purveyors of fake news. But they persist.

I covered all kinds of demonstrations while at The Plain Dealer, but none that affected me like the one I was sent to report on in Forsyth County, Georgia, in January 1987. It drew more than 20,000 civil rights marchers in what became the largest civil rights rally in the south since the 1960s. It was a response to a racial disturbance a week earlier at a nearby Martin Luther King Jr. Day celebration.

The rally also drew about 1,200 white supremacist counter protestors. About 1,700 Georgia National Guardsmen clad in riot gear stood between the groups.

It was the first time I saw the Ku Klux Klan in full-dress and in great numbers. Klan rallies in Ohio generally included a couple a Klansmen with a bullhorn while hundreds of counter demonstrators yelled at them.

This was different. The Klan was certainly outnumbered by demonstrators and law enforcement but their presence in large numbers shook me.

Klansman David Duke, who was later arrested, told the crowd of Confederate flag waving supporters that he had come to Cumming, Ga., as a spokesman for white people. The crowd erupted into anti-black chants, including "No Niggers" and "Go home niggers."

Several hundred counter demonstrators donned Klanswear and military fatigues and made their presence known. Bill Brown, 35, sat in his car outside a McDonald's across from where the march began. His wife and 8-year-old daughter were with him. He made no effort to disguise his hatred for blacks, telling me that he was there because of "these niggers." His daughter sat attentively in the back seat. "I'd rather move out if they moved in," he said.

The Rev. Charlie Greene looked on in disbelief at the scene. Greene, a Cincinnati native, was white and the pastor of the Pleasant Valley United Methodist Church nearby. "I really didn't want to come. But I felt compelled to," he told me. "It's hard to stand up in the pulpit and preach brotherhood and let this go on."

The guardsmen took their positions, gripping their baseball bat-sized riot sticks. "I know a lot of my parishioners would side with the counterdemonstrators. I tell them we are supposed to do as Jesus did. All week I wrestled with it and concluded that Jesus would be here. Jesus is here."

At one point a car pulled up and a family of Klan members, white robes and all, stepped into the street. I was aghast when that included a boy, maybe nine or 10 years old, wearing mini robes and hood of hatred. I stood next to an African-American news videographer and watched as Klansmen and their supporters casually stepped in front of his camera, shouting vile, racist utterances. "How do you handle this?" I asked him. He told me that he just had to concentrate on the job.

One of the saddest stories I covered was the 1986 Berea homicide of a 13-year-old girl, who died at the hands of a 15-year-old boy who strangled her in his home and, with some help, dumped the body in the Cleveland Metroparks Mill Stream Run Reservation. She apparently told him she wanted to end their relationship.

Few stories had me near tears like this one. I talked many times to the girl's mother in the days that followed. Her grief was overwhelming. She invited me to her daughter's gravesite and I watched as she carefully removed dirt and overgrown weeds from the marker. She didn't seem to care that her white cotton gloves had gotten muddy and wet in the process. Back at the house, she showed me her daughter's room, where months after the killing, she hadn't changed a thing.

Her assailant, now in his 40s, is still prison.

And I remember a man getting shot right in front of my eyes in the middle of the day on Cleveland's East Side. Police were standing in front of house where a man was thought to be holding a hostage. I thought it was going to be a long day just waiting out the standoff. But suddenly, a barefoot man wearing only a pair of blue jeans, busted onto the porch holding a sword. He ran from the porch to the street as dozens of cops and neighbors looked on in disbelief.

He ran in the direction away from the cops, his sword swinging before him. Inexplicably, he came roaring back heading into a sea of police officers. One of the officers yelled out, "Don't shoot," but another officer fired a shot, striking the man in the lower left chest. There was momentarily silence as no one was sure what they had just seen.

Amazingly, the man lived. I stood over him and noticed the small hole in his chest. The bullet struck no major arteries. Later, police said he was high on drugs.

In 1972, I hitchhiked with a friend to Miami Beach to attend the Democratic National Convention. I was the editor of The Jambar at Youngstown State University and our administrative assistant had secured the passes. I recently wrote about that experience for The Plain Dealer.

We stuck out our thumbs and hoped for the best. We got rides in the back of a pickup truck, road in the cabs of diesel trucks, crowded into a two-seater sports car and felt the warmth of travelers willing to pick up a couple of rag-tag college kids looking for an adventure.

That experience and others like it that followed became a part of who I was as a person and as a reporter. That sense of adventure continued throughout the years I wrote for The Plain Dealer. Along the way, reporters and editors took me under their wings and I learned from the best of them. I cherish those days and bless those still hammering away at their keyboards, hoping there is someone looking over their shoulders, offering a bit of advice and encouragement.

Journalism is an adventure, a search for the truth and for reliable information. You never know where it will take you until you stick out your thumb. I am forever grateful that I accepted the ride.

The ladies of the press

MARY ANNE SHARKEY

The long, battered table in the middle of the Ohio Statehouse Pressroom was piled ceiling high with yellowed newspapers and magazines. The Pressroom was conveniently positioned between the ornate Ohio House of Representatives and the regal Ohio Senate. It was a frequent stopping place for news-hungry legislators.

The Journal Herald in Dayton had promoted me from Dayton City Hall to the Ohio Statehouse. I followed two legends, Hugh McDiarmid and Keith McKnight, to become the newspaper's first woman Capitol Correspondent in 1978. McKnight gave me a tour of the Pressroom and a smart mouth in the back feigned concern about a female in the locker room: "Oh, no, we are going to have clean up this place, paint the walls pink."

I took a closer look around the pressroom walls and noted they were decorated with scantily dressed women featured in the risqué "Peach" section of the Toledo Blade. Where am I? Is this a pressroom or a greasy garage?

Let the hazing begin. A few days later, I visited the Pressroom and it got quiet, too quiet, when I walked in. I know they were discussing this female interloper. I ignored them and went to my assigned workspace. Finally, one of the "guys" who worked for Scripps Howard offered to show me around and all eyes followed us. We got to the large table and he kicked out a large box overflowing with Playboys and Penthouse magazines. "This is our titty box," he snickered.

Now I understood why all those eyes were following me, it was a set up. "If you think I give a shit, I don't," I said in a modulated voice. A few laughed, and one of the AP wire reporters who would become a favorite patted me on the back and said, "That's the way to handle these clowns."

Relating this reception to my tough-as-Lou Grant city editor Bill Flanagan, he asked me, "How you going to handle this situation?" I responded, "I can handle these guys, I will just beat their ass every chance I get." Flanagan chortled, "That's why I sent you there."

What my male tormenters did not know is I considered the Statehouse light duty compared to covering cops and courts. I competed for traditionally male beats because of my admiration for women like Doris O'Donnell in Cleveland and Annie Heller in Dayton, and national political columnist Mary McGrory.

What a ride it was in a newsy town like Dayton: the deadly Xenia tornado in 1974 that destroyed large swaths of the city and both Wilberforce and Central State universities; the 1975 murder of Charles Glatt, school desegregation planner in the Dayton federal courthouse; the deaths of 165 night club patrons in the Beverly Hills Supper Club fire in Kentucky in 1977, many of the victims from Dayton; striking Dayton firefighters who committed arson to force the city to accept the union's demands; and a serial killer who randomly shot black people during hot summer nights over several years.

Perhaps my most controversial story was on the 1974 death of an Alcohol, Tobacco and Firearms agent who shot and killed another AT&F agent in the Dayton federal courthouse. The two were apparently involved in illegal activities including selling confiscated guns on the black market. A source gave me a transcript of the dramatic testimony. "You are fucking with my family, you are fucking with my future." Charles Alexander, the editor of The Journal Herald, made the courageous decision to run the story with the obscenity because it was a direct quote from the murdered federal agent. However, the publisher of Cox Newspapers, owners of both Dayton newspapers, did not agree and our church-going, straight-laced editor was fired for putting the expletive on the front page.

The editor's firing erupted into a national debate in journalism circles.

So after being in the middle of a national journalism controversy, and covering murders, disasters and mayhem, I thought I had moved to the white glove side of journalism with the assignment to the Statehouse. The General Assembly could not pump up the adrenalin like a call in the middle of the night to cover a major disaster.

My city editor Flanagan, who called me a "broad" much to my unspoken dislike, did not treat me any differently than male reporters and gave me some of the best assignments. For that, I let the "broad" reference slide.

This was decades before the politically correct era. At the Statehouse, the lobbyists and legislators would gather in a smoke-filled, stereotypical political bar across South High Street at the historic Neil House Hotel. It was generally agreed that what went on was off-the-record. Many married male legislators were seen dining and drinking with pretty young women before retiring to a room at the hotel. One Ohio state senator from Cleveland would introduce young women as his "nieces" and we could only conclude that he came from a rather large family.

I decided the bar was much like the scene of a fire. If you were going to cover it, you needed to see it for yourself. After keeping the informal rule of off the record, I gained acceptance by the legendary House Speaker Vern Riffe who rose from being a "hillbilly legislator" – his words not mine – to the most powerful figure in Ohio politics. In fact, the Speaker found that a reporter such as I was useful as a lobbyist repellent. "Here, sit next to me so they will leave me alone," said the Speaker many times trying to swat away a lobbyist.

This gained me a huge reporting advantage through the years. The Speaker fed me a number of scoops on background. His trust also opened the door for other legislators, lobbyists, and members of the administration to call or meet with me.

By 1983, I was recruited by The Plain Dealer's State Editor, Greg Moore, to join the Columbus Bureau of The Plain Dealer. We had worked together in the Dayton newsroom, and as a woman and Greg as an African-American we bonded over navigating the white male world of newspapers. Greg persuaded me to join The Plain Dealer despite the fact the PD had a well-deserved reputation of having a snake pit of a newsroom. Dayton, a non-union newspaper, was a much more congenial place to work without the labor difficulties and the "we-they" management fights that plagued the PD.

When I made the jump, I was serving as the first woman president of the Ohio Legislative Correspondents Association. After I accepted the offer from the PD, my peers joked the only way the PD could get a Statehouse press corps president was to hire one. In other words, no one actually working for the arrogant largest newspaper in Ohio would be elected to a largely ceremonial position in the Ohio press corps.

In the next few years, other newspapers and TV and radio outlets began to assign additional women to the Statehouse. Women remained a distinct minority but there was some comfort in our increasing numbers.

The women reporters decided to band together and for our first outing we invited the colorful Governor Jim Rhodes to lunch. The Governor insisted on going to the exclusively male Athletic Club, and much to our dismay he ordered us all fruit salads and brought flower corsages. We thought it could not get worse but it did. Rhodes ducked all the substantive state budget questions and talked about his daughters and grandchildren. No one took notes. A few of my colleagues were in a rage and tossed his flowers into a trash can.

Prior to the advent of more women in the press corps, I was the only reporter Rhodes refused to take on his China trade mission. I later learned he felt a woman would force him to clean up his language and jokes. His press secretary, Chan Cochran, tried mightily to deny my snub had any correlation with being the only woman in the press corps. Years later, Chan admitted that was his most challenging time as the press secretary for Rhodes, trying to justify why I was snubbed by the Governor on the trade mission. I might add here I got no support from my male colleagues who went on the exotic trip. Some of the reporters who did travel to China with Rhodes accepted expensive Gucci purse trade mission gifts for their wives, leading to what we called "Gucci-Gate" in the Ohio press corps.

As an aside, Rhodes did belatedly admit that it was a mistake not to take me to China and I can only assume that was because by that time I was the bureau chief of The Plain Dealer. I did not give him the satisfaction of saying that's okay because it was not.

Rhodes' fourth and final term was also marked by the fact that he was being covered by those of us who were in college during the 1970 National Guard killings of four Kent State University students after he had ordered the guard to Kent. When he made his final run for Governor, I pinned him down for not apologizing for the deaths of the students at Kent State. "I already apologized." he insisted. I could find no record and told him so. "Look it up," he insisted.

Our women's group of reporters had better luck with Speaker Riffe than Rhodes. He agreed to meet us at a blue-collar bar, Club 185, in German Village. There was a bowling machine and a pool table. Riffe was enjoying himself as we bought him drinks and peppered him with questions that were strictly on background. His candor struck us, and so did the fact that he was taking us seriously. We had taken note that he had a woman for his Chief of Staff.

Maureen Brown, a reporter for Scripps Howard, waited for the pool table to open up so she and Riffe could get in a game. The guys playing pool told her she would have to win the table. So Maureen chalked up her pool cue, tossed off her heels, and hiked up her skirt. She made short work of it, banking shots and clearing the table. After winning the table, Maureen turned to the Speaker to get their promised game going. "Hell, no, Maureen, you didn't tell me you were a pool shark," he said with admiration.

Rhodes' final term (1979-82) was dull. But soon things would get newsier when Richard "Dick" Celeste was elected Governor. His administration was awash in Cleveland-style ward politics and patronage. Scandals erupted in half of the agencies including the Department of Mental Retardation and the Ohio Bureau of Employment Services. Cabinet members were forced to resign due to public corruption charges and convictions. A Franklin County Grand Jury investigated and indicted the Governor's chief fund-raiser and the fund-raiser for the Ohio Democratic Party for shaking down state contractors for contributions.

We had so many front-page stories that a Newspaper Guild representative called us to suggest we slow down because the reporters in the newsroom looked bad by comparison. This made us laugh, or as my bureau colleague quipped, "There is enough dead wood in that newsroom to make a petrified forest."

During the first Celeste administration, I became the first woman Bureau Chief by succeeding Tom Diemer for The Plain Dealer. I drew a choice assignment to cover the national political conventions but even at this late date in my career I had to assert myself. Bob McGruder, Managing Editor of The Plain Dealer, suggested I might want to cover the "wives" of politicians at the convention. I looked him directly in the eye: "I don't do wives." We sat in uncomfortable silence until he laughed.

The Celeste administration was overwhelming our small bureau of reporters. And the more we wrote about scandals, the more stories and tips came our way. I joked about putting a sign on our office door: "Dump here." I actively recruited ace investigative reporter Gary Webb to move from Cleveland to Columbus. "Look Gary, you are going to be like a kid in a candy shop."

Fortunately, I had the knowledgeable and talented Tom Suddes as my colleague who did an outstanding job on the Home State Savings Bank scandal, the biggest banking failure since the Great Depression. Also in the bureau were two talented women I had recruited, Mary Beth Lane who we stole from Dayton, and Laura Jones who was our resourceful and organized office manager. When Gary agreed to join the bureau, I felt we had a murderers' row line-up of reporters.

Meanwhile, we could not ignore the Oho Supreme Court. The court was in a fight with the Ohio Bar Association which had launched an ethics investigation of Chief Justice Frank Celebrezze. The news of the ethics investigation leaked and it started an unprecedented war between the Court and the Bar. As we looked deeper into the Celebrezze-led Court with a multi-part series, "A Law Unto Himself," we found the court was awash in patronage and favoritism. Ironically, one of the key figures in the Cuyahoga County corruption scandal that sent County Commissioner Jimmy Dimora and Auditor Frank Russo to long prison terms was the late lawyer Lou Damiani. Maybe it was not a coincidence because Damiani, as the administrative director of the Ohio Supreme Court, was orchestrating much of the pettiness, patronage, and suspicious court activities.

Associate Ohio Supreme Court Justice James Celebrezze, Frank's brother, sued The Plain Dealer and me over a story that quoted a state legislator comparing the court to the "mafia." Eventually the case was dismissed thanks to the excellent work of PD lawyers but while the lawsuit was pending I was sidelined from covering the Court. Webb, one of the top investigative reporters in Ohio, took over the court coverage and the campaign for Chief Justice. Webb delivered with a series of stories that rocked the Court and contributed to the defeat of Frank Celebrezze as Chief Justice.

Prior to the filing of the lawsuit, the Chief Justice tried to trap me before his brother's libel suit was filed. He called me into his office on some ruse and quizzed me about the new story I wrote quoting the legislator who used the word "mafia." I sensed I was being taped so I dodged his line of questions.

A year or so earlier, the Chief Justice reportedly said in a locker room at the Athletic Club: "I want Mary Anne Sharkey dead." An alarmed member of the Ohio Senate called me after he left the locker room. "I don't think your life is in danger but I feel I should tell you what the Chief said." Bill Woestendiek, editor of The Plain Dealer, placed an angry call to the Chief Justice and told him he better never threaten one of his reporters again. Celebrezze denied it.

Celebrezze lost to Thomas Moyer, a moderate low key and respected jurist, in the 1986 election. Ohio newspapers weighed in heavily on the race condemning Chief Justice Celebrezze and giving Moyer their full-throated endorsements. The Court has remained solidly in Republican hands since then.

Despite the many scandals that marred his administration, Richard Celeste still dreamed of running for President. Gary Hart was the leading Democrat running for the 1988 presidential nomination until his campaign blew up over an affair he was allegedly having with Donna Rice. The Miami Herald had stalked him after Hart had foolishly challenged the newspaper's political team to do so. The result was Hart was forced to drop out of the race for President.

Celeste began an exploratory committee and stepped up his appearances in the national news media. Given the Governor's reputation for womanizing, it was surprising Celeste saw Hart's downfall as his opportunity. It was not a secret in state political circles that Celeste had mistresses including an intern that worked in his office and another one who was on his security detail.

Brent Larkin, long time PD political writer and columnist, and I had separate but solid sources who confirmed these affairs. After Celeste made it clear he was exploring a run for President, I received a call in the Statehouse Bureau from Larkin: "Are you thinking what I am thinking?" asked Brent. "If you are thinking Celeste has a lot of nerve to do this on the heels of Gary Hart – we are on the same page."

Larkin and I began to double-back to our sources with direct knowledge of Celeste's multiple affairs. It did not take long for the Governor's office to catch wind of our inquiries and our publisher Tom Vail was called directly to ask him to get us to back off. Fortunately, Vail kept that political pressure to himself as we continued with our investigation.

In June 1987 Celeste held a press conference on a topic long forgotten, but what happened will be a part of political history. Prior to Celeste's arrival, several of us joked about who was going to ask THE question of Celeste. Tim Miller of the Dayton Daily News pulled out a dollar bill and I added a quarter to the bounty. The intrepid Jim Underwood of the Horvitz newspapers took the money. And we waited for the usual Q & A session after the news conference.

"Governor," Underwood said directly to Celeste, "Governor, is there anything in your personal life that would preclude you from being president, as it has for Gary Hart?" The room went silent as we held our breath. "No", responded Celeste. Underwood pressed again. Same answer "No."

The Governor's staff looked ashen. They knew he had made a huge Gary Hart-like mistake of lying at a press conference in front of a large Statehouse press corps. Later, they admitted Celeste had been prepped for that question and he was to dodge it but under no circumstances answer it.

Larkin and I went to work. We produced a detailed story on Celeste and his womanizing that went back to the days when he was Lieutenant Governor. This was years before Bill Clinton and Donald Trump, and newspapers did not publish such personal and lurid stories about politicians.

Our story was heavily edited by a skittish team of editors and the lawyers who took out all the pertinent details except linking Celeste to three women who were not his wife, Dagmar. The story was definitely not written by Larkin and myself who are known for hard-hitting reporting. Instead it had this tepid lead that Celeste "was romantically linked to three women." The story excluded pertinent details as one woman was a young intern in the Governor's office, another woman was married to a top campaign aide and was placed on the state payroll, and a third woman and her husband were social friends of Dick and Dagmar Celeste. In fact, limiting it to three women was a conservative estimate and Vail stated that in public after the story was in print.

Well, it caused a media uproar. Our story went national and led to a debate on whether Larkin and I should have reported on Celeste's affairs. What did it have to do with his job as Governor? Why now and not earlier? Was the story written because he lied or because of the affairs? All fair questions that we had asked ourselves before publication. But had our full story appeared it would have muted some of the criticism.

And I got some personal sniping from Celeste supporters that he had rejected me and the story was a payback. Now, no one accused Larkin of that motivation, just the woman who co-wrote the story. I also noticed all the stories by other state and national media were about how The Plain Dealer wrote the story rather than focus on the story of Celeste and his womanizing. I thought they were all dodging the real story.

No, it was not personal. The reason it was a story was quite simple. Celeste saw an opportunity to run with the exact same personal baggage as Gary Hart. And he lied about it at a press conference.

For me though, one of the best moments was going into the Statehouse Pressroom feeling beleaguered by all the criticism of the Governor and his mistresses story, and being greeted with "Way to go" and "Good work" by other reporters, who appreciated it was a gutsy and difficult story.

I smiled and remembered my first day in that pressroom, when I felt a need to prove that a woman could be a statehouse and political reporter and compete with the guys. And yes, from time to time, I got to kick ass.

Stop the presses (for the very last time)

DICK FEAGLER

The Press was proud of the way it handled obituaries. When I went to work for it in 1963, it was proud of the way it did everything. Proud of the fact that it paid the estimable Maxwell Riddle to spend his full time as a practicing expert on dogs. Proud of its brand-new building at the end of Ninth Street (a site chosen by Louis Seltzer who was confident that the city would move in his direction which, obediently, it did.) Proud of the fact that Theodore Andrica, who spoke a babel of languages, was sent yearly on a trip to the old country where he would look up relatives of Cleveland's ethnic citizens and deliver greetings from the New World. Proud, indeed, that Cleveland's large Hungarian population was due in part to the fact that Andrica and Louis Clifford (perhaps the greatest city editor in the nation in the fifties and sixties) had traveled to the Hungarian border during the 1956 revolution and greeted and wrung the hands of fleeing refugees.

The Press was proud that it had convicted Samuel Sheppard of the murder of his wife, for the Press saw itself as a righteous instrument of the Almighty's will which could function where the courts might fail. The Press was proud of the rumors of the tunnel from City Hall into its editor's office through which mayors elected by the Press could slip unnoticed to receive instructions. The Press was proud of the fact that it paid the bills for other newspapers in the Scripps-Howard chain...proud of the fact that it scorned those other newspapers...proud of the fact that it paid its own journeymen reporters so much more than union scale that they had forgotten what union scale was (something most PD reporters could learn by merely glancing at their paychecks.). The Press was proud of its power, proud of its skill, proud of its staff, proud of the fact that hundreds of people in town including scores of unendorsed and chastised politicians referred to the paper and its editor as "that goddam Louie Seltzer and that goddam Cleveland Press." The Press was a proud place and it was proud of its obituaries.

"We write them like little human-interest stories," an assistant city editor explained the third day I worked there. "For some people, it's the only time they get a write-up in the newspaper. So write your obit like a story. . .they're all different because people are different. Except, of course, they all end the same way."

I was still on probation and determined to prove myself. The stiff I drew to eulogize was an old tailor who had lived (until the previous day) on Murray Hill. I telephoned his wife.

"Tell me something about your late husband, Madam," I said.

"I'm a tella you, all right," she said. "All hisa life he's a work his fingers to da bone. An what he's a got to show for it? Two no-good kids so rotten they never bother to come anna see him. He's a live his life for nutting. Nutting!"

I scribbled this all down and typed it into the death notice. Then I carried it though the clean, new city room and set it down softly next to Louis Clifford. Then I went back to my desk and peeked at Clifford. In about five minutes, he casually picked up the obituary and read it. His expression did not change (it rarely did, I was to learn) but he stiffened slightly. He peered over at me, crooked a finger and beckoned me to him.

"The thing is," he said, not unkindly, "that I believe this lady said this all right. I believe this is the way she feels now. But what people do with these obituaries is, they cut them out and save them. It isn't how this lady feels now that is important. It's how she is going to want to feel next month and next year. An obit is for memories and memories should be the way you want them to be."

My memories of the Cleveland Press are going to be the way I want them to be. The last look I got at the Press, I will not save. It was Monday of the week after the paper announced its close. I went back to the office to get my clips – walking up the back stairs past the cop that had been hired to make sure that none of us tried to steal "significant" company property like a printing press.

The shabby city room was almost empty. Taped on the glass partitions around the editors' cubicles were typewritten notes telling of available jobs:

"The San Juan (Puerto Rico) Star is looking for two general assignment reporters. Must speak Spanish and English."

Inside one of the cubicles, Dan Sabol, the managing editor, was hunched in his chair looking at his phone.

"I've been on this thing for two days trying to see what I could line up for people," he said.

"What do you think you're doing to do, Dan?"

"I don't know," he said. "There's something in Austin, Texas. My wife says if we got to move, what's the difference if we move to Pittsburgh or Texas?"

(On my first week on the job, nearly 20 years ago, I had gone to lunch with Sabol in one of the Ninth Street restaurants that had been chased out when the office buildings began marching toward Louie Seltzer's Press. "I go in and ask for a raise every six months," Sabol had told me then. "Gee," I said. "Do you get one?" Sabol had smiled, "Usually," he said.)

Out in the city room, kids I didn't know – recent hires – were getting their things out of their desks. They looked sad – they had lost jobs in a business where jobs are hard to get. But their faces did not reflect the stun and shock visible in the faces of the old staff members. The paper had been dying for years, but dying is not dead. A hundred-year-old oak tree in your backyard can be dying. . . but it still stands like a tree and looks like a tree and you know that it stood there before your house did. . . long before you were born. Then one morning there is a crash and the tree is refuse . . messy trash strewn around the yard. It is a mangled corpse of a tree and the *Press*, on the last day I saw it, was a mangled corpse of a newspaper. I put my clips in a box and walked out, past the cop. "You wanna see in here?" I said. "Naw," he said, half embarrassed.

And I went home to shape my memories.

Which are. . .

Learning how to get interviews at the first light of dawn from women who hours before had discovered they were widows; their husbands having been shot or stabbed or killed in auto accidents.

My teacher for this: Bus Bergen, winner of a carton of "Pall Mall Awards" on the old radio program "Big Story."

It was a Bergen technique, standing on the stoop, to apologize for intruding on the widow's grief, then pause, stare at her and say:

"Pardon me, but what was your maiden name?"

"Kmetz," the woman might say.

"Kmetz," Bergen would say. "You look awfully familiar to me. Where did you grow up?"

"Lee-Harvard," the widow might say, or "Miles and 131st" or "St. Clair and 105th."

To any of these responses, Bergen would reply, "Why, so did I. I thought you looked familiar." And curiosity (an emotion more powerful in women than in men) would take over and Bergen would be in the door.

To this technique, I added a refinement of my own. If a new widow offers you coffee or tea, always take it. If she doesn't offer, ask her for some. Get her doing something for you and the interview will go easier.

Memories of . . .

Winsor French, society columnist, who knew everyone in the world worth knowing. "Cleveland is absolutely desolate," French would write, "entirely everybody is in Europe this month." And Bill Rice, feature writer and rewrite man would read this and growl, "Goddammit, French. Everybody isn't in Europe! I'm not in Europe!"

Crippled by disease, French tooled around the office in a wheelchair to the arm of which was affixed a bicycle horn. He and the chair arrived at work each day in French's Rolls-Royce, piloted by a liveried chauffeur named Sam. When French died, we heard Sam got the Rolls. We didn't check it because we wanted it to be true. Memories are what you want them to be.

Memories of . . .

Julian Krawcheck who while writing his graceful column would munch copy paper. He was the only man I ever knew who literally ate the stuff and he only at the cheap kind because the expensive kind has carbon paper on it which, I presume, spoils the taste. . . Jerry Horton, photographer, who taught me how to ring a doorbell. "Nobody home," I said to Horton one day as we stood on the stoop hoping for an interview. "The sonuvabitch doesn't want to talk to us," Horton said. "We'll just keep ringing it. Watch. We'll ring it for half a minute and stop. Now we'll ring it a couple seconds and stop. Now another half minute. Then a full minute. Then a second. Then two minutes. Then ten seconds. It'll drive him nuts and he'll give up and come to the door." He did.

Memories of. . .

Louie Clifford and Louie Clifford and Louie Clifford. Who taught me all the journalism I will every need to know. Who gave me my first byline. Who assigned me my first series . . . a series on closed-chest heart massage. Whom I feared and loved. Who, after a little boy had been killed in a suburb, sent me day after day to talk with a certain neighbor woman he suspected had done the killing.

"What do I talk to her about?" I asked Clifford.

"Just talk to her," Clifford said.

So I talked to her. Every morning. About the weather. About the proper care of her front lawn. About the other children in the neighborhood. . .

Saturday I worked. Clifford didn't. I was hoping for a day of reprieve. There was a note in my typewriter. "Go see your lady, Clif."

We talked about the family of the dead boy. About the police. About all the questions the police had asked. And finally, one morning, she asked me if I thought she should tell police about the bullet hole in her kitchen.

"No," I said. And ran to tell Clifford.

He arranged to have her picked up that day but it was two more days before she confessed. The police were sweating her in an upper room of the police station and our final edition deadline was minutes away.

"You better have something to phone in to Clifford," said Doris O'Donnell, a crack PD reporter.

I set myself like a sprinter and dashed up the stairs and burst through the door of the interrogation room. Startled faces looked up at me. "Get him the f– out of here," a cop yelled. They hustled me down the stairs. At the bottom, I ran into Norman Mlachak. "Call Clifford," he said. I did.

"I can't find out anything," I said.

"Just listen," Clifford said. "Don't say anything. She confessed 20 minutes ago. We have it in the final." He had telephoned the interrogation room and talked to a cop who owed him a favor. He had scooped me from 10 miles away.

Louie Clifford. He called me into the paper conference room and shut the door. "How would you like to go to Vietnam?" he asked. "I think I would," I said. "I know you would," he said. "I'd give my left nut to go."

That was in 1967. Fifteen years have passed and yet, since the Press died, I have found my memory changing tenses (as memories will) so that the past has the freshness of the present and the present seems as hard and stale as a bad roll at a dull banquet. I can see the city room of the *Press* on a summer day in the mid-sixties and in my mind's eye men now dead are resurrected and men now retired are hard at work.

Bob Stafford sits scowling at the rewrite desk, rolling a hand-made cigarette and preparing to take a story from Bergen, Stafford settling in because he knows that Bergen will dictate the story with the length and dramatic flair of an episode of the "Hallmark Hall of Fame."

"Listen to this, Bob," Bergen begins. "You've never heard a story like this in your life. There's this West Side father and son, see–Elmer Monroe, 45, of 677 West 67th Street, and son Dabney, 19–that's D-dog –A-B, boy-N, nellie-E, echo. . . "

On the copy desk, one of the copy editors is humming a tuneless song, which he will continue to hum during his entire shift. Another copy editor is asleep sitting up. He will nap on the rim for weeks until one Saturday a traitorous or perhaps envious colleague will detonate a firecracker beneath his chair and he will awaken to news he is fired.

"...Now get this, Kid. Elmer and Dabney rent a house from a landlord named Henry McCrea. I'm getting the address and spelling. Now they haven't paid their rent so McCrea has the lock changed on the front door while they are away. They come home and can't get in so they get sore. So they go to this cousin's house and they get a couple of shotguns..."

In the darkroom, a pinochle game is in progress. It has been in progress since the day the building opened and is only interrupted, and then grudgingly, when elderly couples are led into the studio to be photographed for the Golden Wedding column.

"... They go back to shoot the lock off but McCrea is inside the house with a .45-caliber pistol and he starts banging away at them. Well, they got their 1958 gray Chevrolet station wagon parked across the street and they crouch down, using it for cover, and begin to return the fire. Both of them are pretty good shots because they are experienced hunters, see?"

"How do you know that?" says Stafford, always suspicious of reporters.

"Hell, kid," says Bergen. "They're from West Virginia. That's all they do down there..."

Ted Schneider, photographer, comes out of the darkroom and waves. Schneider and I recently shared an interesting adventure which, had Bergen been there to report it, would have become an epic saga.

We had been sent to Mannington, West Virginia, to cover a mining disaster and the city desk had telephoned requesting a photograph that would capture the tragic effect of the deaths on the small town. Schneider decided to climb to a cemetery overlooking the village and shoot his picture—with the little hamlet in the background and a tombstone in the foreground. He soon found the perfect spot but there was no tombstone nearby.

"Doggone," Schneider said.

"Let's move one," I said.

We searched until we found a medium-sized tombstone – about the size of an attic shutter. Schneider got on one side and I on the other.

"Lift," I said. And, grunting, we began to move the stone toward the spot he had picked. "Jesus," Schneider said. "Here comes a guy with a gun."

A man was walking up the slope carrying a rifle.

"Put it down," I commanded. "Walk around the front of it, put your head down and mourn like hell."

We stood, heads bowed, expressing a sorrow that was totally genuine. The rifleman passed 40 yards away.

"Rabbit hunting," Schneider said. "Let's get this over with."

"... Anyhow, kid," Bergen says. "Old Elmer and son Dabney are peppering away at the house. And inside the house, old McCrea is trying to get a shot at them, only he can't see around the station *wagon. Bullets are flying back and forth across 67th Street. And then, that's when Dabney... after all, he's just a kid... he panics..."*

"Hurry up," says Stafford. He has an eye on the clock because in these days the *Press* prints five different editions each day and Stafford is hoping to make the late home edition with this story.

"Boy!" he yells. And a young woman hurries over to take the first part of the Bergen story to the city desk so that it can be edited, a fresh page at a time, and hustled into print. Copy aides regardless of sex are called "boy" and will be for another year or so. What will end the practice will be protests, not from women but from blacks.

The copy girl drops the Bergen story on the city desk and scoops up a batch of edited copy and carries that to the horse-shoe-shaped copy desk where a group of copy editors sit around the rim looking like sour-faced Apostles who have been given a bad table at the Last Supper.

A second glance at one of the men sitting there is necessary. Even in this newsroom of nonconformists, he seems out of place. He is and he isn't. His name is Bob and he is a resident of a local mental hospital. For years... at least three days each week... he has reported to work at the *Press* as if he were on the payroll and sat with the copy editors (where it must be admitted he blends best) reading the newspaper. No one has ever asked Bob to leave. Patience wore thin during a period when he was conducting a romance with one of the women patients and would bring her with him from home... her dress buttons askew and her hair unkempt... to sit with him on his glorious perch. But the bloom of romance faded and now he comes alone. "You got to get away from that place where I live," he explained to Bill Dvorak one horribly stormy day when the two entered the *Press* building together. "You stay in that place where I live it will drive you crazy."

(I must break the mood of my summer days here and tell you that Bob kept coming to the paper until the day it folded. Now, like the rest of us, he has lost his shelter. Now, like the rest of us, he must look for another place that will have him. Now, like the rest of us, he must be starting to realize the difficulties of the quest.)

"... OK," Bergen tells Stafford. *"You got the scene. McCrea shooting at the Monroes, father and son. Then the kid panics. He cracks under battlefield conditions. He jumps into the station wagon, starts the motor, and pulls away leaving Daddy standing in the middle of the street except not for long because McCrea picks him off so in a second he's lying there."*

"Where is he now?" asks Stafford.

"At the Morgue, "says Bergen. *"Isn't that the greatest story you ever heard? Listen, kid, I think it's worth about a lead and three pages."*

"Yeah," says Stafford and writes it in seven paragraphs and sends it over to Louis Clifford who is waiting with his copy pencil and who trims it to five.

Louis Clifford. He was the newspaper's field marshal. Louis Seltzer and Norman Shaw were the policy makers but it was Clifford who was in charge of changing policy into type. If the *Press* decided to make a certain man mayor of the city of Cleveland, Clifford would supervise stories that were calculated to make the voters lust for the candidate's leadership. He did this well but he was at his best with the BIG story. Or that story his instincts told him could be pumped up into the BIG story. His editorial judgements on copy were unquestioned as Moses' editorial judgement on the Ten Commandments. Clifford, though, would have trimmed them to seven. And led with the one about murder.

To some reporters, and I am one, he was an entire university. I studied under Clifford the way some composers studied under Beethoven. To a few unlucky reporters, young and not so young, he was a menace to career and self-esteem. One night, on my way out, I passed a newsman whose desk had been positioned far from Clifford's city desk.

"He doesn't like me," the reporter, a man of about 45, said. He was nearly in tears. "I don't know why," he said. "He won't even talk to me." In a few months, the man quit, never knowing just what sin he had committed. None of us knew.

But if, for reasons equally unfathomable, Clifford liked you, then life was a lark—filled with choice assignments and page one bylines. If you loved newspapering, the chances were that Clifford would be on your side. It was his life. "I hear the guild wants to increase the retirement benefits," he told me one day. "A GOOD newspaperman doesn't live long enough to retire."

Louie Clifford. He was on his way to Indiana on a vacation one Saturday morning and he stopped in the office. Five minutes after he left, the operator paged me.

"You're on my list as knowing heart massage," she said. "There's somebody out on Ninth Street who just passed out. I don't know who."

He was on his back sprawled across the seat of his car. The seat was too soft. I pulled him out on the pavement and pumped on his chest, trying to use what I had learned researching the series he had assigned me to write. "One chimpanzee, two chimpanzee," I recited, struggling to get the rhythm right. But I was crying too hard to say it. At the hospital I took the watch from his wrist and gave it to his wife. I got to him too late. He beat me to another deadline.

Years later I told it all to Mike Roberts. "You ought to write it," he said.

"I can't write it," I said. "It's a family story."

But the family is broken up now.

Some of them are dead, except they don't seem dead when you write about them. Clifford, Horton, Dick Maher, the politics writer, who would hold court every election night in the back room of Marie Schrieber's old Tavern Chop House on Chester. Other reporters would be staked out at campaign headquarters hoping to talk to the candidates. When Maher, after dining graciously, visited the headquarters, the candidates wanted to talk to HIM. In Chicago, in the summer of '68, Maher covered the politics in the convention hall; I covered the riots in the street. We would meet in a Loop restaurant after midnight to compare notes. I was a kid and he was a dean but he treated me as an equal. Dead now.

Herman Seid, photographer unflappable. One dawn he went out with Wally Guenther to interview a fracas victim. They got in the door, but the victim appeared at the top of the stairs—a white apparition wrapped in bandages. "Get out, get out, you bastards," he screamed, then tripped and tumbled down the stairs and landed in a heap at Seid's feet. "Does this mean I can take a picture?" Seid asked. Herman is dead.

Stop the presses (for the very last time)

Paul Lilley, Forrest Allen, Jack Ballantine, Hilbert Black (who manned the city desk with a sweet disposition, a sour stomach and a package of Rolaids). These were men who were so good. . . so very good. . . that they could afford to have graces. Associate with them and you would learn about class while you were learning the peculiarities of your trade.

They were knights and Louie Seltzer was King Arthur. They called him "Mr. Cleveland." We didn't. They did. They, the mayors, the governor, the President. To us, he was Louie. He did not strut the office in regal splendor. He popped in and threw a string of firecrackers on the floor of the city room. He hit reporters in the belly. He bought our children presents at Christmas. He sat on the city desk and answered the phone (to the terror of young reporters calling in from fires who were hoping not to get Clifford, let alone Seltzer.)

He had two loves. His wife and his paper. When his wife was dying, it was necessary to prepare a "10th ad"–a story about her life and accomplishments that would be set in type and ready to run when we had learned she had died. Late one Thanksgiving eve, Ray DeCrane, an assistant city editor, approached me. "Take a crack at Marian Seltzer's obit, will you?" he said. "Four guys have worked on it and we don't think it's right yet."

"Can I see a proof?" I said.

"I got one locked in my desk," DeCrane said. "We don't want Louie to see it. We're keeping the type stashed in the refrigerator where the printers keep their lunches." I didn't have to ask him why, I knew it wasn't because Seltzer was feared. It was because he was loved.

I am coming to the end of this story and I see that it is loaded with death. It is a story about the death of a paper, but in telling it, without meaning to, I have written mainly about men who have died and about our preoccupation with the coverage of death.

The wonderful people I worked with who have survived the paper – Bill Tanner, Bernie Noble, Paul Tepley, Milt Widder, Tony Tomsic, Bob August, scores of others – I have barely mentioned. They can speak for themselves. I have tried to speak for persons and a paper who lie mute.

I notice, too, to my dismay, that the truth of the Cleveland Press – all of it – is not captured in this obit. What is captured here, in part – in small part – is my truth. All of us have our own truth and those of us who are left will carry our own versions of the feel and history of the newspaper with us to our own graves. Each one of us will call his version the truth, but none of us will have it all because you don't get it all. In journalism or in life.

The one common denominator for all of us is love. I understand something now that I never understood before. I have read that when a loved one dies, one of the many feelings the survivor feels is resentment. This always seemed strange to me before but now I understand why it is so.

I don't resent Joe Cole or the people, who, at the last minute after it was too late, tried to save the *Press*. I am glad they tried, but the *Press* I loved is not the *Press* they ran. The *Press* I loved gave me adventure, identity, travel, pay, swagger, education, friendship, some measure of fame and fulfillment.

The resentment comes (as it must I now know in the death of anything truly loved) because of what it took from me.

It took nothing by force. It took nothing I would not have voluntarily given, if I had realized I was giving. It took a kind of love that I can never give to another paper because it's all used up. It took the resources of my youth, including that willingness to sacrifice personal dignity for ambition and professional zeal. Any decent man can only offer that once and then he shouldn't.

And finally, it took a dream. My dream of working for . . . of belonging to such a company of heroes. It took my dream and gave it substance—gave it an address and a certain span of years and never warned me that when the address changed and the years were over, the dream would die with the paper.

Dream and paper both will now sink through the depths of the past until they finally come to rest to lie at the bottom of my soul—a vision of wavering outline, there but not there, real but unreal, visible but unreachable. Dead but haunting me.

~*This story was originally published in the August 1982 edition of* Cleveland Magazine, *which granted permission for it to be reprinted in this book. Our thanks to* Cleveland Magazine.

The magic of a city and newsroom full of characters

SCOTT STEPHENS

The seeds of this profession are sowed in the bleak backwoods of Nova Scotia: wood pulp turned into a pale treasure called newsprint that is cheaper than glossy-grade paper, yet strong enough to run through high-speed presses and versatile enough to accept four-color printing. By the midpoint of the 19th century, they're loading giant rolls of the stuff onto freighters and sending it south to eastern seaports. From there it is unloaded and placed on huge flatbeds, which then roll west through the republic to Pittsburgh, Cleveland, Detroit and beyond.

Soon, neatly folded piles of newsprint will land with a thud on front porches in Glenville, Lakewood, Cleveland Heights and Parma.

Just like magic.

Anyone who has worked in newspapers has their own story about that magic. For me, it begins on a warm June morning in Cleveland in 1981. The Plain Dealer newsroom on the corner of E. 18th Street and Superior Avenue is a windowless bunker of clutter and smells that include the pungent exhaust from idling newspaper delivery trucks, clouds of cigarette smoke and the odor, as my colleague John Funk would later describe it, of last week's farts. I have been hired as a summer intern only after a presumably more able candidate reneged and headed off to a more prestigious gig at The Washington Post.

Although I had worked at newspapers since I was 16 and interned at the genteel downstate Cincinnati Enquirer the previous summer, I am not completely prepared for what I am walking into. There's Rosie Kovacs, the taciturn day city editor, shouting into a phone while madly scribbling notes on a legal pad. Darrell Holland, an ordained minister and the paper's religion editor, snatches up one of the three smoldering cigarettes from an ashtray and argues loudly with a caller about a Bible reference. Coffee in hand, reporter William F. Miller holds court in the back of the room, his baritone cutting through the quiet morning like a foghorn. A copyboy places a handful of typed copy into a pneumatic tube and sends it down to composing like a shot out of gun. Bob McGruder, the weight of being managing editor of the state's largest newspaper on his shoulders, greets the new day with a scowl and disappears into his office.

I am guided to the desk of Leslie Kay, one the paper's best reporters, who is out on maternity leave at the time. This is where I will reside. Directly behind me, the desk of investigative ace Walt Bogdanich is covered in a two-foot pile of papers. I soon discover that Walt, who would go on to fame and Pulitzers at The New York Times, the Wall Street Journal and "60 Minutes," didn't really need a desk since he was rarely in the newsroom. To my right sits Judy Pennebaker, the paper's fashion editor. "You're going to enjoy it here," she says in a sweet southern drawl.

And she was right.

I had always wanted to work on a big-city daily. As a kid growing up in Pittsburgh, I'd swing by the local Thrift Drug Store on my way home from school and sneak looks at the New York Daily News. Back then, the News was the best-written newspaper in the country, with Jimmy Breslin and Pete Hamill lurking like a couple of sluggers in the middle of the lineup. The allure of the news business – being where the action was, writing about it, and then talking about it over big drinks in some saloon at the end of the day – was irresistible. I would grow older, of course, and soon realize that my vision of the business – and of The Plain Dealer – were naïve and over-romanticized. But for a 22-year-old, walking into a real newsroom was like entering the gates to a magic kingdom. And – get this – they paid me for it!

So I spend the morning of that first day soaking in the sights and sounds and the people. But even 22-year-olds with stars in their eyes get hungry, and by noon I am on my way to lunch. The Headliner is a nondescript-looking tavern on the corner of E. 17th Street and Superior Avenue, a 30-second walk from the newsroom. Two reporters I have heard of, Bob Daniels and Jim Parker, are seated at a table next to the oval-shaped bar and wave me over.

Parker stares at his soup.

"What the hell is this?" he growls to Lillian Ameen Pigg, wife of one of the Headliner's co-owners and sister to the other.

"Pea," she says. "The soup is pea. It's the special."

"It's special alright," Parker says glumly.

I volunteer that this is my first time in the Headliner.

"Jesus Christ, your first time—that's unbelievable," Daniels exclaims. "When did you start?"

"This morning," I say.

Daniels throws his head back and laughs heartily. More than 35 years later we are still friends.

For better or worse, the Headliner was an integral part of working at The Plain Dealer – even if you didn't patronize the place. A list of the most important telephone numbers on the city desk – the air traffic control tower at the airport, the National Weather Service, the after-hours number for the FBI – included the bar's main line. Copy was refined and repaired over the pay phone near the jukebox. Editors and reporters mixed easily with pressmen wearing newsprint hats and television personalities encased in three-piece suits. The framed coats-of-arms of regulars covered the west wall, glowering over the festivities. On most any early evening, McGruder could be found there poring over proofs of the next day's paper while Parker jammed a couple of quarters into the jukebox to hear Merle Haggard one more time before heading home.

The Headliner was Cleveland's version of a dying breed of establishments that were known collectively as newspaper bars: The Pen & Pencil in Philadelphia, the Billy Goat in Chicago and the storied Lion's Head in Greenwich Village, where the Clancy Brothers sang at a back table, Bobby Kennedy argued with Norman Mailer and a future actress named Jessica Lange was known, back in the day, as the second-prettiest waitress on duty. Like the Lion's Head, the Headliner could be called, with some degree of accuracy, a bar for drinkers with writing problems. Decades later, I have mixed emotions about the place. In its warm confines, friendships blossomed and conversation flowed as easily as the 65-cent Stroh's drafts. There were, as they say, a million laughs. It could also be a place in which marriages died, health declined and careers were derailed. "If you're a man and you drink a lot, I can see the appeal," my friend and fellow intern, Elaine Rivera, confided late one night. "If you're not ..."

The significance of the Headliner extended beyond a social spot for the newsroom. The bar had evolved into the de facto office of the Newspaper Guild, the union representing newsroom writers, photographers, copy editors and support staff. J. Stephen Hatch, a former Plain Dealer reporter, was the union's executive secretary. Although many of us are hard-pressed to remember Steve being intoxicated, he was a fixture on a stool in the Headliner, and many a Guild strategy was hashed out as the clock crept toward closing time. Some in the newsroom complained, with some validity, that's Steve's fondness for the tavern unintentionally cut some members out of the union's decision-making process – especially women. But as a young guy new to collective bargaining, I spent hours with Steve drinking beer and talking about unionism. His gruff exterior belied a keen intelligence and passion that would have a large impact on my life a decade later.

Cleveland was a lot larger back in those days, and living and working downtown put me in the center of the action. While glitzy new stadiums and fashionable restaurants were a futuristic fantasy, we made do and had fun. On Sunday mornings, you might spot Bogdanich and reporter Stephanie Saul whacking a tennis ball back and forth on the pavement of E. 14th Street, in front of the Reserve Square apartments where they lived. The Indians and Major League baseball were on strike that summer, but the music scene in the Flats provided ample entertainment. And while nobody was winning any James Beard culinary awards back then, nobody was going hungry, either. We had fun grabbing drinks and grub at Captain Frank's, a creaky seafood house perched on the Ninth Street Pier, Chung Wah's, a Chinese dive at E. 39th Street that stayed opened until 4 in the morning, or the Mardi Gras, a late-night joint near the paper that had live music, cold beer and customers of dubious repute. When the Headliner was closed on a Saturday night there was the 2300 Club, a no-nonsense gin mill at E. 23rd Street and Payne Avenue. One late night, a buddy of mine asked Nunzio, the aging proprietor, whether he worried about getting robbed. "Not at all," he said, pulling out a sawed-off shotgun from under the bar and putting the question to rest.

Nunzio's security system was probably a good idea: there were more than 300 homicides in Cleveland in 1981, a product of the toxic gumbo of drugs, guns and economic downturn. The nine blocks I walked every night from the paper to my apartment on E. 9thStreet was an adventure I do not wish on anyone. Once, I was at a housing project with then-Mayor George Voinovich for some sort of ribbon-cutting news conference. Despite our police escort, anger begin to boil over, and the crowd was becoming increasingly loud and hostile. "Get in," a worried-looking Voinovich said sharply as he pushed me into the backseat of his car and sped away.

Appropriately, I spent a good deal of my summer at the police beat, a cramped room on the first floor of police headquarters in the bowels of the Justice Center. Here I had access to a steady stream of scanner noise, cigarettes, bad coffee and the police beat car – a junker sedan with a two-way radio, squeaky brakes and air conditioning that was on life support. There were two main reporters on the beat. John Coyne, a guy who had been doing this since the police pulled the plug on the Beatles' Public Auditorium appearance in 1964, was a just-the-facts, Joe Friday kind of character. The other guy was Ed Kissel, a quirky and mysterious loner who was good on skates and has a piece of hockey equipment he gifted to a future pro player in Toronto's Hockey Hall of Fame.

Both were incredibly well-sourced. While competitive to the point of not speaking to one another, both men were generous and kind to me with their tips, guidance and support.

On my first day on the beat John sent a tip my way about a hit-skip fatal that was botched by prosecutors, allowing the driver to walk. The victims were understandably outraged, and the authorities were embarrassed. After a half-dozen phone calls, I called in my notes to the rewrite desk. I was fortunate that William C. Miller, a young reporter with a nice writing flair and movie-star looks, happened to be working. To my amazement, Bill crafted my disjointed mess of reporting into a page-one story – my first in The Plain Dealer. To this day, it's one of the best stories "I" have ever written.

Competition from the afternoon Cleveland Press, as well as the city's television stations, cast a long shadow over work at the beat. The sight of another reporter asking for an accident report was cause for panic. Missing a story that the competition broke resulted in a lump in your stomach and an uncomfortable phone call from the city desk. Consequently, snippets on the scanner about a shooting in West Park or a collision in Hough caused you to jump into the police beat car and pray that it got you to where you were going. When I began the summer, there was no Sunday edition of The Press, meaning that we at The Plain Dealer got a bit of a break Saturday night. That changed on Aug. 2. Struggling to stay afloat, new Press owner Joseph Cole launched a splashy color Sunday edition, spoiling our quiet Saturday nights and cutting into valuable socializing time at the 2300 Club.

But The Press' last gasp didn't last long. On June 17, 1982 – almost exactly one year after my internship began – the paper closed. I'm sure it made life a little more relaxing for other reporters in town, but relaxation never produced good journalism. The demise of The Press softened the edge of competitive journalism in Cleveland. It causes other effects as well, none of them good. For a couple of decades, The Press and The Plain Dealer had been battling for circulation. Although the Press was named one of the nation's top 10 newspapers in 1964, The Plain Dealer surpassed it in circulation in 1968 – a product, in part, of the impact television was having on afternoon dailies. During the circulation wars, the two papers vied for talent, driving up salaries and benefits. The Plain Dealer even instituted a bonus "night differential" pay to help it attract or steal reporters, photographers and other talent. And, with The Press' demise, there was one less authoritative news source for radio and television, diminishing the scope of news they reported.

My internship at The Plain Dealer prepared me well for a career in the journalism that would last nearly 30 more years. After stints at other newspapers in Ohio and Florida, The Plain Dealer hired me as a full-time reporter in 1990. At 32-years-old, I had a more jaundiced view of the business of journalism. The seeds planted during those long nights at the Headliner took root and I became more and more involved in the Newspaper Guild, the largest media union in North America. The turning point came in 1996, when my friend and colleague, Jack Hagan, then the Guild's chair of The Plain Dealer bargaining unit, asked me to serve on the union bargaining team. The 10-year contract we negotiated – unheard of at the time – proved prescient.

At the time the pact was signed, The Plain Dealer was highly profitable, hired top-flight talent and built both a new, palatial newsroom downtown and a sprawling printing plant in the suburb of Brooklyn. The publisher threw parties for the staff at the Cleveland Zoo, passing out unlimited Dove bars to the kids and wine and hors d'oeuvres to their parents. In the 1990s, The Plain Dealer was one of a few newspapers that brought a "help wanted" sign to professional conferences. Interest in jobs at the paper was so intense that during a gathering of the Investigative Reporters & Editors Inc. in Chicago, the editor in charge of hiring switched her room to an anonymous hotel a half mile away to avoid being buried in resumes. John Griffith, an affable city editor at the time, held court in the lobby bar, buying drinks for any reporter who stopped by and running up a tab that exceeded the budgets of some small weeklies.

But the digital age was closing in. Craigslist was killing classified advertising, and media consolidation was putting profits over people and product. Newspapers were caught flat-footed, unable or unwilling to respond to a rapidly changing world. Soon, the salad days of the 1990s were becoming a fading memory.

My work with the Guild increased. I was elected to the union's International Executive Council, a position I held for six years. I worked on organizing and contract campaigns at other locals. At The Plain Dealer, I succeeded Jack as unit chair, a position I held for 10 years.

When I think about this period, I am reminded of the tides at the Bay of Fundy. At low tide, you can walk for miles on the ocean floor and you think you can walk forever. But once you are a mile or two out and the water starts engulfing your ankles, you realize that you'll never get back alive. The kicker is that you never really saw it happening.

Two events define the era for me. Just before Plain Dealer editor Doug Clifton retired in 2007, we went out to lunch together. We had a long conversation but one thing Doug said really stayed with me.

"I don't want to end my career dismantling a newsroom," he told me.

A little more than a year later, I would discover that Doug knew what he was talking about. For the first time in its history, the newspaper laid-off people. A total of 27 writers, photographers, copy editors and support staff were given pink slips. Harlan Spector and Karen Long, two dear friends and Guild stalwarts, came into the office to be there for the 27 on the Saturday they were told to clean out their desks. It was the saddest day of my professional career.

These days, the profession I entered in the early 1980s is barely recognizable. Cleveland.com, the digital sister of the print Plain Dealer, touts nonsense like where to find the "best taco nights" or the smartest place to shop for "gluten-free hot dog buns." The Plain Dealer staff, which still does real reporting, has been decimated by attrition, buyouts, layoffs, and theft of talent by the non-union digital product. In a final indignity, they were exiled from their own newsroom and consigned to office space elsewhere. The Headliner, of course, is also gone, its coats-of-arms, jukebox and colorful characters replaced by a low-end sandwich chain.

I'm gone as well. Ten years ago, my wife, the photographer Christine Stephens, and I accepted buyouts. She had worked there for more than 25 years. One morning, looking down the business end of 60, I am returning from a workout at the Lakewood YMCA when I stop to pick up The Plain Dealer at a nearby convenience store. It is about 9 a.m. and the rack was empty.

"Any newspapers?" I ask the young woman behind the counter.

"Never came," she says. "I'm on the phone with them now."

It is at least the third time in the last six weeks this has happened. The paper of record is missing in action.

So what about that magic, anyway. Is it gone?

It is tempting to say that it is.

And then there is this:

On a warm spring night a year ago, I walk into Nighttown in Cleveland Heights. The Society of Professional Journalists has gathered to give a young woman named Rachel Dissell a Distinguished Service Award for her amazing reporting on rape testing kits and other groundbreaking work. Rachel interned at The Plain Dealer when I was an established reporter there, and we became colleagues and friends. I would be inflating my own importance to say she was a protégé – Rachel didn't need me or anyone else to succeed – but I like to think I had some positive influence on her career. This same night, SPJ is giving its annual Philip W. Porter Scholarship to Nora Spadoni, editor of the high school newspaper in the school district in which I now work. It's the same scholarship Rachel received when was a high school senior. Together, these two women represent an inspiring and hopeful future for journalism, and seeing them together makes me feel good. But before the formal program begins, I have an odd sense that it's time for me to go, so I get up to slip out the back door.

I slip out the back door. Rachel didn't slip out. Rachel held her ground.

The road to a big-city daily and life at Ohio's largest newspaper

EVELYN THEISS

In the 1980s, the dream of most journalists was fairly simple: get a reporting job at a major metro, preferably a union paper where the pay was excellent.

The Plain Dealer was one of those papers, and solidly among the top 20 largest daily newspapers in the country. Here's why wages mattered so much: a reporter would be paid about 3½ times more than at a small paper, where 20 hours of unpaid overtime was not unusual, and you might have less than eight hours off between work days.

You worked at these smaller papers to pay your dues and get better at reporting and writing. You hoped and planned for something bigger and better.

As a journalism student at Kent State University, I hadn't been sure that it was realistic to think of getting *any* reporting job. Thankfully, a journalism professor told me I was good enough to make a living as a reporter, and that I could work my way up to a metro. For me, that was a huge 'wow.' Most of us didn't have the confidence in our worthiness that college kids today do.

We also knew it was pointless to apply at the PD until you had at least five years of experience at a smaller paper. The PD was the reward for proving your mettle, and the quality of the stories it ran seemed proof that the system worked.

Those small-paper years were also a way of learning if reporting was what you really wanted to do, because you were being paid so little for it. I got a reporting job at the Record-Courier in Ravenna, and I loved it – just driving my red Renault Alliance down rural roads to cover township meetings in Portage County was a blast. You never knew where you'd find a great story, but I found them everywhere.

Besides the exhilaration of being young and independent, my life felt full of professional possibility. I could accept making only $10,000 a year just starting out (even while a friend who was a mortgage loan secretary was already making $36,000, without a college degree.)

In 1984, $10,000 was enough for living in – literally – a garret apartment in Ravenna, where the rent was $125 a month and the furniture was extra small to fit under the eaves. It felt cozy, and I was happy.

~

I'd been reading newspapers since I was 8. The Cleveland Press was delivered every afternoon to our home in Lakewood, right about the time I got home from school. We weren't a morning-newspaper family. My dad preferred to read the paper after work, and that meant The Press.

But actually, wanting to be a newspaper writer would have been on par with saying I wanted to make a living as an actress. Ridiculous. I didn't have any connections, which I thought you needed. Reporters and writers were exalted figures to me. I remember being 12 and going to a friend's birthday party where guests flocked around The Press' aviation writer, Charles Tracy, because he was a celebrity. I'd read his columns even though I had no interest in aviation.

I read everything: crime news, politics, Dick Feagler, and niche local and syndicated columns, such as Carole Turoff's Feminesque, and Nancy Stahl's Jelly Side Down. (When you fall in love with newspapers as a kid, you remember such details.)

The Press had been killed off in 1982, and The Plain Dealer was it in the mid-1980s and I was on my way. I got a reporting job at the Record-Courier (circulation about 20,000) before I even graduated from Kent State. After a year I moved up to the 70,000-circulation Lake County News-Herald, and then a few years later to Cleveland Magazine as a staff writer.

One cover story I wrote at the magazine had people warning me, "Now you'll never get hired by the PD." It was titled "The Violent Side of Your Morning Newspaper," and it involved a Teamster boss at the PD, a death threat and Mafia ties.

Don't believe people who say "never."

So, my initial newspaper foray was from 1984 to 1989, then I briefly became a media relations manager at the Cleveland Electric Illuminating Co. That job, with mind-numbing writing that barely took me two hours a week to do, ridiculous office rules and blatant sexism, sent me into a depression. I mention this because I had a Scarlett O'Hara moment: "As God is my witness, if I just get a chance to be a reporter again, I will never, ever take it for granted – or give it up."

Someone heard me – because I got a break. (You can have talent, but you always have to get a break, too. Some people never do.) My former News-Herald editor Ted Diadiun had been hired to staff a new bureau system at the PD and he remembered my work, so I was going to be brought on as a feature writer for the Lake County bureau. This was it – my second chance at journalism and I was so grateful, and wired, I could hardly sleep.

A pre-employment aside: Several of us had heard how one local woman was offered a PD job and gave her employer notice. The PD reneged, and she ended up jobless. So, I bought a special device at Radio Shack and tape recorded the PD's job offer on my office phone. I was dead serious – this was crucial to my future. I got the offer and I accepted. This all might sound crazy now, but my soon-to-be PD colleagues totally understood my fear.

This was in 1990, when the PD was going through an historic hiring frenzy. Nearly 70 reporters and editors were brought on to staff three new bureaus, in Mentor, Medina/Summit and Lorain. We couldn't have known it, but it was the PD's peak; after that, the paper eventually contracted, too slowly at first for us to notice.

Fast forward a few years, to the late 1990s at a publisher's luncheon for a group of reporters, held in a room just off the dreary cafeteria in the old 1801 Superior Ave. building. There was talk of news going "online," though that may not have been the word used then. Publisher Alex Machaskee said he knew one thing for sure: "The future is paper." We reporters didn't necessarily believe that – but we thought the future was further away than it turned out to be.

~

The 1990s and 2000s were glorious years for reporting at the PD, when management put serious resources into reporting – sending a team of reporters to Oklahoma City, for example, when the federal building there was blown up by a home-grown terrorist and assigning half a dozen people to each of the national political conventions. I myself was sent to England to report a feature story on Dennis Kucinich's new wife, Elizabeth. Five other reporters and I were sent to various spots around the world in 1999 (in my case, Ireland) to report on features that related to the upcoming millennium. And, incredibly, a reporter and editor were sent to Kathmandu to report on the beheading of a Jesuit priest from Cleveland.

Back to my PD beginnings, though, during which felt like I'd been let out of a career jail for a fresh start. When I began working in the Lake County bureau in Mentor, I had a 90-mile round-trip commute between the office and my home in Strongsville. I was so grateful to be a reporter again, I would have driven to Erie, Pennsylvania, each day. I even bought a car phone the size of a brick, so editors could reach me as I drove. My most memorable scoop out of the bureau was the story of a Colombian drug ring being run out of Chardon. I was told that was the story that got me moved downtown after eight months.

My new assignment was covering Cleveland schools – mostly to do investigative stories. The Sunday night before I started, I went to my new desk in the newsroom with a small box of my bureau belongings. I looked around at the dingy space with its battered furniture – where two reporters had to share one "computer/word processor" the size of a dorm refrigerator, where the police scanner constantly squawked, and a switchboard of receptionists answered calls.

Euphoria. This was what I'd worked for, to be in a city room, where you'd write on deadline while the presses thundered two floors below.

I was 28, and I was ecstatic.

~

The Cleveland schools beat in the 1990s served up a cornucopia of craziness that was just waiting to be exposed by a motivated reporter making her bones. I cultivated sources by spending several hours each day at the administration offices on East Sixth Street, where you could walk in and out at will and where people were dying to talk, behind closed doors anyway. (This is of course no longer possible in the secured warren of administrative offices now housed on a few floors in a downtown office building. Today there also is no one PD reporter, let alone two, dedicated to such a "narrow" beat. Also, the Cleveland schools have about one-half of the students they had then, and almost no one knows who the mostly-powerless board members are.)

By hanging around the administration building and meeting people, a reporter would become a familiar figure, one to whom people would inevitably pass on tips about one outrageous thing or another. This was the era when, on school board meeting nights, the Cleveland TV stations showed epic fights among the members of a politically divided board or the board versus administrators. Patronage jobs were regularly doled out, tax dollars were wasted, and absurd practices – business and otherwise – ruled.

For example, a teacher once took me up to the attic of the E. 6th Street administration building, an attic that few people even knew existed. There, in piles taller than I was, were old student records, dating back to the early 1900s. Their general categories were identified by a piece of paper hanging on a string over them – a certain fire hazard and a terrible way to deal with historic records.

Sometimes, when I told my editor about a tip or the details of the story I was working on, he'd say, "You've got to be shitting me." I never was.

Some of the stories that got me on Page 1:

- finding out about a theft of computers from a warehouse, the twist being that district leaders at first had no idea someone had even purchased these computers, or the 60-plus computers that remained.
- learning that a dozen schools didn't have working fire alarms, so "human fire monitors" were used. "Human fire monitors" were substitute teachers being paid $150 a day to walk the halls and sniff for smoke. The district had already spent $250,000 on this over several years, instead of simply fixing the fire alarms.
- finding out that school cafeterias were overrun by cockroaches because the district had only one exterminator for 127 buildings.
- learning that one administrator, a well-known political hack, had been on paid sick leave for nearly three months, but that his boss had not asked for documentation, or even an explanation. I got a tip that I'd find the "ill" operative hosting a political fundraiser at a restaurant and, yes, there he was, seemingly healthy and suddenly very angry.
- on the classroom front, finding out that students were not being allowed to take home textbooks to study – there were so few books that students had to copy notes from shared books during class time to study at night.

Eventually, Cleveland Mayor Mike White ran a slate of hand-picked candidates who took over the school board – they were called the Four "Ls – but that didn't end the craziness. One new board member – a minister – resigned after accusations of sexually assaulting a Head Start parent at his church; another board member, also a pastor, was a no-show for the commencement speech he was to give at a high school and was seen at a Blockbuster video store during a crucial school board budget-cutting meeting and lied about it; another married board member was audiotaped while having extramarital sex by a board adversary in a possible extortion attempt. You *couldn't* make this shit up.

Today, it would be impossible for a reporter at the PD (or Cleveland.com) to find so many stories regularly exposing wrongdoing or negligence. Reporters aren't given time – years, as we had – to develop a beat or the sources who will tell you what is really going on behind the scenes. That's where the important stories are, and that is how corruption and stupidity are brought to light. For today's "beat" reporters – and I use the term loosely, because they are given a disparate range of subjects to report on and have to crank out stories or re-write press releases every day – the emphasis is on short and fast, on feeding the machine.

Certainly, you will still see in-depth stories and special projects on Page 1. But the stories of local malfeasance are a tiny fraction of the number they used to be. They simply aren't done, because the watchdogs are gone. There aren't enough reporters to cover suburbs, schools and government agencies. (I'll leave out the economics here. Let me just say that back in the days when the PD was investing in journalism, profit margins for the owners were well into the double digits. As of now, there's still a profit at the PD and other papers, but not like there used to be. Hedge funds are buying local papers, and they wouldn't bother if there wasn't money to be made.)

In any case, the idea of what is now happening to public dollars without reporters' oversight is mind-boggling.

~

After three years, my beat changed to Cleveland City Hall, where the mercurial and vindictive – but often effective – Mike White was still mayor. Before a year was over, I was suddenly and unexpectedly moved up to become the PD's politics writer.

That meant covering the 1996 Republican and Democratic conventions in San Diego and Chicago, respectively; interviewing President Bill Clinton in 1998 in a several hours long meeting during which, for the first time, he blamed the National Rifle Association for costing Democrats the House and Senate; and covering the race that turned out to be the comeback of Dennis Kucinich, who ousted incumbent U.S. Rep. Martin Hoke, to Hoke's considerable and everlasting shock.

To me, one of best things about being a reporter was that after a beat felt wrung out, or if I got a lousy editor on that beat who seemed to have no news sense about Cleveland (a flurry of these were hired in the 1990s, all from out of town), I simply looked for another beat that interested me.

That's how I went from being the politics writer, to feature writer for the Arts & Life section, to a five-year stint as fashion editor and then, before I left in 2013, a medical reporter. I loved the hell out of all those beats, until a subject began to feel stale.

Being the fashion editor was a definite highlight – and I was lucky enough to be part of the last hurrah of the PD's investment in this beat. I was named fashion editor in 2000, after the retirement of longtime Fashion Editor Janet McCue. What a job she had! In her day, she flew business class and stayed at five-star hotels in Milan and Paris. She also didn't have to file stories while she was traveling, but rather wrote them several weeks after she came back, which allowed her take European vacations after the shows.

When Editor Doug Clifton came to lead the PD, he made it clear that those days were over. Janet decided to retire from a job she'd been identified with for 20 years. And I, who had studied fashion and its history, was asked if I was interested. I certainly was.

Happily, the PD was still willing to invest in this coverage – and there was plenty of local advertising to support the stand-alone fashion section we published each week. So, it was a logical business decision.

In 2000, I covered the ready-to-wear shows in Milan and Paris. No business class or five-star hotels for me, but I was immensely grateful to travel to Europe to cover the shows and, yes, I filed stories as quickly as the ancient Radio Shack laptop sending stories via phone modem from Europe would allow.

I covered the twice-a-year shows in New York, too, staying at first at the Marriott Marquis, where I had nine or 10 days to immerse myself in the city, report on fashion feature stories, and file stories each evening about that day's shows, or at least the eight or so I went to. File story, sleep for a few hours, and do it all again the next day: it was exhausting, but I knew how lucky I was.

In 2001, I covered the New York and Paris shows in the spring, then went to New York again that September. That's why I was on the 42nd floor of the Marriott Marquis on Sept. 11. My editor called me that morning and left a voicemail, saying something nonsensical to me about "Fashion week is obviously over," and something else about a plane crash. Since I hadn't turned on the TV, I had no idea what she was talking about. I called her back, and within a half-hour, I was down at Times Square, interviewing people who stood motionless as they read the rolling news ticker to learn something unimaginable had happened a few miles away. I then walked toward the World Trade Center on Sixth Avenue, before and after the buildings collapsed.

I didn't get far, because I had to file a story in a few hours. So, I interviewed people who were walking back from what we later called Ground Zero, and they told me shattering stories of near-misses, of how they were not far from the buildings when they collapsed and of friends and family who worked nearby – or inside.

That night, the city shut down as it never had before. I looked down on Times Square at about

1 a.m. when not a single car, or person, could be seen. No movement at all. Every storefront and restaurant had its walled gates down.

An empty Times Square – that was unprecedented, at least in the past two hundred years. I was desolate, alone in my room, unable to make calls on either the hotel phone or my cell, which were not working.

The next day, several of my PD colleagues drove into the city. We unexpectedly met at the barricades near West 10th Street and became a team.

We were doing something we never thought we would in our lifetimes: reporting from an American city that had been under attack, where nearly 3,000 people had died. The family members of the missing and dead now were lined up outside the Lexington Armory to provide DNA samples from combs and toothbrushes, hoping the bodies of their loved ones would be recovered and identified.

I reported the saddest stories I ever had to write, talking to bereft families, or people who'd been walking down the stairs of the buildings as the firefighters who gave them encouragement headed up to their deaths, it would turn out.

I left the city four days later, riding back with my PD colleagues, reporter Michael Heaton and photographer Marvin Fong. We had an emotional debriefing in the car. I am sure it helped a little.

The news business, and the PD, changed immediately. As far as my beat, the trips to Europe were over, understandably, and who wanted to travel anymore? But the PD continued to send me to New York for the shows and remembering the trauma of being on the upper floors of the Marquis, I moved to the historic Algonquin.

I think I'm safe in saying the PD or Cleveland.com will not have a reporter staying anyplace like the Algonquin, on their dime, ever again.

Kim Crow became the fashion editor after I stepped down (at five years, it was my longest stint on a beat ever). She soon had to deal with the belt-tightening of this new era, which meant staying in NYC budget hotels and paying for her own meals on much shorter trips.

And then the PD stopped sending her even to New York for the shows. During the glory years, dozens of regional newspapers' fashion reporters and editors would meet in New York twice each year, and even competed for a special fashion writing award. That ended long before 2010, as bloggers – who could sell merchandise through their posts – replaced the reporters whose papers no longer sent them.

~

In the scheme of what's happened to newspapers, the fact that the PD scrapped fashion coverage seems trite. And compared to the bread-and-butter local news that's no longer being covered, it is indeed minor. Yet it's also hard to believe it all went away so quickly.

But of everything I miss since I left the paper for a TV producing job in 2013, and then soon moved to a nonprofit writing job, it's losing my colleagues and not working in a newsroom that is the hardest.

Reporters, for the most part, are well-read, scathingly witty, smart and irreverent – in short, delightful company. And because of the intensity of covering breaking news and tragedy and exposing wrongdoing, you have shared emotional experiences, and nothing connects people more strongly. Also, you get to be yourself – we were members of a tribe, one that included mostly interesting or downright eccentric people, and even weirder ones who would account for the bizarre anecdotes we still remember.

The Harvard grad who nearly caused a fire by heating his wet socks in the newsroom microwave. The high-level editor who assigned a reporter to write a feature on the woman he was having an affair with. The desk editor who was a ranting know-it-all who sometimes slept in his car after drinking with colleagues at the nearby Mardi Gras bar.

And the theater critic who vandalized a colleague's car with a military-grade slingshot under the security cameras in the PD parking lot – in daylight. The sweet old-timer who covered the scent of his daily lunchtime vodka with after shave. A graceful writer who wrote less than a handful of stories each year – and kept getting away with it, editor after editor.

There were tragic stories too: a longtime reporter whose mental illness led to drugs and homelessness and the jazz-loving writer who was hopelessly miscast in the newsroom, and later killed himself.

Very few boring people work in newsrooms. If they were lackluster they didn't fit in or last long (mostly), though some became low-level editors. Other people left and were only dimly remembered. Which made sense, because for a long time, we had about 300 people in the news department alone. It seems like a dream, but we did, and it wasn't all that long ago.

And then there were your friends – who remain your friends, and even if you lose touch, you easily reconnect when you see them. Because you are all former reporters, and that makes you different and quirky, and probably an entertaining storyteller.

Most of us have moved on and the lucky ones – I am one – continue to work with smart, irreverent people in our new jobs.

We former reporters were there for the magnificent final years. I am sad for all the journalism graduates who will never be able to have this abundant of a newspaper experience, let alone make a decent wage at it. Like blacksmiths, the jobs we had are gone and will never be available in the same way again. The reporters who remain – outside of New York or Washington – may work at newspapers or lame websites with annoying pop-ups but will not make much of a living.

Next year – 2019, when the Newspaper Guild contract expires – will bring the final bloodletting of talent and experience.

Yes, the world always changes – in this case, for the worse. For all the reporters who might have been, for all the readers who will never know as much about their towns and cities and government as they would have, the days will never be as rich as they were in the last, great days of the Cleveland newspaper.

For those of us who know what we loved is gone, there will always be sadness. I am not just speaking for myself when I say that if you were meant to be a reporter, and you were a good one, you knew it. Your curiosity was insatiable, you knew what your purpose on this earth was, and that you were born for this role. Your adrenalin pumped just the right amount when you wrote on deadline, the words flowed from your fingertips, and you knew your story might change something for the better.

This is what is almost gone. Those who remain newspaper reporters, for now, are "beating on, against the current," in F. Scott Fitzgerald's words in "The Great Gatsby." Eventually, soon, the current will overtake them.

And the stories that "old" reporters share will last as only as long as we do.

Health care, the "sleeve," and life in The PD newsroom

JOAN MAZZOLINI

The Plain Dealer experience is a kind of Rorschach test. Reporters who sat side by side with the same editors for years have vastly different experiences, different stories, different opinions of editors and co-workers.

But for those from a certain era, there's one commonality: Interviewing for a job at The Plain Dealer is still the stuff of legends. People sat for days, sometimes never being interviewed, or being interviewed on their way out at a bar. When I came up from Birmingham, Alabama, I didn't realize until I was ready to leave that my return trip, arranged by the paper, was to Birmingham, Michigan.

I arrived in late October 1991 at the tail end of the great expansion years, when nearly one hundred were hired to add and beef up suburban bureaus.

I left a small paper and walking into that dark, dirty-looking newsroom stuffed with people and energy, I knew I had landed at a big city paper. But with that came issues that were a surprise. For example, I learned that the Newspaper Guild had just taken a strike vote. It was a little freaky to think I might be on strike days after starting.

There also was a generational fight going on at the paper over pensions and these new things called 401ks, where companies were not on the hook for guaranteed benefits. Some of the younger, newer reporters wanted them as they were being sold to Americans as great things. But older reporters, specifically Dick Peery, spoke of the dangers of getting rid of defined pension plans.

Ultimately, we had both, but the paper never contributed a dime to our 401Ks – and people didn't realize then their shortcoming. At the same time, our pension payouts were small – especially compared with our high pay – though they were slightly increased after much wrangling. Before I left, the company contributions to them were frozen, meaning you weren't accumulating more years for retirement.

I was hired to take over the vacant Metro medical beat – which differed from the health care beat in Features and the health insurance and medical beat in Business.

I came from a small paper, the Birmingham (AL) Post-Herald, where reporters worked together amicably and there wasn't a lot of inner-office competition. That wasn't entirely the same at The PD.

Soon after arriving, like nearly every other PD reporter, I worked the November elections. Reporters were sent to the board of elections in each of the seven counties with phones to plug in so that those writing stories back in the office could be in constant contact with them. Every update was called in until the final tally came through, sometimes too late for the first edition. We had stories on every election in the seven-county region. The PD was the largest paper in Ohio and thought of itself as the paper of record. What a change.

So except for a skeleton day crew, all the reporters were involved in the election coverage. It was a camaraderie-building event and afterward everyone went over to the Headliner, one of two bars near the paper. Reporters from TV and radio stations all joined us for a giant, rowdy but happy crowd where everyone talked shop about surprise wins and losses, and newly minted elected officials. (The other bar, the Mardi Gras was a favorite of the editors. So favored that the desk would call the bar to reach editors with questions on stories that were being readied for the next day's paper.)

A week or so on the job, I started calling around to hospitals and other organizations to introduce myself, suggesting a meeting, asking about what new things were happening. Typical beat building. Much to my surprise the business reporter had started doing the same thing, calling the same people.

There wasn't a shortage of medical or health care news. The Features department reporter covered health news –outbreaks, new discoveries and treatments and any local researcher or doctor publishing articles in medical or science journals.

My understanding of the beat – from the little direction I got (The Plain Dealer was a swim or drown sort of place) – was to cover the business of hospitals and health care, the competition of the facilities, in the region and Ohio. And there was no shortage of either. Ohio was still a "Certificate of Need" state, meaning that for a hospital to add a service, such as transplantation or a specialized piece of equipment, they had to show that there was enough population to warrant adding something that other hospitals already had and wouldn't diminish the procedure at the other hospital. The old practice makes perfect – that if a surgeon does a lot of kidney transplantations they are better skilled than one who does one occasionally.

These CON documents gave me a great look at the hospitals' plans for the future. At that time, the great consolidation hadn't occurred. Most hospitals were stand-alone facilities, even the Cleveland Clinic and University Hospitals. There was one group of smaller hospitals that had joined together – the Meridia Health System – that included the hospitals Euclid, Huron Road, Hillcrest and Suburban (which became South Pointe).

I had a great time. I remember spending hours waiting outside an office at a hospital to get a look at their 990s – the IRS documents that nonprofits had to file and which had to be available for anyone to look at. (Today, they're all online at GuideStar.) But in those days, nonprofits had to show them. But they didn't have to make copies so I had a legal sized yellow pad on which I would write down all the important items found, such as salaries for the highest paid employees and contractors. It took hours. I just sat there reiterating my right to see them, lawyers were called and ultimately I was shown into a conference room where I was watched while I reviewed the documents and wrote down the information.

I did that for the Greater Cleveland Hospital Association – now the Center for Health Affairs – and was shocked to see the executive director making over a quarter of a million dollars.

The hospital ground shifted a bit after a report came out showing that Cleveland area companies could save money by flying employees to the Mayo Clinic for certain treatments and surgeries. Seems illogical but all things considered – cost of the flight, the cost of the treatment at Mayo, and amount of time off work – was much better than at Cleveland hospitals, it worked out in the end.

After that, a local business group forced hospitals to come together and be part of a report card of sorts that would allow them – and patients – to compare the quality of certain medical procedures and surgeries. They agreed, begrudgingly. Companies felt the info would help them steer employees to the better-quality hospitals and that in the end it would be cost effective.

It fell apart – but not without the first report cards showing some surprises, including that Mt. Sinai Medical Center, now closed, had the best heart surgery outcomes of all. That revelation might have helped kill the reports.

The hospitals fought over everything. The report – which we got in advance copy to prepare our stories – used odd symbols to show whether they had done as expected, better or worse. We decided to use up, down and sideways arrows instead, so readers could understand. Hospitals freaked.

Hospital officials, and the executive director of the hospital association (the one making over $250,000) would come to see the editor, David Hall, who backed me completely. Hall noted that they thought talking to the "parent" would more easily control the story and me.

Not long after, the start of the merging and consolidation of hospitals began. More great stories to cover.

Health care was an issue inside The PD, too. A few months after starting, I was asked to join the health care board as one of two union reps. Management had its own health plan, but all the union members – which at that time included all reporters, copy editors, photographers, editorial board writers and assistant editors in Metro, Sports, Business, and Features, had a different plan that was jointly overseen by a guild and management board. The two sides jointly hired an attorney, an insurance consultant and other specialized consultants for advice.

Our health plans were in a crisis. When the Guild negotiated – it was for a lump-sum increase that would be divided up for wages, health insurance and pension funding. We were so big then, insurance companies bid for our business, and we offered several plans. But it had been many, many years since the amount of money for medical insurance had been increased, despite rapidly increasing health care costs.

We got out of the jam. But my position on the board for more than 15 years grew increasingly contentious – first with the management side as they replaced their board members with hard asses and later with the Guild when, after years of great insurance, the decline in staff and surge in prices meant some tough decisions about medical benefits had to be made.

The PD was known for having a number of married couples on staff. As out-of-pocket costs rose, some clever couples chose different health plans, so that whatever one plan didn't cover fully, the other would pick up the difference.

The management reps were probably surprised, but myself and my compatriot on the board,

Don Rosenberg, stopped that practice and required married couples to pick one plan for both of them. It wasn't popular with all, because a set amount of money went to health care for each employee, so they felt they were being penalized and subsidizing others.

At the same time, unmarried staff were subsidizing families because more money went in monthly than the cost for a single person's plan. The extra went to shore up the plan.

The changes and other cuts helped stave off for a good while the need for PD staff to reduce their pay to cover insurance.

But there was many a contentious guild meeting where health care and pensions were hotly discussed. Don and I sat and answered for the decisions we made.

I left the newsroom in 2010. My last few years at the paper, guild staff made tough choices, including transferring wage increases to health care. Ultimately, we voted to take a pay cut and 10 days of furloughed time off, which combined amounted to a 12 ½ percent pay cut. Those left at the PD are still taking the furloughs.

It seems crazy that a decade or so earlier, I marveled at how the paper was flush with money, sending reporters all over the globe, and more importantly flush with space, enough for everyone to write stories that were as long as they wanted. Reporters' opinions, what they saw and knew from their beats, were respected, for the most part.

The Plain Dealer still had a society writer, Mary Strassmeyer, who wrote a column called "Mary Mary," but the paper also hired freelancers to go to parties she didn't want to attend. People vied to get into her column. I sat near Mary, and saw the near daily floral arrangements and gift baskets delivered to her and placed on her assistant's desk for later decisions on which would go into her car.

It was a different time.

Our renowned rock critic, Jane Scott, was there. By the time I started, she was a senior, with a funky haircut and big, red glasses and a small, sweet voice. But soon a younger features reporter was there, to begin shouldering the load.

We still had a night police reporter who'd didn't write stories but called in information. When it was your turn for nights, you'd answer the phone and Ed Kissell would start giving information mid-sentence.

I learned quickly about the "sleeve." If you found out your story was holding, or it had already been edited around 4 p.m. or so, you might stand up and pull at your sleeve, making sure at least one person saw you. Then you'd get up, coat left behind, walk and talk to people as you made your way to light out the front door and walk half a block to the Headliner. The PD building was virtually windowless, by virtue of previous strikes, so there was no one to see you go for a beer. Soon enough, as others started tugging at their sleeves, a good number of other reporters would follow.

In the opposite direction, was the Phoenix coffee shop that PDers would amble to throughout the day. There was always someone from the paper there. For a small shop, it offered great people watching. It had a parking lot and enough on-street parking to draw politicians, business people and others for impromptu meetings.

It was a better time.

Woe to the reporter who wanted to meet up at the Headliner but got the conspiratorial line editor who barked orders when the story was done to find some offbeat, non-existent angle or link to something. Male reporters bristled over one particular editor, fighting over this last call he wanted.

Others simply agreed to find out (but didn't) and then reported – nothing to report. But then there was the small number of copy editors who read each word and expected it to be literal. A hot day mentioned might get the question, what was the temperature?

The paper was big enough that you might not meet or really know people in other departments for years. The sports department was nearly vacant. Business was in a different area, Features, Business, all had big robust staffs. Metro, of which I was a part, was the biggest and the queen bee at the paper, which rubbed some the wrong way.

But no department had better work stations than the others. Two to a terminal (now computers). Fights did erupt when someone wanted to take notes on the terminal, hogging it for hours.

No windows. Only the library had a small window so we could see whether there was a giant snowstorm or a beautiful day.

Looking back, it was definitely the time to be a reporter at The Plain Dealer, maybe everywhere. When the new building opened in 2000 and we moved in with a new editor, a new vibe took over. More insurance-like for sure. But we tried to keep the things that made working there great and added to your knowledge and skill as a reporter and writer.

Some editors saw reporters walking around talking as loafing, and a bad thing. I can't tell you how many times someone came up to talk to me or vice versa and in mentioning the story you were working on that they or you didn't know some fact, big or small; I can't tell you how many times casual newsroom conversations about stories and other things led to learning information that would provide a new angle for a story or improve it in some way.

Institutional history. We had it in spades for a while.

The new vibe included moving people around if they thought they were too chummy with their cubicle mates. After having no windows, the new building had giant floor-to-ceiling windows looking out on Superior Avenue. But sun glare for those sitting nearby, and complainers, meant these giant shades were rolled down blocking out most of the view. I got into a fight over the shades.

Reporters were moved around to different beats, sometimes because their fortunes were rising, or sometimes as punishment. In that newsroom at that time, someone always knew and had the phone number of a person you needed to reach. We were wired in; covering beats, developing sources, and coming back and telling editors this is the story I have.

For my first 15 years there, I now feel fortunate. Reporters are the biggest bitchers and moaners but love the work, love knowing things and love trying to get that insight into stories that would help, or inform, or shock readers.

Readers would call. Some reporters didn't like to talk to them. I loved it, even those who were complaining. I met an elderly gentleman by phone who had gone to elementary school with my father and my aunt, his twin sister. (Yes this was my hometown paper).

Reporters now working at the two companies that once were The Plain Dealer don't see each other much. For younger reporters, this is a real loss. Based on reading (I still have the paper delivered even though they keep giving away their product online for free), they don't seem to avail themselves of the library system to see what's happened before and include some actual context. And there are no older reporters there to tell them the back story on a politician or a topic of any kind.

Beats have almost disappeared and with them the power of the reporter to stop an editor from dictating a BS story – because your sources, your reporting, doesn't back that up. That may be the greatest loss of all.

Covering Cleveland neighborhoods: these streets talk - if only we'd listen

MICHAEL O'MALLEY

Creativity in the journalism business is not necessarily in the writing of stories, but in the finding of them – observing and pulling together compelling narratives out of ordinary human happenings.

It's about finding the stuff of color, character and emotion – the stuff that rarely comes from a press release, a politician's mouth or a news conference.

It could be the story of Cynthia Lawrence, an elderly homeless woman working all night in a labor crew, cleaning up trash at Jacob's Field after a ballgame.

Or the underground economy of poor and disabled people doing piece work out of their homes, slipping thousands of plastic washers over metal screws for less-than-minimum wage.

Or the underpaid, half-starving Filipino sailors working and living in poor conditions on a ship unloading steel wire in Cleveland.

These stories, published in The Plain Dealer, didn't come from official channels. They came from me, snooping the environs of Cleveland with an open notebook.

They are stories featuring places and people; stories of who we are. The story of Bob Woodworth, a distinguished looking, white businessman who dressed in conventional suits and ties and voted Republican. When he died, he willed a rental property he owned to his tenant, Hilda Rojas, a Latina single mother struggling on little income.

The story of a black Catholic congregation that moved into an abandoned Bohemian church on Cleveland's East Side and painted the faces on the statues of Christ and the saints black.

The story of Kate Kearny and Norma Rodriquez, friends since the second grade, who never left the tough, impoverished, Cleveland neighborhood in which they were raised. Kate, whose ancestors came from Ireland in 1911, is one of the last of the Irish in the area of Bridge Avenue and West 65th Street. Norma, whose family came from Puerto Rico in 1960, is of the earliest Hispanic families to move into the once heavily Irish neighborhood now dominated by Latinos.

I found the story in 1996 when I spotted an Irish flag flying on a pole in the front yard of a house on Bridge Avenue. Odd, I thought, in this neighborhood?

I stopped the car when I saw a woman on the front porch. It was Kate, a good talker who dragged her friend Norma into the chat.

I soon learned that the two women were in their 40s. Irish Kate spoke street Spanish and knew merengue and salsa steps; Latina Norma knew Irish step dancing – "slap, hop, heel toe" – taught by the Irish nuns at St. Colman's where the two women met as kids in the second grade.

And Kate's dad used to call Norma "Chiquita." She called him "Old Irishman."

They kept talking. I listened.

As kids, they played kickball in the street until dark. As teenagers, they were a winning team in dance contests. One night, they got tattooed together. Another night, drunk on cheap wine, they threw bricks through the windows of a white supremacy group's headquarters at West 96th and Lorain Avenue.

At this point, I'm already writing in my head.

And the story of Kate and Norma soon appears on the Metro cover of The Plain Dealer with a color photo of the two women in a pew at St. Colman's.

Unfortunately, we see too few of these kinds of stories today in daily newspapers – stories of inner-city history, poverty and culture told in slice-of-life narratives.

One reason, I believe, is that newspapers are looking away from covering urban life, in favor of suburban news. A PD editor once said about the city's Hispanic community: "Those people don't read."

Also, stories like Kate and Nora would take too much time, editors would say, to find and flush out.

Daily newspaper reporters in 2018 – sadly too few of them left – are under tremendous pressure to feed websites, whether the feeds meet the standards for quality news or not. Few reporters have the freedom to wander and hunt selectively for stories as I often did during my 23 years at The Plain Dealer, beginning in 1990.

One late night in August of 2000 (having sneaked into Jacobs Field after an Indians game), I discovered hundreds of homeless people with plastic bags and leaf blowers picking up postgame litter under the tens of thousands of seats.

They were hired by a temporary work agency and were earning take-home pay between $25 and $30 for a seven-hour shift. Most of them were African-American, some wearing bandanas, bent over as they moved through long rows picking trash by hand – a vision of early American slavery.

I found 60-year-old Cynthia Lawrence taking a break, sitting in a box seat that would have cost her $35 during a game. The Trinidad native, who had no bank account or address, told me she was saving her money and hoped to get off the streets soon. "Not much longer," she said.

On this night, she worked 7.25 hours, grossing $37.34. After taxes were taken out, she got a check for $30.81. The temporary job agency charged her $1 to cash her check.

This story came to me from a tip by my colleague Dale Omori, a Plain Dealer photographer. In the days of film cameras, Dale and photographers covering Indians games had to leave about the seventh inning to get back to the photo lab and process the film.

Dale, on his way out of the stadium, noticed people, many of them looking impoverished, gathering around the closed media gate.

He assumed, rightly, that they were cleanup crews waiting for the game to end. He told me, "Maybe we can find a homeless person" in the group who we could follow for a possible story.

So, on an August night, we gathered with the tattered crew and discovered they were all homeless. We waited with them as the fans filed out of the other stadium gates. And when the media gate opened, we shuffled in with them.

Dale had two cameras strapped around his neck along with media credentials, so when a security guard walked by us, he assumed we were doing some postgame coverage.

But then the main stadium lights went down. To avoid any possible inquiries, we hid behind a concession stand until the coast was clear.

Eventually, we mingled with the cleanup crew and, fortunately, the big boss, Mike Justice, had no idea we snuck in. We told him we were from The Plain Dealer and he figured we were interested in how the massive stadium is cleaned, so he gave us all the details, including how the workers are divided into color-coded teams, each wearing a numbered sticker the color of his or her team.

The Red Team works the lower box seats from foul pole to foul pole. Blue works the upper deck; Green the bleachers.

Mike Justice told us that sometimes workers are given free hot dogs if there are any left over from the concessions. "They're leftovers. They're going to be thrown out anyhow," he said.

Dale and I stayed all night with the workers who were being paid by Minute Men, a temporary work service. With the job done and the sun rising, we followed the workers as they shuffled up Carnegie Avenue about a mile to the Minute Men office where they would get their pay for an all-night shift of back-breaking work – about $27 clear.

Dale had shot 17 rolls of film that night. We never told the editors we snuck in.

Our story, featuring six pictures, hit the front page, but not before a debate among editors about the newsworthiness of it.

My immediate editor, John Funk, saw the story as a "Holy shit!" Poor blacks barely out of slavery conditions picking up peanut shells and trash at a major league ballpark attended mostly by white fans.

Others were not so moved. "At least they're getting some money," was the argument by those trying to kill the story or keep it off Page 1.

The debate was not unusual. Over three decades of newspaper reporting, I often focused on urban poverty and social justice issues and those stories often drew debates among editors.

In 2000, I received an award for social justice reporting from Greater Cleveland Community Shares, a nonprofit agency helping needy people.

The recognition prompted the executive editor, Doug Clifton, to give me a kudo in writing, but I believe he did it out of a professional sense of duty, not for my work, for he eventually pulled me off urban coverage and put me on a beat in the suburbs.

Exposing local institutional poverty, exploitation and social injustices can make some newspaper editors – and some readers – uneasy.

A story I wrote in 1996 about poor and disabled people in Cleveland doing piece work out of their homes, snapping metal screws and plastic washers together for way less-than minimum wage, was met with the same editorial criticism as the Jacobs Field story:

"What's the story? At least they're getting some money."

Well, here's the story:

A local company, RP Coatings Corp., dropped off boxes of screws and washers weekly at dozens of households on the city's lower West Side. The assembled pieces were used by automobile manufacturers throughout the world.

The piece workers earned $1.50 per 1,000 screws they assembled with washers, earning less than $1 an hour.

The story, published on Page 1, triggered the federal Department of Labor to investigate, resulting in the company being charged with violating minimum wage and child labor laws. The screw workers were reimbursed with back pay and the story received an Excellence in Journalism Award for Public Service from the Society of Professional Journalists. That's the story.

Back in the 1990s, The Plain Dealer hired a consultant to study its news operation for possible improvements. Overdramatically, the consultant said she had never seen a paper like this. "You are a reporter-driven newspaper," she said, noting that we were the last of a breed of dinosaurs. "You need to be editor-driven."

Oh?

Soon, editors on all levels were jotting "ideas" on legal pads, assigning "stories" and hunting for "sources."

How the hell, I thought, would an editor find the stories I write? Reporters find stories and write them. Editors edit.

How would an editor find a story I once wrote about a neighborhood saloon that was closing after a half-century?

I happened to be driving along West 105th Street when I spotted a very clean picture window lettered "Glunz Café." Just the outside neatness of the place, nestled in a declining neighborhood, told me there was a story in there.

Here's my lead and what I saw when I entered: "At the corner of the bar near the big picture window, Sparky the electrician lights a long, black cigar as 'Father Rick,' raising a beer goblet shaped like a chalice, offers a toast to a chorus of laughter.

"It's a typical Friday night at Glunz Café on Cleveland's West Side. Fred and Irene Glunz are working the taps and coolers; the bar top is cluttered with bottles, ashtrays and elbows; and laughter as thick as incense hangs like the smoke from Sparky's cigar.

"But there's also a sadness here that touches the hearts of Glunz regulars."

I learned that night that Fred and Irene Glunz, husband and wife, were selling the place they opened 46 years earlier and retiring.

Now I've got a story, no thanks to an editor.

Editors need to edit. Reporters need to dig.

How would the story of Watergate have happened without the digging of two hungry reporters?

During my days at The Plain Dealer, I had the good fortune of working with one of the best investigative reporters in the business, Dave Davis, who now teaches journalism at Youngstown State University. Dave and I, through sources, digging and old-fashioned shoe-leather journalism, nailed down award winning stories of inner-city residents being exploited by ruthless contractors and slum landlords.

We exposed a shady scheme by a company that sold and installed home alarm systems, duping hundreds of inner-city homebuyers into buying systems they couldn't afford.

The homes, some new, some rehabbed, were part of an affordable home program that gave lower-income families a piece of the American Dream.

The ruthless company approached contractors when the homes were under construction, saying it would install the systems' wires while the walls were open at no cost to the contractors.

Once families moved in, the company said, they could decide whether they wanted the alarm systems activated at a monthly cost.

But we discovered that a family that refused the system was told by the company that it wanted its system back and to get it back it would have to break holes in the walls and rip out the wires. Most families signed a contract with the company to avoid tearing their new homes apart. And most of them soon discovered they couldn't afford the systems and they ended up in Small Claims Court. A number of families were slapped with liens on their homes.

Following our series of stories, a Cleveland court ruled that the company's business practices were "unconscionable" and "illegal."

And the scam was halted.

Dave and I also exposed the crooked workings of a giant slumlord, Associated Estates, which owned three inner-city apartment complexes subsidized by tax payers through the U.S. Department of Housing and Urban Development.

The company had been sucking subsidy payments from HUD for years but failed to put any money back into the places, resulting in deplorable living conditions, including infestations of roaches, high levels of lead (which were poisoning children), no smoke detectors, no window screens and leaking pipes. Associated Estates even collected subsidies on empty apartments, telling HUD that they were occupied.

The three properties – Longwood Estates, Rainbow Terrace and Park Village – were all on Cleveland's East Side, housing thousands of low-income African-Americans.

In 1996, the city cited Rainbow Terrace and Longwood for more than 8,500 sanitary and safety code violations. And, eventually, living conditions at the properties got so bad that HUD declared Associated Estates in default of its contract with the government.

Dave and I kept these stories on the front page for months and in our reporting we discovered that HUD in Washington, D.C., was working on a secret deal to oust Associated Estates from its ownership of the properties.

The deal, which we discovered through a leak in the Cleveland HUD office, was that HUD was paying Associated Estates $1.7 million of taxpayers' money to walk away from the properties.

Dave and I kept digging, exposing a large criminal scheme operating at the peril of poor people, while fleecing taxpayers. HUD was embarrassed. Associated Estates threatened to sue us.

William C. Apgar, an assistant director at HUD in Washington, D.C., called The Plain Dealer editorial page editor Brent Larkin, asking for a conference-call.

Dave and I and Brent took our seats in Brent's office where we hooked up with Apgar through a plastic voice box on a small table.

Apgar cackled away at how our stories were unfair to his agency and to the bad landlord that was getting paid in taxpayers' dollars to walk away.

"You guys are writing all this stuff," Apgar groaned. "But those places are not that bad."

That's when Dave Davis stood up, walked over to the little plastic box and spoke. "Mr. Apgar, this is Dave Davis. Have you ever seen these places? Have you been to Longwood or Rainbow Terrace or Park Village?"

Apgar responded "No, but. . .

Then Dave let loose. "Hold it! Mr. Apgar, are you saying these places aren't that bad when you have never seen them? I suggest, Mr. Apgar, that you get your fucking ass to Cleveland and I'll show you these places, Mr. Apgar.

"How the fuck can you say these places are not that bad when you're sitting in fucking Washington?"

Brent and I looked at each other nervously as Dave went nuclear in the room.

I can't remember how our meeting returned to a more normal decorum, if it did at all.

But I can still see Dave's blood-pressured face, his jabbing finger and the fire in his eyes.

A ferocious blast at a blow-hard bureaucrat.

Reporter driven.

Welcome to The Plain Dealer

HARLAN SPECTOR

I started working at The Plain Dealer on Nov. 2, 1990. The windowless, second-story newsroom was hot, noisy and jammed with people. My early conversations with new colleagues established there were two tribes of people: Guild and management.

Local 1 of The Newspaper Guild represented more than 300 news staffers at the PD, including reporters, photographers, editors, librarians, graphic artists and clerks.

Over decades, Local 1 had negotiated one of the best pay scales in the industry relative to cost of living. When they hired me as an assistant metro editor, the PD was flush with cash. They sent reporters across the country and overseas routinely, with no apparent limit on the travel budget. As population shifted to counties surrounding Cuyahoga, the newspaper spent big money chasing readers and advertisers. They opened three new bureaus in the outer counties in 1989-90. That's how I got hired. The paper aimed to out-local the local papers, and they needed dozens of new journalists to do it.

Each local bureau had nine or 10 people and a bureau chief, plus the PD needed additional editing staff downtown to move copy and crank out zoned metro sections.

New hires at the newspaper competed with veterans and management favorites to get noticed. Most bureau reporters wanted to be transferred downtown where the action was. Some complained they were ignored. My boss used to say, "There are worse things around here than being ignored." He was right about that. You could have a target on your back and not even know it.

If you wanted face time with a boss, sometimes the best bet was to pull up a barstool at the Mardi Gras, a PD hangout on E. 21st Street. A lot of business got done there, which troubled some staffers who felt it was a boys' club.

A co-worker described the newsroom as the Island of Misfit Toys. Journalism attracts characters, and the newsroom was democratic in the sense that there was tolerance for weirdness, crankiness and dissent, even the occasional tantrum. Editors yelled across the newsroom. Reporters argued with editors over assignments and rewrites. Clashes spilled into the managing editor's office all the time. To management's credit, you could disagree, and they didn't hold a grudge.

So many oversized egos populated the newsroom it was hard to count. Old school reporter Lou Mio, who pecked away on the last remaining newsroom typewriter, had a cartoon taped to his desk: "If assholes could fly this place would be an airport."

Then there were people like Ed Kissell. He quietly did his job for years as a night cops reporter from a press office at police headquarters. He called in his notes from crime scenes and fires but would not take a byline. He told a co-worker he thought it would be taking advantage of someone else's misfortune. He died shortly after he retired.

"He craved secrecy," an obituary said. "About the only times he appeared in the newspaper's newsroom were on paydays, when he would quickly grab his check and be out of the office before anyone realized he was there. Some of his bosses did not even know him."

Among stories PD veterans liked to tell was one about Don Bean, a police reporter who sent out a newbie on the beat to interview the mother of the unknown soldier laying flowers at the Soldiers and Sailors Monument on Public Square. The reporter apparently walked around the square until she realized she'd been pranked. The story was good for a chuckle. But an account published in a book about Cleveland journalism reminded me that was not such a great time for women at the PD. Many women who came on board in those years had their own stories to share about blatant sexism.

Before voicemail and email, editorial clerks stationed at the front desk of the newsroom answered calls, stuffed phone messages into mail slots and made announcements on a loudspeaker. Almost daily, they announced that a recipe prepared in the test kitchen, located off the newsroom, was ready for consumption. Staffers scurried to the front of the newsroom for samples.

My first week, I met Roma, our metro desk clerk. She sat in the middle of an oval ringed by city desk editors. She had an Elvis shrine on her desk. Roma was biting and irreverent and took no bull. She especially liked to needle newsroom bloviators.

Roma stopped me and asked if I was Guild or management.

"Guild," I said.

"Good," she said. "Then they can't fuck with you."

(Actually, they could. But there were limits).

At that moment, I wondered what I got myself into.

Goodbye Plain Dealer

Tuesday, July 30, 2013, 5:45 p.m. The newsroom email said, "Important Message" from sender "admin."

We all knew what it meant in an instant.

The PD had announced the previous December it would lay off 50-plus members of the Guild, the second major layoff in five years. We waited months for the bomb to drop. Here it was. But nobody could click open the attachment. Admin had to send out a corrected one.

The attached letter told us we should wait by our phones the next morning between 8 and 10, for notice whether we are being "separated" from employment.

The letter ended by saying, "We sincerely regret having to go through this process and we thank all who are impacted for their years of service and wish them all the best for their future."

There was no immediate sign of upset in the newsroom. Several people chuckled over the tortured "all who are impacted" line.

It sunk in this was my last day in the newsroom.

A few weeks earlier, I had volunteered to be put on the layoff list. Ever since they announced the job cuts, a steady stream of Guild members walked into the glass offices and volunteered to leave so they could take advantage of the severance package being offered.

PD owner, Advance Publications, was making big changes at its newspapers, in favor of a cheaper, digital business model designed to maximize clicks online. The fact that so many staffers volunteered to leave was telling.

My reasons for walking away were complicated. It's hard to think about sometimes. I loved the business. We all did – at least the journalists I know. People lucky enough to have worked during better days of newspapers reminisce like some people reminisce about high school. The best experience you'll never have again.

I had moved to reporting after nine years on the metro desk. My editor, Bob McAuley, encouraged his reporters to be dogged. He was a hard-ass newsman and one of the nicest guys around. Bob, and a few other editors I worked for, believed the best journalism came from enterprise work, not from editors cooking up ideas in meeting rooms. I looked forward to coming to work in those days.

But the rewarding part of the job became increasingly marred by economic turmoil. It stops being fun when you see workers pay dearly for owners' bad decisions. Newspapers for years had no real competition, and they were arrogant. When the internet became a thing, they failed to grasp what was happening. I remember a top editor standing in the newsroom and declaring the internet would never replace newspapers.

It was obvious soon enough the newspaper business was in big trouble. I had been a union officer since the 1990s and was elected Guild chairman at the PD starting in 2008. The first round of newsroom layoffs happened that year. They fired 50 Guild people a few weeks before Christmas but didn't touch any managers. We would do more with less, they said. Renowned Channel 3 reporter Tom Beres, who did a phenomenal job covering the PD's slow-motion collapse, often called out the company on the air. "You don't do more with less, you do less with less," he said.

A year after those layoffs, the company came to the unions for a 12 percent wage concession. Either we accepted, or they would lay off 60-plus more people from the Guild, Teamsters and printers union.

You learn a lot about people in that situation. The Guild urged the membership to take the wage cut to save jobs. Some members had come out against it. Nerves were frayed. We called a meeting for the vote and weren't sure what to expect. We were nervous.

But the membership voted overwhelmingly to take the pay hit in exchange for job security. Afterward, people came up and shook our hands. Some had tears in their eyes. I was never so proud of our union.

I naively thought at times that after owners got their pound of flesh that maybe they would leave us alone for a while. Employees ask year after year how much more can they cut? But then I got it. It doesn't end.

The loss of staff through attrition alone was remarkable. The PD shed about two-thirds of its Guild-represented news staff from the time I started until I left. Important beats went uncovered. They shuttered the suburban bureaus and the Sunday Magazine. They idled the fleet of PD delivery trucks that used to line up at the loading docks on E. 18th Street. As revenue declined year after year, the company increasingly did not deal with the Guild in good faith. They lied to the union and violated our contract left and right, tying us up in an endless cycle of paperwork, grievances and legal procedures.

PD staffers were anguished about the decline of journalism as we knew it – a decline not just in staffing, but also in standards.

It became clear to me by 2013 that experienced journalists had fallen out of favor under the owners' new click-driven, cost-cutting "model." Management needed just enough seasoned journalists to claim respectability, but they didn't need many. They were enamored with people who were younger, cheaper and nimble in digital space, regardless of whether they had journalistic chops. Being a savvy newsperson or a graceful writer was not valued so much, and contrary points of view were no longer welcome at all.

Advance was moving people and resources over to the non-union Cleveland.com. The changes became big news in town, and in other cities where the company owns newspapers. Clevelanders were shocked to learn the PD was going to cut home delivery days. The outcry in New Orleans over the company's plans to cut jobs and reduce print days at the Times-Picayune thrust Advance into the national spotlight, prompting a report on "60 Minutes." In Cleveland, a group of Guild members launched a "Save The Plain Dealer" campaign. It generated widespread news coverage and a public backlash that may have influenced ownership to back off on plans to reduce print days like they did in New Orleans.

The company would not reveal when Plain Dealer layoffs would happen. Many co-workers were sick with stress during the first half of 2013. *I wish they would just get it over with.* I heard that every day.

We fought year after year to preserve journalism at the PD. But it never was about the journalism to people on the other side of the bargaining table. Sometimes I had a hard time convincing colleagues of that. Owners have a number in mind, Local 1 Executive Secretary Rollie Dreussi would point out. How much they want to make, how much they want to cut.

You can't reason with a number. You can't talk owners into doing what's right for journalism. You certainly can't shame them into it.

The Guild and other unions didn't have power to stop layoffs. But we got the best terms we could in a six-year contract that expires in 2019: A decent severance for laid off employees, more money for health care and pension, and job protection for those who remained.

One of my co-workers quipped afterward, "It's a shit sandwich, but at least it has lettuce and tomato."

The email of July 30, 2013 arrived as many staffers were getting ready to leave for the day. People started gathering, huddling and talking quietly. Even when you know it's coming, it stuns. I didn't quite know what to do with myself.

I walked around the newsroom in a daze for a while. I said goodbye and shook hands. I hugged people I had never hugged before.

It was a good way of life while it lasted.

A prize-winning columnist leaves The PD

STUART WARNER

The Plain Dealer newsroom is solemn on Saturday mornings. The soaring two-story ceiling, the light refracting from the massive bank of windows and the rows of empty desks make the space feel almost like a cathedral awaiting Sunday's Mass. A few reporters and photographers scurry off to assignments. A couple of editors answer phones, hoping the next call isn't about a plane crash that they have no one left to cover.

Connie Schultz knew that's what it would be like on Saturday, Sept. 17, hardly anyone there, no one with time to ask what she was doing, a question that might make her cry.

She started cleaning out her desk, filling canvas bags with books and mementos.

She stopped to remember the day six years before when her colleagues had stood applauding at their desks or leaning over the mezzanine rail above. Her columns had won the newspaper its first Pulitzer Prize in more than 50 years. Tears filled her eyes as she saw their shared pride.

There were tears this Saturday morning, too. The empty room came to life for her, bustling with the memories of the people who, 18 years earlier, had given a 36-year-old single mother with no newspaper experience a chance to be a reporter.

She was leaving The Plain Dealer, this time for good.

The next night, she let editor Debra Adams Simmons know. Debra asked Connie to stay. But on Monday morning, Sept. 19, Connie submitted her resignation.

And I'm glad she's gone.

I'm not glad for the waitresses, steelworkers, teachers and countless other blue-collar workers who heard her voice as their own. And I'm not glad for the legions of young women, including my three grown daughters, who found her work empowering.

But for those who planned to pile even more bile onto her from behind the cloak of a personal computer as the man she loves seeks re-election to the U.S. Senate – I'm glad you lost your favorite target.

I was her editor for six years; I am her friend still. So don't expect total objectivity here. In 2006, when her husband, Sherrod Brown, challenged Mike DeWine for his Senate seat, I recommended that she take a leave of absence. She resisted until articles and comments by people inside and outside the newsroom helped change her mind. It was the smart thing to do. She became a tireless and effective campaigner for Brown.

She came back to the newsroom after he was elected. It seemed awkward. I jokingly wondered if a senator's wife could have me disappear for trimming three paragraphs off her column. But there were more serious issues to deal with. She was popular in the newsroom, but not universally beloved. People inside and outside The Plain Dealer began to question whether she was a cipher for her husband's views.

I thought that was ridiculous.

I spent almost every day with her for months before she met Brown, working on her narrative series "The Burden of Innocence," which became a finalist for the Pulitzer Prize in feature writing. I got a regular dose of her opinions on women, minorities, workers' rights, the right to choose and gays. Marrying Sherrod Brown did not change her views one bit.

But when she returned to The Plain Dealer after the election, it got so tense that management admonished her and me for mentioning his Christmas stocking in a column on Nov. 30, 2007. It humanized Brown, Connie was told. Soon, her column was moved from the front of the features section to the opinion pages. For a long while, the only reference to her husband allowed was the tag line at the bottom of her column that she detested so – *Connie Schultz is the wife of U.S. Sen. Sherrod Brown.*

The tension eased when Debra Adams Simmons became editor. In August, she decided to move Connie's column to the front of the Metro section.

But on Sept. 7, Connie wrote about attending a Tea Party rally in Avon. In the column, she neglected to mention that state Treasurer Josh Mandel, her husband's likely challenger in 2012, had spoken there.

Something else happened that she didn't write about. A videographer known to be a "tracker" for the Democrats was escorted out of the building. These "trackers" follow the opposing party's candidates everywhere, hoping to catch a glaring gaffe like former Virginia Sen. George Allen's "macaca" moment.

Connie was indignant about the decision to oust the videographer from a public event, at a venue funded by taxes in the town where she lived. So she pulled out a Canon PowerShot that she has been packing since she was assaulted by an angry Republican a couple of years ago.

She started recording as Mandel was speaking – a move she later described as "making an in-your-face point about public forums."

Kevin DeWine, chairman of the Republican Party and cousin of the man defeated by her husband, called it a "blatantly political act," implying that she was serving as a tracker for the Democrats.

Hogwash.

It was a blatantly journalistic act.

But on Sept. 8, Connie wrote a column apologizing for the Tea Party column. She acknowledged her editors' concern that some could have construed that she was filming her husband's likely opponent for *The Plain Dealer*.

Now, she regrets that apology.

If it was a mistake to film Mandel, Connie tells me, "I would rather be a journalist who made that mistake than the coward who has to ask for permission."

Connie agrees with me that she made one error in covering the Tea Party event: She didn't tell her editors everything that happened. If she had, they could've decided whether she should write the column.

A prize-winning columnist leaves The PD | 173

But the Tea Party incident didn't trigger her departure.

On Friday, Sept. 16, she learned that a volunteer for Brown's Senate campaign had posted an erroneous item on her personal Facebook page, saying that Connie would be raising money with Brown at an event in Akron. Connie was planning to attend the event, but not speak.

Word reached her editors again. She heard another meeting would be scheduled. Instead, after calling me and others for advice, she decided it was time to go.

Part of her reason was selfless.

"I realized I was putting my editors in a terrible spot," she says. "They've been so supportive. They wanted to make this work. They deserve more than the ugliness that's heaped on them."

But in the newsroom that Saturday morning, she knew there was a more pressing reason to go.

On her final trip to her desk, she picked up a bumper sticker mounted on a plaque with a message that she had cherished for years: "Well-behaved women rarely make history."

I was with her at Harvard when she tracked down the author of the quote, historian Laurel Thatcher Ulrich. I know that to Connie, "well-behaved" means playing by someone else's rules.

"I'm a 54-year-old woman," she says now. "I'm not going to start playing by a new set of rules."

She stuffed the placard in the bag. And a few moments later, a part of Cleveland's journalism history walked out of The Plain Dealer's doors.

~Connie Schultz left The Plain Dealer in 2011. This story was originally published by Cleveland Magazine. It is used with permission.

Those were the days in Rubber City ... but they had to end

STUART WARNER

I felt like crying when I first sat down to write this, only three days after it was announced that the Akron Beacon Journal had been sold to Gatehouse Media, another vulture capitalist group picking over the remains of the industry I love.

But perhaps the good intentions of the newspaper's patriarch, John S. Knight, had indirectly created the monster that was devouring the Beacon.

Akron was the first of Knight's newspapers. He inherited it from his father, and then he and his brother James transformed his family's hometown publication into a journalistic empire. JSK wasn't the first to create a newspaper chain – Scripps, Hearst, the Pulitzers all preceded him – but nobody did it better, as he proved that you could produce both profits and Pulitzer Prizes. Knight-Ridder newspapers had won 85 of journalism's most coveted awards by the time the chain was sold for $4.5 billion in 2006, when the value of daily newspapers already had begun their steep decline.

Knight had been dead for 25 years by then, but his legacy still oozed from the walls at 44 E. Exchange St., in downtown Akron.

"Passing by the John S. Knight Room every day where his typewriter sat in that glass case was powerful for me," said Regina Brett, a two-time Pulitzer finalist and New York Times best-selling author. "We were a Knight paper, and writing was all that mattered. To see that instrument that he hammered out editorials on made me appreciate the great foundation he laid for us all."

Now, that foundation has crumbled. The new owners have gobbled up around 150 daily news organizations and hundreds more weeklies, consolidating where they can, selling property and parts and pieces to the highest bidder. They are owned by a hedge fund. They have one mission: making money. Their first order of business in Akron was to fire the remaining staff – a newsroom that once numbered 190 had fewer than 50 members at the time of the sale – effectively disbanding the union. Quality be damned. They did end up rehiring all of the reporters, a group of talented veterans, but there were plans to consolidate page design, copy editing and digital functions elsewhere. Two photographers were lost. We'll see what happens.

But journalists aren't allowed to shed tears. We must stand back without emotion as we report on the misery of others. And I've had the opportunity to view the Beacon from many perspectives – as executive sports editor, religion writer, columnist, assistant managing editor for features, assistant managing editor for the region, deputy managing editor for news, deputy managing editor for operations, associate managing editor, acting managing editor, spurned lover, competitor and, finally, as an aging, nostalgic journalist.

So, from the latter point of view, I will look back at the good times, the best of the best for me, the 1990s, when the Akron Beacon Journal was doing things that no paper its size had any business doing. We won the Pulitzer Prize Gold Medal for Meritorious Public Service in 1994 for "A Question of Color," our groundbreaking series on race relations in Akron. We produced a 52-week series on the history of rubber in Rubber City then turned it into a 100,000-word book, "Wheels of Fortune." We cultivated a remarkable crop of authors. And we made lots and lots of money.

There was a sense in Akron then that there were no limits to what you could accomplish through journalism, acclaimed author Thrity Umrigar told me during a 2011 interview.

"You felt you could take chances, try anything," added Umrigar, who reported and wrote columns in Akron for 15 years.

Longtime friends Umrigar and Brett, who both came to the Beacon from the Lorain Morning Journal in 1987, were among a group of writers who worked at the paper during the '90s that is probably unmatched at any newspaper in the country outside of New York, Washington and LA.

Journalists who worked at the Akron Beacon Journal during that decade have produced somewhere close to 150 books – I keep losing count because it seems every time an angel gets its wings, either Terry Pluto or Mark Dawidziak have published another.

Those two word machines have written more than 50 books between them. Pluto's "Loose Balls" about the defunct American Basketball Association is considered a classic among sports readers. Dawidziak is equally prolific writing about Mark Twain or TV detectives like Colombo or Kolchak.

Among the other celebrated authors who came out of Akron in that decade are New York's literary bad boy Chuck Klosterman ("Sex, Drugs and Cocoa Puffs, But What If We Were Wrong"); the Bard of Boston sports Michael Holley ("Belichick and Brady, War Room"); Michael Weinreb ("Bigger Than the Game, Game of Kings").

Umrigar ("The Space Between Us, Story Hour"), Brett ("God Never Blinks, Be the Miracle") and David Giffels ("All the Way Home, The Hard Way on Purpose") all earned an international reputation without leaving Northeast Ohio.

Two writers from the Beacon's powerhouse sports department in the 1990s, Brian Windhorst and Chris Broussard, have turned their writing skills into national TV gigs at ESPN and Fox Sports.

Current columnist Bob Dyer and former columnist Steve Love both wrote successful books with sports legends Omar Vizquel and Gerry Faust, respectively. Former copy desk chief Kathy Fraze has published nine mystery novels featuring detective Jo Ferris. Longtime reporter Bill O'Connor just finished his fourth novel. Investigative reporter Roger Snell, who won a Silver Gavel for his reporting on the Ohio Supreme Court, has written two non-fiction books, including a biography of Chicago Cubs pitcher Charlie Root. James Beard Award-winning food critic Jane Snow wrote the definitive book on Akron cooking.

But none of them, perhaps, have received any more attention than a man who wasn't even a writer at the paper. Artist John "Derf" Backderf's graphic memoir "My Friend Dahmer" has been translated into dozens of languages and the movie version was an indie house hit.

It was almost as if good writing at the Beacon was infectious.

"I know that working around all those people inspired me and challenged me," said Giffels, whose latest nonfiction book, "Furnishing Eternity," was called "a page-turning drama" by The New York Times. "You looked up to those other writers ... and had to rise up to their quality."

~

The quality writing in Akron during the 1990s had its genesis in a corporate decision made in 1980.

The Akron Beacon Journal had long been a quality newspaper. Knight won a Pulitzer for his editorial writing in 1968 and the paper's remarkable coverage of the Kent State killings in 1970 won the 1971 Pulitzer Prize.

But after the retirement of legendary Executive Editor Ben Maidenberg, "Mr. Akron," in 1975, the paper's stewardship suffered from rapid change at the top.

At the same time, Editor Gene Roberts was transforming the Philadelphia Inquirer from a bloated local rag to one of the most respected newspapers in the country. The company took notice and began dispatching some of Roberts' young guns.

In 1979, hotshot war correspondent John Carroll was sent to the Lexington Herald-Leader, a mediocre paper where I was the sports editor. In 1980, Knight-Ridder vice president Jim Batten sent Inquirer Associate Managing Editor Dale Allen to Akron, telling him he wanted the city to have a newspaper that Knight could be proud of before he died.

During the 1980s, both Lexington and Akron won Pulitzer Prizes. Carroll, of course, went on to lead the Baltimore Sun and the Los Angeles Times. Allen settled in Akron for 17 years, where he developed one of the best mid-sized newsrooms in the nation.

But it took some work. I was hired as executive sports editor in Akron in October of 1979. I was only 27 but I saw a newsroom that seemed behind the times. Allen noticed the same thing when he arrived a few months later.

"I had already concluded the paper was deplorably out of date. It looked like a newspaper from the late '50s or early '60s, and it read the same way," he wrote in an unpublished memoir that he shared with me. "The bulk of the news columns were filled with rather simplistic news stories, usually involving single sources for the material presented. The writing was pedestrian, too, sadly reciting facts with little effort to put them in a context that might make them meaningful to readers. The logical reaction to a daily edition was one big yawn, followed by a nap."

Allen brought some of Roberts' philosophies to Akron, which was an editor-dominated paper when he got there. "If all ideas are coming from the top, then you're going to have a very limited newspaper," Allen told me in a 2011 interview. "If they are welling up from the bottom, the breadth of your coverage is going to expand."

He was also an avid reader and had an eye for writing talent. When he saw writers he appreciated, he found positions for them.

Brett was hired as a business writer, even though she had no business writing experience. Dyer and Sheryl Harris, who were key reporters on the Question of Color team, were both brought in as copy editors until Allen could find reporting jobs for them. Giffels was hired as a part-time society writer. He covered gardening for a while, too.

They, like others, were attracted by the paper's reputation.

"I had received job offers from both the Plain Dealer and the Beacon on the same day and as a young reporter, didn't quite know how to decide," said Umrigar, a native of India who moved to the U.S. in 1983 to study at The Ohio State University and pursue her dream of becoming a writer. "My former editor (Rich Osborne of the Lorain Morning Journal) ordered me to accept the job at the Beacon because of its reputation as being a hothouse for cultivating writers. And that truly was the case."

Giffels said that reputation is also what got Klosterman interested. Of course, he was working in Fargo, North Dakota, at the time, so even Akron's weather was also an incentive.

They also enhanced their own writing climate in Northeast Ohio.

"When Chuck came, he and Mike Weinreb and I would go out drinking, talking the whole night about books, projects, ambitions," Giffels said. "We fed off each other."

Brett, Umrigar and some of the others often organized brown bag lunches for any reporters who wanted to attend. They would bring in speakers or discuss writing topics among themselves.

"Bill O'Connor used his pen like a paintbrush," Brett said of her former reporting colleague. "He was my first mentor. I still have the fountain pen he gave me with his initials on. He always said, 'Don't set out to tell a great story. Just tell the story. Release it like Michelangelo released the figures from the marble.'

"Everyone raised the bar and set it so high, you wanted to be better," she added "But it never felt competitive. There was a rare organic camaraderie. Everyone cheered for you when you hit one out of the ballpark."

Not always, though.

"As someone who cared a great deal about writing about marginalized communities, I never quite felt a full-throated support extended to me by the powers-that-be about unearthing these stories," Umrigar wrote in an email to me. "In fact, it was often the opposite – I felt marginalized myself for wanting to write about forgotten people, like I had to beg to do those stories and even when permission was granted, support could be pulled out at any time."

~

Dale Allen believes that Knight-Ridder's push for diversity helped him recruit a wide-range of writing and reporting talent.

"We ... made good use of the Knight-Ridder minority hiring program, which was overseen by Al Fitzpatrick, the former deputy editor in Akron who had taken the job as assistant vice president for minority affairs at corporate headquarters," Allen wrote in his memoir. "Working with Al, we secured three minority-hiring positions on our staff, which were paid for in the first year by Knight-Ridder. After the first year, we absorbed the staff members within our own budget."

However, he was cautious about making the minority hires too obvious to everyone in the newsroom.

"I instituted a new policy of *not* making the distinction known to employees. In that way the new minority hires became part of the *Beacon Journal* family, irrespective of the hiring method used," Allen wrote.

The Beacon became an island on the way to bigger things for many of the minorities Allen hired.

Bob Fernandez, Vernon Clark and Rich Henson all went on to work for the Philadelphia Inquirer, Lornet Turnbull moved to the Seattle Times, Leona Allen became a top editor at the Dallas Morning News and Glenn Gamboa is the voice of Music in New York at Newsday. Chris Broussard earned a measure of TV fame at ESPN and Fox Sports. Andale Gross is an editor for The Associated Press in Chicago.

Glenn Proctor became the first African-American editor of the Richmond Times-Dispatch in the former capital of the Confederacy. He's also written several books, his latest a self-help missive: "750 Questions: Worth Asking Yourself or Your Significant Other."

Mizell Stewart rose to become managing editor in Akron and then a top executive in Scripps-Howard and Gannett. Holley and Cindy Rodriguez both became stars at the Boston Globe. Carl Chancellor became a fellow at the Center for American Progress and Cristal Williams Chancellor is the Director of Communications for the Women's Media Center, a nonprofit founded by Jane Fonda, Robin Morgan and Gloria Steinem.

David Lee Morgan Jr. is the author of seven books, including "LeBron James: The Rise of a Star" and "More Than A Coach: Jim Tressel." Andrea Louie, author of a novel, "Moon Cakes," has been awarded artist residencies at Yaddo, the MacDowell Colony, Djerassi, Hedgebrook and the Fundacíon Valparáiso in Spain and is the executive director of Asian American Arts Alliance in New York City.

Thrity Umrigar, art directors Susan "Mango" Curtis and Terence Oliver all pursued careers as academics.

Later minority hires like Betty Lin-Fisher and Malcolm X Abrams remain stalwarts in the newsroom today.

And more than a dozen minority journalists – Curtis, Oliver, reporter/editor Yvonne Bruce, reporters Chancellor, Holley, Leona Allen, Carol Cannon, Holley, Collette Jenkins, Kevin Johnson and Will Outlaw, and photographers Jocelyn Williams and Mike Cardew – were major contributors to perhaps the paper's seminal moment, winning the 1994 Pulitzer Gold Medal for Meritorious Service.

They gave the project a diverse and distinct voice.

~

On a Saturday night in early May 1992, a young assistant city editor named David Hertz took a report about an incident near Canton. Apparently, a black man had attacked a white man who yelled, "That's for Rodney King."

Only two days before that incident a white jury in Los Angeles found four white city cops not guilty of beating King, even though the whole world had watched the video of King getting almost thrashed to death.

Hertz saw a story that touched the place where we lived.

"We've got to do something," he told me the following Monday morning.

"What?" I responded.

"I don't know. Something," he said.

"Why don't you call a meeting and ask people to talk about it?"

"Nobody will come"

"Sure they will."

They did.

Twenty to 30 staff members showed up in the John S. Knight room to talk about race and the implications of the conflict we'd seen. Many told personal stories. Some wept.

We called another meeting a week or so later. And even more staff members showed up. And the conversations got even deeper.

"Race is tough to talk about. It's real touchy," reporter Carole Cannon said in an interview in 1994 and. "It got difficult because I'm black, and I felt the same way a lot of them did. It was one of the most difficult topics to deal with."

And the topic was immense. How could we get our arms around it?

Managing Editor Jim Crutchfield, an African-American, was skeptical we could. He had seen so many attempts to approach the topic. None had been successful, he said.

Nevertheless, he suggested forming a committee of six staff members, and let them attack the topic out of view of the top editors and the rest of the newsroom.

So we put Hertz, Weekend News Editor Deb Van Tassel and Investigative Editor Bob Paynter, who are all white, together with editorial writer Laura Ofobike, reporter Yalinda Rhoden and columnist Carl Chancellor, who are all black, and let them have at it behind closed doors.

They debated for two weeks how to approach covering race relations in Akron. I had some insight into their discussions because Van Tassel is my wife. Let's just say the talks often got heated, sometimes personal.

Yet they emerged with a plan as bold yet focused as anything I'd ever seen in journalism. A team of two reporters and a photographer would be assigned to each of five topics, which ultimately emerged as:

- Thirty years After the Dream: Where race relations stand in the 1990s.
- The Streets Where We Live: How does skin color affect where we live.

- School Daze: How race influences where our kids go to school.
- Jobs and Progress: Does skin color play a role in who gets them now, who'll get them later.
- Crime and Punishment: How race impacts the commission, investigation and prosecution of crime.

Each team would spend up to three months on their topic, overlapping the previous team by a month. The series would be rolled out over a year in three-part segments, 15 days of 4,000 to 5,000-word stories in all. In addition we would poll extensively and use focus groups on each topic.

(We later added a 16th day of the series with an internal focus group that examined attitudes on race within our own newsroom. As with every focus group, we offered the participants the option to remain anonymous. The newsroom focus group was the only one in which no one would go on the record. It also shows that there was as large a divide in the newsroom about race as there was in the community at large.)

That was all very expensive but Publisher John Dotson, an African-American, wasn't fazed by the cost. Just do it, he said. Or something like that.

But who would lead it? Hertz had sparked the initial conversation and brought us all to the table, but he was inexperienced ... and had just been promoted to deputy business editor. We selected Paynter to lead the reporting effort. He was a whiz with databases, winning national awards for his groundbreaking work on campaign contributions. Could he put a face on those numbers? His work that freed an innocent man from prison convinced us he could.

Assistant Managing Editor Doug Oplinger was selected to direct the focus group operations, working with Chancellor and Dyer. Oplinger had been a key editor working with Managing Editor Larry Williams and Metro Editor John Greenman on the 1987 Pulitzer-winning coverage of the attempted takeover of Goodyear Tire and Rubber.

Van Tassel directed the production process, working with the photo department and designers and Bruce, who copy edited the entire project.

The teams were ready to go immediately. But other editors reminded us that we had made a commitment to cover the 1992 election, both national and local, like never before, devoting a full-page to politics five days a week.

So we decided to delay reporting until 1993 even though we knew through a spy in the Cleveland newsroom that the Plain Dealer was embarking on a similar project and had two to three times the resources that we did.

The PD published its eight-day series of long stories and lots of graphics and photos in late 1992. "Race: Attitudes Divide Us" took a second place in the state The Associated Press contest for community service.

We published our first story in the "A Question of Color" series on Feb. 28, 1993. The last story was published on Dec. 29.

It wasn't easy. Our newsroom was strained. Twenty-nine reporters, editors, photographers, artists and page designers worked on the project. But so many others helped in ways that made the in-depth coverage of race possible.

And there were legitimate disagreements within the newsroom about our approach. We focused on Akron and Summit County, excluding Canton plus other more rural communities in our circulation area. We also limited the discussion of race relations to blacks and whites.

"One other thing that has always struck me is that as one of the only Asian reporters at the paper, I was not recruited to work on the Question of Color series," Umrigar, a native of India, recalled recently. "In those days, race was so narrowly defined that it only included blacks or whites. I could've brought a whole different perspective to that debate. Even if we'd done just one story about other races that made up the Akron community, it would've broadened the conversation so much."

We knew going in we had our limits and made our decisions based on them. But undoubtedly she is correct. We could have been more inclusive. And better. Besides the commitment of time and resources, though, one other decision made our series stand out. We didn't stop with just reporting the problem. We facilitated an effort to do something about race relations.

That came out of an argument between the men and the women on the team before we published the first installment. After discussing the initial stories, the women, led by Van Tassel and Curtis, insisted that we weren't doing enough, that we needed to go beyond the reporting. The men said that wasn't our job. Our job was to report the facts.

"Mango and I felt very strongly that the project had to make a difference, have community impact, go beyond the traditional news package of photos, infographics, and stories that largely confirmed what we already suspected about race relations," Van Tassel said.

The debate ended when the women stormed out of the room.

I sat back and watched it all without comment, then reported to Allen what happened.

The next day he had a Solomon-like brainstorm. We brought in a group of community leaders and activists and asked their advice. They suggested we facilitate a larger conversation. "Don't tell us what to do," Akron Deputy Mayor Dorothy Jackson said. "Just bring us together and let us decide what needs to be done."

And that was the beginning of totally separate second phase of the project, Coming Together, which evolved into a community organization by the same name that worked on improving race relations in Akron and several other cities until the newspaper was sold in 2006.

The dueling projects .... A Question of Color and Coming Together ... were awarded the Pulitzer Prize's Gold Medal for Public Service on April 12, 1994.

There was great joy in the newsroom that day.

"This goes way beyond my dreams and expectations," publisher Dotson said as he popped the cork on some nonalcoholic Champagne in the newsroom. "The community deserves a big piece of it, the way it responded and got all wrapped up in this."

Added Hertz: "The project changed the lives of the people who worked on it."

How much did it accomplish?

"I'd like to hope we made a difference, but I don't think we did," copy editor Yuvonne Bruce said. "But maybe we touched one person and changed one opinion."

Well, the project certainly did touch at least one person – President Bill Clinton.

On Dec. 3, 1997, Clinton cited A Question of Color/Coming Together as the reason he selected Akron as the site for his first national town hall on race.

"The reason we came to Akron, as – as was said earlier, in part is because of this Coming Together Project you've done here," Clinton said. "And I believe if we can find constructive ways for people to work together, learn together, talk together, be together, that's the best shot we've got to avoid some of the horrible problems we see in the rest of the world, to avoid some of the difficult problems we've had in our own history, and to make progress on the problems that we still have here today."

Seems like a long time ago.

~

The beginning of the end of the 1990s at the Beacon came for me in early 1997 when Allen took early retirement. He never explained why. I never asked.

But he left us with one last item on his bucket list ... a 52-week series on the history of the rubber industry in Akron. It was a project he had been talking about for years. Few newspapers had ever tackled anything of that kind of depth and breadth.

He even had a name for it: "Wheels of Fortune."

He selected Van Tassel to direct the effort. She had left the paper before the completion of A Question of Color to become business editor of the Seattle Times and I followed her to the Pacific Northwest, without a job, as soon as Coming Together was underway, fully funded at first by the Beacon and Knight-Ridder. Allen enticed us to come back in 1995, me as deputy managing editor of operations with the promise that I would get first shot at managing editor should that job become available and Van Tassel as special projects editor.

And this was some special project. Managing Editor Glenn Guzzo was named interim editor after Allen's departure. He made sure Van Tassel had a squadron of reporters rotating on and off her team, anchored by David Giffels and Steve Love, two of the paper's most accomplished writers, with many others rotating in like Glenn Gamboa, Katie Byard, Charlene Nevada and Jim Carney among others. Art director Mango Curtis coordinated the design before she left for a position at Northwestern University. Deputy photo director Susan Kirkman Zake unearthed hundreds of historical photos.

Looking back, I'm not sure how they accomplished it. Fifty-two weeks, four open pages per week, more than 300,000 words in all. They gave us stories about people like Violet McIntyre White, a scrappy, 100-pound woman who worked in the factories while the men were away fighting World War II, as well as those of the industry giants, the Seiberlings, the O'Neils, the Firestones and E.J. Thomas.

And after all that, they weren't finished. Van Tassel, Giffels, Love and Zake spent several months revising and refining the initial series down to a 100,000-word book published by the University of Akron Press. It sold almost 15,000 copies, the most ever by the university press, won a national university press award for the use of photos and led to a four-hour community forum.

"'Wheels of Fortune' ... unpacked the history of Akron's rubber industry and laid it out for better understanding," Love said. (It also) allowed me to work with the best of the best, fellow writer David Giffels and project editor Debbie Van Tassel. It did not win a Pulitzer, but it remains, in my mind at least, the most important and lasting work of my career."

As "Wheels of Fortune" was in progress, sucking up resources, the Cleveland Indians, who only won 86 games during the regular season, surprised the baseball world by reaching the seventh game of the World Series before losing in extra innings to the Florida Marlins.

The Beacon Journal newsroom never flinched, producing a special section for each of the 29 days, including off days, of the playoffs. The sports staff, built by editors Tom Giffen and Bill Eichenberger and led then by Larry Pantages, proved why they were not only regarded as the best in Ohio, but one of the best in the nation year after year. Their playoff team included beat writer Sheldon Ocker, who later would be awarded one of sports journalism's most prestigious honors, the J.G. Taylor Spink Award; author and columnist Terry Pluto, Chris Broussard, Greg Couch, etc. They provided unmatched coverage of the games. Michelle LeComte, editor of the quick response team, led a group of reporters who followed the baseball team's fans. Michael Good's photo team and Terence Oliver's art department provided not only game coverage but produced a full-page poster for A-1 every night.

As associate managing editor, it was my job to pull it all together for each edition. That included reconfiguring the section each time the Indians won to allow for additional advertising.

It was exhilarating. It was exhausting. And it was deflating, when the Indians lost the final game in the 11th inning after blowing a 2-1 lead in the ninth.

But we sold lots of papers and made lots of money.
Newspaper chains generally don't publicly reveal the profits of its individual units, but I was privy to the numbers that year. We made 27 percent profit on $100 million in revenue in 1997, an all-time record for the newspaper. Daily circulation was at a 30-year high of 165,000 even though the Plain Dealer had made a major circulation and editorial push into northern section of the Beacon's prime territory.

We were all giddy. So giddy in fact that corporate gave us $1 million over budget for 1998 to redesign and expand the Sunday newspaper, a project for which art director Terence Oliver, assistant managing editor Geoffrey Gevalt and I spent long hours producing the prototype. Knight-Ridder's acceptance of the proposal meant hiring seven more full-time journalists, bringing our news room full-time employees to 189.

But none of us saw what was coming. In hindsight, it was obvious.

Almost 50 percent of our profits that year – $12 million – came from the Sunday classified ads section. It was almost like printing gold. Yet most of the newspaper industry badly underestimated how competition from the internet would affect classifieds.

Actually, Knight-Ridder had been a pioneer in digital journalism. "K-R was quite aware of the threat posed by the internet, warning those of us who were editors and publishers on many occasions that hard times were ahead," Dale Allen said.

The company's emphasis on the Merc Center in San Jose, California, and its push for database dominance through subsidiaries like VuText made it one of the nation's leaders among newspapers. But much of that died when CEO James Batten died in 1995 and was replaced by Tony Ridder.

"The sombitch (Ridder) had no appreciation for anything Batten and his folks had done trying to move K-R into the 21st century," Allen recalled. "From my perspective, Batten had the right ideas but was at least a half-decade ahead of the technology available to carry them out."

As a personal aside, I almost died from pneumonia in early 1998. The stress of the playoffs and the Sunday redesign project had left me with the immune system of "a 90-year-old," doctors told me. I was in the hospital for 10 days, out from work for a month.

By the time I returned in February, an outsider from Gannett, Jan Leach, was named editor even though just before I got ill, Publisher John Dotson had promised me an interview for the job. Soon it was apparent I was not going to be part of Leach's management team even though I had been lured back to Akron with the promise I would be promoted into top management. After I declined a demotion, I was given a buyout of 13 weeks pay for 29 years of service with Knight-Ridder and "the opportunity to pursue other interests."

So I only know the paper's financials for 1998 through hearsay. Profits dropped to ONLY 21 percent that year, I was told, and the bean counters began slicing and dicing. All of the jobs from the expanded Sunday section – and more – were eliminated.

That same year, a piece of all of us died, when Fran Murphey, a reporter and columnist for 55 years, passed away. "... she had something they can't teach you in journalism school," Thrity Umrigar wrote in Murphey's obit. "She had a passionate heart. And a love for people and this community that never dimmed."

Meanwhile, several months after my dismissal, I returned to journalism with the The Plain Dealer, first as a reporter in 1999 covering Akron and Summit County. That left me in the weird position of competing against two of Ohio's best, Bob Paynter and Margaret Newkirk, on the investigation of corruption in Summit County government, which had begun near the end of my watch at the Beacon. I was no match for those two, but proud still that eight people connected with the county were convicted.

Later I became the paper's writing coach. New Editor Doug Clifton, also a refugee from Knight-Ridder, arrived a few months after I did and began raiding the Beacon Journal's talent bank, recruiting Van Tassel as business editor, Paynter as an investigative editor/reporter, columnist Regina Brett and consumer reporter Sheryl Harris among others. At least 15 in all made the

45-minute trip north. Columnist Pluto and basketball writer Brian Windhorst were among the last to leave for Cleveland after they were hired by Clifton's replacement, Susan Goldberg, in 2007.

Steve Love and longtime art director Art Krummel, who had designed the award-winning Page 1 graphic for Question of Color, were among a dozen or so who took hefty buyouts from Knight-Ridder. Umrigar left to write books and teach at Case Western Reserve University. Stars like Chuck Klosterman, Gamboa, Mike Weinreb and Broussard pursued careers in New York City. Giffels eschewed big-city offers, choosing to become the literary voice of Akron while also teaching at the University of Akron.

In 2006, after a decade of Ridder's leadership, Knight-Ridder was sold to the McClatchy Corporation. McClatchy shed itself of several papers in aging cities like Philadelphia, Detroit and Akron. The Black Press Group of Canada paid a reported $160 million for the Beacon Journal, 10 times what the paper would sell for 12 years later, when GateHouse Media bought it.

Layoffs and buyouts continued until the number of full-time employees dipped below 50. Circulation fell to around 60,000.

On Nov. 11, 2013, Beacon printed its last paper in-house in favor of printing at The Repository in Canton, now also owned by GateHouse.

My hat is off to Editor Bruce Winges, former Managing Editor Doug Oplinger and veterans like Bob Downing, Jim Carney, Katie Byard, Jewell Cardwell, Paula Schleis, Doug Livingston, Yuvonne Bruce, Betty Lin-Fisher, Cheryl Powell, Amanda Garrett, photographers Lew Stamp and Cardew and many more who maintained the paper's high standards of journalism despite the many downturns. In fact, as I was finishing the last words on this chapter, the Akron Beacon Journal was named the best newspaper in Ohio for 2017 by the Press Club of Cleveland.

Columnist Bob Dyer, one of the key writers in the Question of Color series, is among those still standing. His investigation of televangelist Ernest Angley should have received Pulitzer consideration. He survived the first round of cuts by GateHouse. He speaks for a lot of us when he reflects on his 30-plus years in Akron.

"We thought we could do anything and everything – and we had the money to try," Dyer wrote in in an email.

"The reporting, writing and editing were superb across every department. We were considered one of the best mid-size papers on the continent, for good reason, and I was damn proud to work at the place.

"Although comparing today's newspaper industry with what we had in the 1990s is extremely discouraging, I feel fortunate to have lived through what I consider a golden age of journalism. We did things right, and we would spend whatever it took – in terms of both time and money – to bring a major story home."

It wasn't a perfect time, of course. Women managers didn't get the same bonuses as men until the middle '90s. The threat of a strike in 1993 almost derailed the race project. A dispute between Dyer and Carl Chancellor over the word "niggardly" divided the newsroom and became part of The New York Times' Pulitzer-winning project on race in America.

But it was a damn fine time to be a journalist in Akron, Ohio. And that's why I'm sad that so much of that is gone.

Newsgathering in the new millennium: boom and then bust

KAYE SPECTOR

I started working at The Plain Dealer in August 2000 as a Metro reporter.

I was a journalist who had worked at a string of smaller dailies and weeklies in the Greater Cleveland area for about 15 years. I was always envious of The Plain Dealer reporters I met on the job and so longed to work with them. I had unsuccessfully sought a college internship and several jobs at the PD. Finally, in 2000 I got the paper's attention.

The Plain Dealer was an odd and endearing place from the moment I first walked in the door for my interview.

Everyone who worked in editorial has a hiring story. They are told humorously in retrospect, with elements of exasperation, miscommunication, desperation or bewilderment.

Like many job candidates, I had to do a "tryout," a rite of passage in the hiring process in which the editors would give you an assignment and then judge your work.

My assignment: Find and write a story – any story – that had to do with the suburb of Brooklyn. It was a sleepy suburb that no one at the PD had written about in months, from the looks of the clips. I was desperate. I called the mayor's office and tried to enlist the help of the secretary by explaining my situation. She HAD to help me come up with a decent story or I wouldn't get the job.

The only thing she could offer was that it was the first day of a hockey skills class taught at the city ice rink by a semi-pro hockey player who grew up in the community. It didn't sound like much, and I didn't have a clue about hockey. But I had a moment of sudden inspiration. I would call a PD reporter whom I'd worked with at another paper. He was a rabid hockey fan. I would pick his brain and come up with another story.

I thought my friend would be happy to help me get on board at the PD. But when I reached him, he heaved a big sigh. He was really busy with a story, sweating it out on deadline and clearly did not want to talk.

I pressed him anyways because I knew the guy, and I was determined to get a job offer. After many more sighs, he did reluctantly talk to me, and even warmed up to the subject. Because of his insight, I was able to broaden the story to include the struggles of older communities to keep expensive ice rinks and hockey programs running. It was a better story than a quick feature on a semi-pro hockey player. But it felt like pulling teeth to get it. Welcome to the Plain Dealer, I thought.

Last batch of hires

I came to the Plain Dealer during what would be its last big hiring spree. I didn't realize it then, but I know now that I was hired at the beginning of the end of the fat days for the Plain Dealer – what would become a long slide of decline and painful contraction that continues to this day.

Although a hiring freeze was announced a few weeks after I came on board, no one thought it would last. In that era, it seemed like the paper was constantly hiring people, sometimes groups of them at a time.

The paper had expanded greatly in the 1990s, opening three well-staffed bureaus in neighboring counties and beefing up the copydesk, layout desk and metro desk downtown to handle the influx of copy and the multiple zoned editions the paper was putting out every night.

When I came on board, Editor Doug Clifton had been gradually expanding the staff in the year and a half since he had arrived, much of it on the suburban desk.

The goal was to increase readership in the outlying areas by doing stories that were intensely local. That meant assigning reporters to cover more than 75 cities and townships. Be at every council meeting. Write about every city hall, school district, police force and fire department.

The plan was to zone page B3 four ways in the Cuyahoga County edition of the Metro section. B3 would be like a second front page, filled with suburban news originating from groups of northwest, southwest, northeast and southeast communities that ring Cleveland.

The goal was to have four to five local stories in each zone every day, which took a significant amount of news staff to accomplish. I was among a group of five reporters hired during that period and was assigned to Metro, covering a group of southwestern suburbs.

Although the paper hired editorial employees after the year 2000, never again would the staff see large numbers of reporters and editors hired at the same time. And when people left, positions began to go unfilled.

The non-management editorial staff, which peaked at around 350 when I was hired, had shrunk greatly through buyouts in 2006, and then layoffs and buyouts in 2008. Vacant positions went unfilled. By 2012, the non-management editorial staff numbered around 170. Almost another 70 positions would be gone through buyouts and layoffs in 2013.

The New Building

When I joined the PD, though, it appeared the paper was continuing on a wave of expansion and prosperity it had been riding since I moved to the Cleveland area in the mid-1980s.

There was the massive staff hirings, of course. But perhaps the most visible expression of what appeared in 2000 to be a bright, prosperous future was what we called The New Building.

In 1994, the company built a $200 million state-of-the-art printing and distribution plant on Tiedeman Road in the suburb of Brooklyn. When I joined the paper in mid-2000, the company was preparing to move in a few months into another new building, this one constructed downtown, which eventually would rise four stories in parts and span three city blocks. The building was to provide a modern, spacious home for about 1,000 employees who worked in the paper's news and the business divisions.

Since 1960, Plain Dealer employees were crammed into a multistory building at 1801 Superior Ave. The newsroom was dark, cramped, windowless and airless and had a jerry-built feel to it.

For example, the metro desk, where the editors sat, was a string of desks arranged in a circle atop a raised floor that concealed the cables and wiring necessary for computers. The metro reporters' small desks were arranged nearby in narrow columns of two desks each, and pairs of reporters seated closely together shared a computer.

If you had a desk mate who liked to read on the internet like I did, you had to find a vacant computer somewhere else to write your story. I usually sat up on the metro desk rim nearby so I could hear my desk phone ring. Working on deadline one afternoon, I was puzzled why I wasn't getting any calls back. I checked my desk phone to make sure the receiver hadn't been knocked off the hook.

"What the hell? My ringer is off."

"I shut it off," asserted the old-timer reporter who sat in front of me. "It was too loud."

Stringers

When I joined The Plain Dealer, its editorial reach was extensive: Anything north of Columbus was considered fair game for coverage. Stringers were an important part of making this happen, and the paper had a wide network of them.

Stringers were freelancers who were the eyes and ears of the paper, paid to attend government meetings and check police and fire logs. They could earn more money if a tip turned into a story and even more depending on where the story ran – like on the Metro cover, for example. Stringers also worked on Election Day, calling in updated results from outlying boards of elections and providing quotes for stories that reporters would put together at the office.

Most of the stringers did this work as a side job. One of the more industrious stringers was able to do enough work to make it a full-time job. Either way, when I joined the paper, the Plain Dealer was relying heavily on its vast stringer network to keep its ear to the ground throughout Northeast Ohio.

A few weeks after I started, the suburban reporters were called into a meeting in a small conference room by the assistant managing editor for metro. He told us that the paper was no longer going to pay stringers.

The reaction among the reporters was surprise, disapproval and a bit of disbelief. Most of the reporters were assigned to cover a number of communities and several wondered aloud how they would cover them properly without stringers. Some worried about taking earnings away from people they had worked with for years. And why was the paper making these cuts when we were getting ready to move into a state-of-the-art multimillion-dollar building?

The AME couldn't answer that but suggested we keep in touch with our communities through follow-up phone calls. Still, the reporters worried about missing out on news that might not be in a local official's interest to reveal.

Elimination of the stringer network was a money decision that eventually affected the paper's editorial reach, influence and quality.

Other money-saving cutbacks would come later, some of them quite devastating. But this, I believe now, was my first glimpse of what the future would bring.

Leaving the paper

When I started working at the Plain Dealer, I truly thought I would retire from the paper. It had been such a long-held goal of mine to work there. And I loved it so.

There was the absorbing, challenging, endlessly fascinating and often frustrating work of newsgathering. I liked the huge responsibility of reporting the news accurately and fairly, and I enjoyed the visibility that working at a large metro daily brought.

Then there was the delightfully varied mix of people working in the newsroom. Some were friendly and funny, some were kind and warm, some were whip-smart and others were petty, arrogant or competitive. Almost all were well-read and had an enduring interest and awareness of what was going on in the world. Many were great storytellers or people who loved to laugh. It was a culture that valued that question Why? even in the workplace.

I left the paper at the end of 2010. With the advent of the internet in the 1990s, then the rise of social media in the early 2000s, I had become convinced the paper would not be there in another 10 years.

The Plain Dealer's parent company had already started an online affiliate, called cleveland.com, with a separate, growing staff. I felt a shift was coming.

I left to work for a local news company owned by AOL, and, three years later, was laid off. That was it for me and the news business. With the industry clearly in contraction, I felt lucky to get an offer to join the marketing division of a Cleveland-based health care system as a writer and editor.

I was at a large gathering of former Plain Dealer staffers recently. At these get-togethers, we tend to do what other people do who have been through an intense shared experience. We tell stories.

I was standing next to a woman who had been a Plain Dealer reporter and had left the paper long before I arrived. She turned to me after one of a long string of tales from the old days and said, "I think we all tend to romanticize the paper."

And I said, "No, it really was that way. And I miss it terribly."

Misfit

DAVE DAVIS

I'll begin this essay as any good reporter would, with a story I shouldn't tell. In fact, it's a story that I've never told.

I arrived at The Plain Dealer under a cloud on Aug. 6, 1990, believing that my career in journalism was over. A few days earlier, I had been forced to resign from the Dayton Daily News amid allegations that I may have broken the law in pursuing stories about Dr. James C. Burt, a Dayton physician who called himself the "Love Doctor."

Burt was performing what he called "love surgery" on dozens of women supposedly to improve their sex lives. In it, he would surgically rearrange their vaginas. I don't want to get too graphic here, but the problem was that Burt wasn't a surgeon and "love surgery" didn't work. His waiting room was crowded with the proof – dozens of women who could no longer have sex, their lives shattered. (One of my close sources had undergone 18 unsuccessful reconstructive surgeries trying to reverse the damage.)

I'm going to be careful here so as not to make you an accomplice to any crimes I may or may not have committed in my pursuit of the Dr. Burt story.

But let's just say that someone was picking up his trash, going through it one coffee-stained paper at a time, looking for scribbled notes, telephone messages, leads for the stories that would eventually play a role in the state revoking Burt's medical license.

The county sheriff and prosecutor got involved.

So when The PD's Maxine Lynch called I almost didn't accept the job. What was the point? But I had a wife, a baby daughter, and absolutely no money. "Yes," I heard myself saying. "I can start next Monday."

The Plain Dealer hired me to help cover environmental issues with Tom Breckenridge, "Breck" as we all knew him, an ace reporter with a steady hand in journalism and in life.

I remember walking into the newsroom at 1801 Superior Avenue for the first time on that August day. It was on the second floor, or, I should say it pretty much was the second floor, a huge open space with the editors' desks arranged in a horseshoe in the middle. A waist-high wall formed the perimeter of the horseshoe and it made it look almost like an ice-skating rink. More than one hundred reporters sat outside, divided into groups according to what they covered, their desks facing the editors to whom they reported.

The newsroom was dingy and like a bar had no windows, so you completely lost track of time.

And it was hot, very hot, because there really was no air conditioning, at least it seemed that way. (I remember Editor Thom Greer bringing in trash cans filled with iced soda one day when it reached 90 degrees and we all complained.) Papers were piled high on every desk. Reporters sat two-to-a-computer. Phones rang. Assistant Metro Editor Jim Darr yelled, "Where the hell's that story."

My first week is a blur – I remember Gary Clark, the managing editor, a reporters' editor who fought for good journalism, coming out and welcoming me to the newsroom. I was nervous. I was on probation. I hadn't lied to The PD about anything; I wasn't really asked about Dayton. How long is this going to last?

As he walked away, Betsy Sullivan, who I knew by the excellent reputation of her reporting but had just met, leaned over and whispered, "He's one of the good guys." This made me feel good, for a moment. I was glad to be working for the good guys, and I felt that Betsy had shared this with me because I was one of the good guys, too.

Sometime later, perhaps even the next day, Bill Barnard, assistant to Publisher Alex Machaskee, came down from the executive suite, holding a piece of paper, an AP story about me. He was standing off to the side in the newsroom talking to Clark and John Griffith, the city editor. The story said that I now worked for The Plain Dealer.

I didn't hear what was said, and it was one of the few topics that really wasn't discussed, even at the Headliner (the nearby bar frequented by PD people). But Barnard left. (Years later, I learned from someone on the newspaper's business side that I was one of only two reporters ever hired without a background check, though I filled out the paperwork for one during my tryout. Given the colorful cast of characters that walked through those doors, I took this as a badge of honor.)

Barnard came down a few more times, and each time he left, and I waited to be summoned. Finally, I decided to come clean with Griffith, a no-nonsense editor who had a reputation for being equally trusted by both mobsters and law enforcement. Griff didn't have an office, just a desk in the horseshoe. So we stood in there in the midst of the chaos and talked, for less than a minute. "We know that you were picking up trash," he said bluntly. "That's why you're here."

This was my introduction to America's 16th largest daily newspaper, a reporters' paper. People argued, fought over stories. They disagreed, even threw things. But it was all a part of chasing the news. If you had the ability and the will, you could get a story and get it published. Sometimes, seemingly, against the wishes of the people at the top.

I resolved that my first story for The Plain Dealer would be a good one, so I stayed late every night that week working on it. Early in the evening, I'd run out to pick up Chinese food. The sun would be going down and the PD delivery trucks would be lining up. More than a hundred of them, it seemed. The smoke from their diesel engines was so thick you could taste it. Later, about 10 o'clock, the desks in the newsroom would begin to shake and you could hear the rumble from the mighty presses in the basement as they began rolling.

On Saturday evening, I stopped in late to look over my story – a front-page, above-the-fold Sunday piece about PCBs being found in a sprawling abandoned auto plant in an East Side neighborhood. Residents in the area hadn't been told about the contamination, which was making its way to the water. Now they knew.

An editor looked over my tweaks, probably scoffed, then waved me over. "Come with me." We hurried down the stairs to the basement and wound our way through The Plain Dealer's massive, block-long maze of printing presses – dangerous territory for outsiders, who could easily get lost forever. The editor knew the way.

We walked fast for a few minutes, past the grimy men in worn overalls, past the huge steel structure with its never-ending roll of paper that was wound around printing plates and would move a hundred miles an hour when the presses were rolling. (At this moment they were stopped.)

We stopped at the end of the line, the place where the papers roll out. "This is Dave Davis," the editor said. "His first story is in tomorrow's paper."

The pressman, who, splattered with ink, looked like a coal miner, pulled a paper off the press without emotion. He handed it to me. "Welcome to The Plain Dealer."

This is how ink gets in your blood.

~

I attended high school in genteel Cincinnati, a nice enough place but too conservative for my liking in its Procter & Gamble sort of way.

I began my journalism career phoning in sports stats to the local newspaper for high school basketball, wrestling and track events. I didn't ever get a byline, but occasionally The Enquirer would use a quote I got, and that was a big deal. My mother was supportive of my desire to be a writer, as long as I took typing in high school. It was what she thought of as a fall-back career.

I longed to escape Cincinnati. Early on, Cleveland captured my imagination.

I was drawn to the city's grit and grime and the fiery steel mills with flames leaping skyward, to the labor unions and the politics and the place that had so many immigrants with names that I couldn't pronounce. Cleveland was so very different from my WASPy, white-collar life in Cincinnati.

It was a far-off place, with alluring images and, yes, names. I was drawn by "The Plain Dealer." Winston Churchill, on a visit to Cleveland, said, "Oh, there's the Cleveland Plain Dealer. I think that by all odds, the Plain Dealer has the best newspaper name of any in the world." That's quite a compliment in a state with newspaper names like The Vindicator and The Blade. And let's not forget the Eagle-Eyed News Catcher, which was one of six papers in Cleveland in the 1840s. "The pity of it all, of course, is that the Eagle-Eyed News Catcher was not able to survive," George E. Condon wrote in "Adventures in journalism." "It had a name that deserved to live."

I worked at The Plain Dealer for 24 years, for five different editors and three different managing editors. When I look back at those years, as I am in this essay, they have merged and condensed into a highlight reel. As Dick Feagler says in "Stop the presses," they are not the truth of the place, at least the entire truth. They are my truth, my memories.

Memories of—

~High School sports reporter Dick Zunt giving me the best piece of reporting advice I've ever received, "Work a lot of names into your stories."

~Griff's wisdom, "Never give your word lightly, and when you do *always* keep it" and "Act as if the whole world is watching."

~Exposing the worst radiation accident ever in medicine – when 28 patients died from radiation exposure in the mid-70s at Riverside Methodist Hospital in Columbus, Ohio. The tragedy was part of a five-day series with Ted Wendling. It had never been disclosed, leaving families angry and uncertain. "I didn't realize until I read the articles how hard it was" on them, said Ivan Selin, chairman of the Nuclear Regulatory Commission. Selin then set out to overhaul the regulation of nuclear materials in hospitals.

~Publishing the average waiting times and mortality rates for every transplant center in the nation, information that had never been made public but that we got because of PD reporter Joan Mazzolini's dogged efforts. With our partner Ted Wendling, we found patients who were told they would die within six months at transplant centers where the wait was measured in years. We followed a patient though a heart transplant and looked at smaller hospitals that were turning away donor organs for nonmedical reasons.

~Receiving a standing ovation at The National Press Club when we received the Heywood Broun Award for our stories about inequities in the nation's transplant system and patients who were waiting for transplants that would never come – patients like Teddy DeWalt, a Kansas City firefighter who died after enduring months of poking and prodding with the hope of getting a new heart, a second chance at life. His wife Loetta never left his side. No one bothered to tell the DeWalts that a political struggle within the University of Kansas Medical Center had already shut down the heart transplant program, that the surgeons were turning away all of the donor hearts matched to the hospital's 38 waiting patients. In the acceptance speech, Joan talked about the important role of journalism, words that I often recall today:

> *We are especially honored to receive the Broun Award because we believe it stands for the very ideals that brought us into journalism, the ideals that keep us going: That news organizations should give voice to those who cannot be heard, those who have fallen through the cracks; and that our work, in some small way, should promote the dignity of ordinary people who find themselves struggling in difficult times.*

~Along with reporter Mike O'Malley, going after sleazy landlords and rip-off security companies that preyed upon the poor, and, with consumer reporter Sheryl Harris, documenting shoddy home repairs by contractors who had received $21.5 million in tax dollars in a Cleveland program meant to help residents improve their homes.

~The "sleeve," our not-so-secret signal to meet at the bar next door.

~Going after the Federal Aviation Administration with reporter Mike Sangiacomo over misleading the public about a faulty radar system that had cost billions of dollars and sometimes did not work.

~Working with editor Stuart Warner on "From flowers to fear," an investigative narrative piece about a local doctor who was being stalked by her former fiancé, Rick Simon, whom she had met through a dating service.

~Rushing back to the newsroom on Sept. 11, 2001, the day planes hit the twin towers, the Pentagon and crashed in Pennsylvania, trying to contribute to our coverage, worrying about my family and what lay ahead.

The truth is that even on the worst days – and there were a few – it was an honor to be a journalist at The Plain Dealer. It was a sacred public trust. I was honored every day I walked through the doors at 1801. On many days our stories helped people in small ways, and on big days, they changed lives.

Like everyone in this book, I have thought much about the future of the profession I love. I don't have an answer for the problems we are facing, and I haven't heard one that I think will work. Sure, there's a lot of good reporting being done now, but not in the volume that we need. And who's going to stay in a profession that can't sustain them. Things seem to be in a continuing state of decline. It's not that I want things to return to the good old days. That wouldn't be progress. And I know that it's important to make money.

Seventy-nine years ago, in 1939, Heywood Broun founded the Newspaper Guild in Cleveland. I was an active member of Local 1. Broun believed, I think, that if reporters received job security and decent pay, the profession would improve and society would benefit. I believe we are back at this point today.

Our country needs good journalism now more than ever. As I write this, there is growing concern about local journalism. Cleveland.com has just downsized again, and there is a question about whether The Plain Dealer will be dismantled next year when the contract with the Newspaper Guild expires. It's mind boggling to think of Cleveland as a no-newspaper town, but we seem to be headed that way.

~

I worked on many big stories for The Plain Dealer over the years, but it's a smaller one that I carry with me and most often recount.

I was sitting at my desk in the newsroom on Oct. 15, 2012, drinking my second afternoon cup of coffee, when the phone rang.

On the other end was a woman, Joan Grace, whose voice was polite, perhaps too polite, and measured. She was a member of the Gethsemane Baptist Church and the Wings Over Jordan Choir. She was in charge of promoting the group's 75th anniversary concert. It was just five days away, and things weren't going well. She was worried that no one was going to come. And they were holding the concert at a larger church, Holy Trinity Baptist Church, because everyone thought they would draw a large crowd.

"That's not what I do," I remember saying.

"I was given your name. They said you might be able to help. We've got a rehearsal tomorrow."

I paused and carefully thought about it. "What time?"

I arrived at the Gethsemane Baptist Church on E. 79th street the next day to beautiful, melodic chaos. It seemed like all 100 members of the a cappella choir were there, dressed in their Sunday best, laughing, singing. I was the center of attention.

I've been buked and I've been scorned
I've been buked and I've been scorned
Children, I've been buked and I've been scorned
Tryin' to make this journey all alone
You may talk about me sure as you please
Talk about me sure as you please

As PD photographer Lisa DeJong took pictures, I talked to people. Teretha Settle, whose grandfather started Wings Over Jordan, told me about how the choir traveled the country during the Jim Crow era, drawing tens of thousands of people, black and white, at each stop. The Rev. Glenn T. Settle refused to sing to segregated audiences, so everyone listened together.

Children, talk about me sure as you please
Your talk will never drive me down to my knees
Jesus died to set me free
Jesus died to set me free
Children, Jesus died to set me free
Nailed to that cross on Calvary

Others told me about how, for nearly a decade, America listened to the Wings Over Jordan choir, the first black singing group on national radio. Their distinct voices emerged in the days before television, when families often sat around on the front porch listening to the radio together on Sundays. The choir was an early voice in the civil rights movement.

Back in the newsroom, I put together my story – words, a photo gallery, audio and hyperlinks would be published online and a written story with Lisa's pictures would go in the print edition. It had been picked for the Metro section cover.

Saturday evening, I found myself in my car driving down to Holy Trinity. There were cars everywhere and no available spots to park. So I pulled up in front of the church and stopped for a moment, watching what seemed like hundreds of people filing in.

My career at The Plain Dealer was coming to an end. I thought about the power that reporters hold, the power of storytelling, the power to fill churches. And I thought about Joan Grace, who when I prepared to leave the choir rehearsal gave me a big hug, whispering into my ear. "Thanks. It means so much when The Plain Dealer shows up."

Yes, it does.

PHOTOGRAPHS

Covering Cleveland - 1946 to 2013

There have been many memorable photographs taken in Cleveland, but this one by Plain Dealer photographer Christine "Chris" Stephens captures the city's beauty, daring, and optimism as it entered the 1990s. For journalists, the image brings mixed emotions. It shows an iron worker atop the 20-story North Point Office Tower at E. 9th Street and Lakeside Avenue, the former site of the Cleveland Press. The Press building was demolished after the newspaper closed in 1982, and it was replaced with an office building and tower. Cleveland Public Library Photograph Collection.

Happy Clevelanders crowd the lobby of the Cleveland Press on Feb. 6, 1946, to buy copies of the first edition printed since a pressmen's strike began Jan. 7. It was the first of four newspaper strikes in Cleveland, and it stopped publication of Cleveland's three daily newspapers. Cleveland Public Library Photograph Collection.

The Plain Dealer offices on Superior Avenue and E. 6th Street. This picture was taken on Feb. 6, 1946, the day a 32-day strike by the pressmen ended. "Presses Roll And City Lives Again," the Plain Dealer declared. "Coffee Was Flat Without Morning Paper." Cleveland Public Library Photograph Collection.

The Plain Dealer city room in 1947. The PD's daily circulation stood at 220,618 two years earlier, ranking it the second highest among Cleveland's three daily newspapers. The Cleveland Press led in daily readers, and the News ranked third.* Cleveland Public Library Photograph Collection.

George E. Condon in 1949. He worked at The Plain Dealer for 42 years, beginning in 1943. He was a reporter, the newspaper's first radio and television critic, and a columnist. Cleveland Public Library Photograph Collection.

Plain Dealer Sports Editor Gordon "Cobby" Cobbledick in 1954 at a Golden Gloves boxing tournament. He wrote a column called "Plain Dealing," and his writing style was just that – short and to the point. Special Collections, Cleveland State University Library.

Regis McAuley was sports writer and sports editor at the Cleveland News. Later he was baseball writer and executive sports editor at The Press. Courtesy of Robert McAuley.

Covering Cleveland – 1946 to 2013 | 203

A pressman for the Cleveland Press changes a printing plate in 1953. Cleveland Public Library Photograph Collection.

A Plain Dealer pressman checks the flow of ink in this undated picture. The photo caption reads: "The papers are streaming out of the presses while the news is still red hot." Cleveland Public Library Photograph Collection.

The Cleveland Press city room on Sept. 18, 1953. The Press was leading in the circulation war, and would grow to 314,247 daily readers within two years.* Cleveland Public Library Photograph Collection.

The Plain Dealer city room in 1954. The newspaper's daily circulation by 1955 was 299,297 – 14,950 below the Press'. * Cleveland Public Library Photograph Collection.

Journalists prepare for a day in the 1954 Sam Sheppard trial. Sheppard was on trial for killing his wife, Marilyn. Photograph by William Ashbolt. Special Collections, Cleveland State University Library.

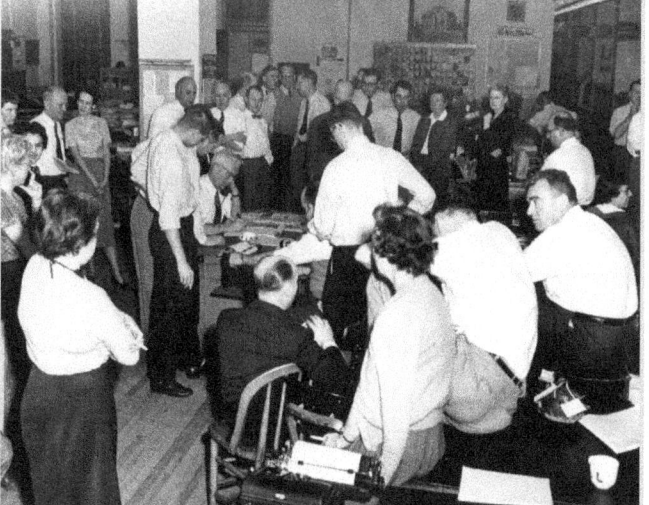

The staff at The Press gathers in the newsroom to hear the jury's verdict in the 1954 Sam Sheppard murder case. Sheppard was found guilty and later sentenced to life in prison, which was overturned on appeal. Special Collections, Cleveland State University Library.

The Plain Dealer presses in the 1950s were nearly a city block long. Cleveland Public Library Photograph Collection.

The Plain Dealer presses seemed to roll non-stop in 1954. Cleveland Public Library Photograph Collection.

The Plain Dealer plating press in 1961. Plain Dealer photograph by William "Bill" Nehez. Cleveland Public Library Photograph Collection.

The Plain Dealer presses in 1954. Cleveland Public Library Photograph Collection.

The Plain Dealer is assembled and ready for distribution in 1956. Cleveland Public Library Photograph Collection.

The Plain Dealer is loaded on trucks for delivery. Cleveland Public Library Photograph Collection.

The Plain Dealer's legendary rock 'n' roll critic Jane Scott, right, began her career as assistant society reporter. Scott is pictured here in 1956 with her boss, Louise Davis. Cleveland Public Library Photograph Collection.

Actress Jayne Mansfield poses with Plain Dealer photographers in this undated picture. Back row, from left, Bill Ashbolt, Dudley Brumbach, Marvin Greene, Bill Wynne. Front row, from left, Karl J. Rauschkolb, Mansfield, Ray Matjasic. Special Collections, Cleveland State University Library.

Editor Louis B. Seltzer stands in front of the Cleveland Press building located at E. 9th Street and Lakeside Ave. in 1960. Special Collections, Cleveland State University Library.

Seltzer reads an issue of The Press in 1960 with his feet propped on one of the desks in the city room. Special Collections, Cleveland State University Library.

Plain Dealer copy editor Robert Manry entering the harbor in Falmouth England, Aug. 17, 1965. Manry was completing a 78-day trip across the Atlantic in Tinkerbelle. Special Collections, Cleveland State University Library.

Robert Manry and his wife, Virginia, are piped ashore as they arrive at Fesitval Hall in England in August 1965 for a luncheon in their honor. Photograph by William Ashbolt. Special Collections, Cleveland State University Library.

Robert McGruder, pictured in 1966, The Plain Dealer's first black reporter. McGruder rose to become The PD's managing editor before leaving for the Detroit Free Press, where he became executive editor. Cleveland Public Library Photograph Collection.

Reporter Donald Barlett in 1969. Barlett left the PD and eventually landed at The Philadelphia Inquirer, where he won two Pulitzer Prizes with his partner, James Steele. Cleveland Public Library Photograph Collection.

Plain Dealer reporters Joe Eszterhas, left, and William F. Miller in 1968. Eszterhas went on to Rolling Stone and Hollywood, where he wrote scripts for several blockbuster movies. Cleveland Public Library Photograph Collection.

Plain Dealer editorial cartoonist Ray Osrin in 1967. He held the position until his retirement in 1993. Photograph by William "Bill" Wynne. Special Collections, Cleveland State University.

Joe Eszterhas, left, in November 1969 interviews former Army combat photographer Ronald Haeberle, whose pictures of the My Lai massacre shocked the nation and helped change the direction of the Vietnam War. Photograph by Richard T. Conway. Cleveland Public Library Photograph Collection.

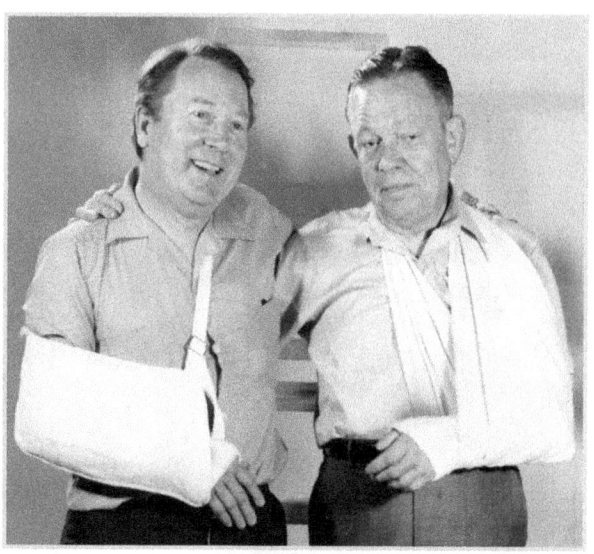

Posing with broken arms (really) in 1971 are Plain Dealer staffers George E. Condon, left, and Peter Bellamy. Bellamy, longtime drama critic, was the son of legendary Editor Paul Bellamy. Courtesy of Cleveland Public Library Photograph Collection.

The Plain Dealer team that exposed horrifying abuses at the Lima State Hospital included, from left, Ned Whelan, Richard Widman and Bill Wynne. This picture was taken May 31, 1972, when the team received the Heywood Broun Award. Special Collections, Cleveland State University Library.

Dennis Kucinich stopped by The Plain Dealer on Nov. 8, 1977, the evening he was elected Cleveland mayor. The newspaper had endorsed him. The photo caption read: "Mayor-elect Dennis J. Kucinich, once a copy aide at The Plain Dealer, returned to the city room last night to send the story of his election up the pneumatic tube to the composing room. With him are his wife, Sandra; Plain Dealer publisher and editor, Thomas Vail, and copy aide Ron Patterson, whose job Kucinich temporarily usurped." Plain Dealer photograph by William "Bill" Wynne. Special Collections, Cleveland State University Library.

Cleveland Press columnist and television personality Dick Feagler with singer Eric Carmen in 1981. Cleveland Public Library Photograph Collection.

Cleveland City Council President George Forbes tosses Roldo Bartimole out of special council meeting on Sohio project in March 1981. Special Collections, Cleveland State University Library.

Photographer Paul Tepley waves goodbye on June 15, 1982, the day The Press folded. Photograph by William "Bill" Wynne. Special Collections, Cleveland State University.

A picket line outside The Press on E. 9th Street and Lakeside Avenue on June 15, 1982, the day it stopped publishing. The newspaper had been overtaken by the Plain Dealer in the circulation war. Photograph by William "Bill" Wynne. Special Collections, Cleveland State University.

Plain Dealer journalists, from left, Jack Hagan, Don Bean, and Robert McAuley. Courtesy of Robert McAuley.

Journalist Terence Sheridan at the Sarajevo airport in 1993. Photograph by Elizabeth Sullivan.

Harlan Spector with deskmate John Petkovic in The Plain Dealer newsroom in the 1990s. Courtesy of Harlan Spector.

A "Save the PD" rally in 2013 in front of the PD offices at E. 18th Street and Superior Avenue. A group of Newspaper Guild members organized the campaign to try to preserve jobs and what they saw as the the quality of journalism in Cleveland. Despite their efforts, the newspaper's owner laid off one-third of the editorial staff, about 50 people, on July 31, 2013, the same day they ended 7-day home delivery in favor of a "digital first" strategy. Photograph courtesy of Harlan Spector.

*Circulation figures provided by historian John Vacha.

About Our Authors And Contributors

Tom Andrzejewski.

Tom Andrzejewski began his 25-year career at The Plain Dealer answering the call of "Boy!" – the term back then for copy aides – while attending Cuyahoga Community College then Cleveland State University. Over the years, he covered several major beats as a reporter and, for more than a decade, wrote about neighborhoods and the joys and travails of Clevelanders in his City Life column and a regular op-ed column. He received numerous national, state and local awards, ranging from the Silver Gavel Award of the American Bar Association to the Good Neighbor Award of the Association of Neighborhood Councils. In 2004, he was inducted into the Press Club of Cleveland Journalism Hall of Fame.

For nearly all his years at the PD, Tom was an officer and executive board member of Local 1 of the Newspaper Guild and a delegate to the Cleveland AFL-CIO Federation of Labor.

Tom's Plain Dealer career was interrupted by service in Vietnam with the 101st Airborne Division field artillery, where he served as a cannoneer then a public information specialist. He was awarded the Bronze Star Medal, Air Medal and Army Commendation Medal.

He left the newspaper in 1988 to start a public relations practice, The Oppidan Group Inc. Occasionally working in politics, Tom orchestrated issues and media in the successful underdog mayoral campaign of then State Sen. Michael R. White in 1989. He also directed publicity, paid media and community outreach for the campaign to build Gateway and played roles in several other city, county and statewide campaigns. Since leaving the PD, Tom has served as board president and a board member of Community Re-Entry and as a board member of the Center for Community Solutions, among other civic activities.

Tom is married to former PD reporter and editor Leslie Kay. They have one son, David.

Roldo Bartimole, known simply to local journalists as "Roldo," has forged his own career in journalism. He worked for a series of newspapers in Connecticut, then in Cleveland at The Plain Dealer and the Cleveland bureau of The Wall Street Journal, before founding his newsletter, Point of View, in 1968. He published Point of View for 32 years. Roldo was the subject of a Cleveland Scene profile by reporter Sam Allard in April 2018. (See: https://tinyurl.com/CLESceneRoldo).

Margaret Bernstein is the Director of Advocacy and Community Initiatives at WKYC Channel 3. In 2017, she received the top award for promoting Diversity & Inclusion from TEGNA, WKYC's parent company. A devoted champion of literacy, Margaret earned a 2016 Emmy for her #WeReadHere campaign at WKYC, which encourages parents to read every day with their children. She serves on the national board for Little Free Library.

Margaret Bernstein.

A Los Angeles native, she earned her bachelor's degree in journalism from the University of Southern California. She worked as a reporter, editor and columnist at The Plain Dealer from 1989 to 2013.

Well known for her passion about mentoring, Margaret was named National Big Sister of the Year in 2000 for her work with two Cleveland girls, Cora and Ernestine, through Big Brothers Big Sisters of America.

She is also the writer of The Bond, a memoir on fatherlessness by the famed Three Doctors. That experience led her to write her most recent book, a storybook titled "All In A Dad's Day," which is designed to tighten the bond between fathers and their young children.

Margaret is married to Shaker Heights Chief Prosecutor C. Randolph Keller, and is the mother of two children, Randy and Alexandria.

Carrie Buchanan arrived in Cleveland from Canada in 2006 after a career in newspapers, primarily at the Ottawa Citizen, the major daily in Canada's capital. Born and raised in Montreal, Buchanan attended Bryn Mawr College in Philadelphia, returning after graduation to Montreal where, despite a double-major in biology and psychology and no background in politics or writing, she decided to take up journalism. Turned out she had a "nose for news," as one public official put it after she broke a steady stream of stories, often from events that took place entirely in French, for the weekly North Shore News in Montreal's West Island suburbs.

In 1978, she gave it up and moved to Ottawa with a new baby, in support of her husband George's high-tech career. Within a year, she was a regular stringer for the Ottawa Journal, that city's morning daily, where she was known for breaking page one stories despite her sleepy suburban beat. She had just been asked to come on full-time when the Journal suddenly folded in August 1980, leaving Buchanan without a journalism job for eight long years. "I felt like they cut my arm off," she often told friends of that time in the wilderness.

In 1984, she enrolled at Carleton University's School of Journalism, where she earned her master's and, even before graduating, a new job at the surviving daily newspaper, the Ottawa Citizen. Twelve happy years ensued, covering suburbs at first, then four years at Ottawa City Hall, then a Quebec-based beat where she covered politics during the second referendum on Quebec separation, when the province voted 49.7 percent in favor of seceding from Canada; native affairs during a major standoff in Oka, Quebec, between Mohawk Indians and the Canadian Armed Forces; and many other stories that called upon her skills in French, politics and environmental science. (Yes, she did finally get to use that biology major!)

By 2000, weary of constant staff cuts and declining quality at her beloved Citizen and jealous of her husband and two children, all of whom were in university at the time, she took a buyout to return to Carleton and complete a doctorate while teaching journalism part-time. In 2006, she moved to Cleveland in support of her husband's new career as Unitarian Universalist minister, then landed her dream job at John Carroll University, where she is now a tenured professor in the Tim Russert Department of Communication and Theatre Arts.

Gary Clark is a career journalist; he worked as a reporter and editor at four newspapers over 34 years.

He and his wife, Caryn, have two kids: Jessica is a college administrator and Brian is an engineer. They no longer fight like they did as kids.

Gary's oldest brother, Brian, was killed in Vietnam in 1966. His second-youngest brother, Rory, died in 2015. Duff still lives in Cleveland Heights and Kevin is a patient at an adult foster care home.

Gary has written thousands of pieces, but never one about himself, as he half-jokingly says is "evidenced by the essay he wrote for this collection." His piece, "Dig deep...," is his first-ever account of the inner workings of The Plain Dealer during his time there.

He also still loves rock 'n' roll and remains a huge fan of Bob Dylan. He agrees with Dylan's lyric: *"You don't need a weatherman to know which way the wind blows."*

Marjorie and George E. Condon, who is goofing off again.

George E. Condon (1916-2011), originally from Fall River, Mass., began his career at The Plain Dealer in 1943 as a general assignment reporter. He became the paper's first television and radio critic in 1948. After 14 years on that beat he moved to the editorial page, where he wrote a daily column until his retirement in 1985.

Besides covering the city for The Plain Dealer, George wrote nine books, among them "Cleveland: The Best Kept Secret," a portrait in essays in 1967; "Laughter from the Rafters," a collection of columns in 1968; "Stars in the Water: the History of the Erie Canal," in 1974; and "Yesterday's Cleveland," a photographic history, in 1976.

He wrote seven days a week as a television critic and then five days a week as a general columnist. Taken as a whole, his columns provided a picture of Cleveland in both its high and low periods.

George's parents immigrated from Ireland. His father was a foreman at a textile mill in Fall River. After they moved to Cleveland, his mother was a maid at the Clevelander hotel downtown. George attended St. Patrick Catholic School and West Technical High School. After graduating, he majored in journalism at Ohio State University. It was there he met his future bride, Marjorie Philona Smith. They married in 1942 and moved to Cleveland the following year, when George joined The Plain Dealer.

The couple had seven children in 15 years. George outlived two of them. His wife, Marjorie Condon, a teacher in the Cleveland public school system for 20 years, died in March of 2001.

George won numerous awards during his career. He was given the Ohioana Award for history, the Women's City Club of Cleveland Award for Literature, the Burke Award for Literature as well as the Sigma Delta Chi Award for Distinguished Service He is also in the Cleveland Journalism Hall of Fame.

In his acceptance speech for the Ohioana Award, Condon wrote, "What I oppose is the hushed, carpeted fearful approach to history and those who made history. There is the air of the funeral parlor in most of our history books, and perhaps the sound of some rinky-tink piano is what we need to break the sad spell and bring history to its feet again. Only in life is there any hope for history."

You can read George's book, "Cleveland: the Best Kept Secret," online at https://tinyurl.com/CLEBestKeptSecret.

Susan Condon Love.

Susan Condon Love is the daughter of George E. Condon. She knew from grade-school on that she wanted to be a journalist – and to travel throughout the United States pursuing that career. After graduating from The Ohio State University with a journalism degree, Susan started her career at a daily in Escondido, California, called the Times-Advocate.

After three years learning the ropes, Love was hired at the Las Vegas Review-Journal as a features writer and food editor. Las Vegas at the time was booming and Susan was able to hone her feature-writing skills covering Las Vegas shows and the quirky people. Her favorite stories were the newly minted millionaire entrepreneur who invented the ubiquitous "dice" clock with dice as the numbers, and the man devoted to using his pilot skills to fly ill children to needed medical treatments out-of-state.

Looking for more adventures, Susan took the leap from Las Vegas to Savannah, Georgia, as the assistant feature editor at the Savannah News-Press. Reeling a little from the culture shock, Susan soon embraced the history and gentleness of the sleepy Southern town that was on the brink of becoming a tourist destination. It was in Savannah that Susan met her husband, then-sports-writer Brian Love. They married at the magnificent Cathedral of St. John the Baptist in Savannah and came home from their honeymoon to a letter saying one of them had to find a new job because of the paper's nepotism policy.

The journalism adventure continued as Susan was hired as the entertainment editor at The Capital newspaper in Annapolis, Maryland, while Brian snagged a job on the sports copy desk of The Washington Times. Soon, Savannah called again – Susan received an offer for the features editor position at the News-Press – and they moved back to Savannah. Brian decided at that point to become a teacher.

After several happy years in Savannah (and the birth of their daughter Kelly Anne), Susan decided to pursue her dream of working at The Plain Dealer and return to her home town. Hired for the features copy desk, she also worked on the design/layout desk. Soon after coming back from maternity leave with her son Brian George, Susan was named assistant homes editor and, mere months later, homes editor.

The homes beat turned out to be a dream job. Happy with the duties of a Sunday Homes section and a Saturday Real Estate section, Susan soon pitched the idea of combining the homes news into a home and garden section called Inside&Out. The section was a huge success for more than a decade. Susan was both the editor, writer and main columnist ("Full House") for the section.

Susan left The Plain Dealer in 2011 but returned to her first love, journalism, in 2016 when she assumed the duties of managing editor for three suburban weeklies on the West Side – The Press, the North Ridgeville Press and West Life. She is thoroughly enjoying community journalism and would urge every single journalist to get a subscription to keep grass-roots journalism healthy.

She currently lives in West Park with her husband, still a teacher, and her two college-going children.

Dick Feagler (1938-2018) is a Cleveland journalism legend. He worked at the Cleveland Press as a reporter and then columnist. After the Press closed, he wrote columns for the Willoughby News-Herald, the Akron Beacon Journal, and the Elyria Chronicle-Telegram. He did commentary, and then was an anchor, at local television stations before joining The Plain Dealer in 1993, returning to his first love as a columnist until retiring in 2009. He continued his "Feagler & Friends" show on WVIZ (PBS) until 2013. Dick, who died on July 1, was the subject of a recent piece by Ideastream's David C. Barnett and Annie Wu. (See https://tinyurl.com/IdeastreamFeagler).

Janet Beighle French, center, with Michael O'Malley and Mary Strassmeyer. Photograph by Jane Scott.

Janet Beighle French worked as the Cleveland Plain Dealer's home economics/food editor from 1963 through 1986.

Her work covered a variety of food-related topics, including the advent of supermarkets, which led to the decline of locally produced food, the development of more modern appliances and quick meal preparation techniques correlated to the movement of women from the domestic to the professional realm, and the increasing interest in ethnic cuisine as the U.S. moved toward a more multicultural society.

Janet reported on government regulation and food standardization, health research, poverty and nutrition, and the emergence of the natural foods market. She also acted as a food stylist, arranging food and props, for most of the photographs in the collection.

Dave Davis teaches at Youngstown State University (hence the bow tie), where he is the first-ever Journalism Fellow, a sort of journalist in residence. He worked for 24 years at The Plain Dealer, mostly as a reporter, before leaving the newspaper in July, 2013, with about 50 colleagues.

Before that, he reported for the Dayton (Ohio) Daily News and The Charleston (W.Va.) Gazette, where he began his journalism career under the crusading publisher W.E. "Ned" Chilton III, who was known for his practice of "sustained outrage."

At The PD, Dave wrote extensively about the nation's widening racial health divide, aviation safety, inequities in the nation's transplant system, among others. He has been honored with an Investigative Reporters & Editors Inc. Medal, a Polk Award, and the Heywood Broun Award, among others. He was twice a finalist for the Pulitzer Prize.

Co-editors Joan Mazzolini and Dave Davis.

Dave received a bachelor's degree in English from The Colorado College and a master's degree in journalism from Columbia University. He is an author and co-editor of this book. He is married to co-editor Joan Mazzolini.

Jack Hagan worked as a reporter and editor at The Plain Dealer for nearly 30 years. He covered a variety of beats including the courts, suburban communities, the environment and as a general assignment reporter. He also spent a short time as an assistant Metro editor where he supervised a team of reporters. After leaving the newspaper in 2005, he worked as the student media coordinator at Cuyahoga Community College for nine years. Jack is retired and lives in Lakewood, Ohio. He attended Youngstown State University and is a graduate of Cleveland State University.

Leslie Kay.

Leslie Kay is a former Plain Dealer reporter and editor who joined the the Plain Dealer after earning a bachelor's degree in journalism from Penn State. She held numerous positions at the newspaper, including suburbs reporter, beat reporter covering courts, general assignment reporter, assistant state editor and finally assistant metro editor, and won national, state and local journalism awards, including the Silver Gavel Award of the American Bar Association.

After leaving the PD in 1990, Leslie joined the Oppidan Group Inc. public relations firm, where she provided editorial, crisis management, media and community relations and media training services. She has also worked on numerous freelance editing and writing projects and was editor of and chief contributor to the 1992 edition of "A Citizen's Guide to Cleveland."

Leslie is married to Tom Andrzejewski, a former PD reporter, columnist and editor. They have one son, David.

Joan Mazzolini.

Joan Mazzolini worked for nearly 19 years at The Plain Dealer, where she won numerous national awards. While at the paper she covered different beats including the business of medicine and hospitals, was on the investigative team, and covered the Cuyahoga County Board of Elections, when the voting machines failed. She previously worked at the now closed Birmingham (Al) Post-Herald, where she wrote a series of stories on private country clubs that ultimately forced the PGA to change its policy and only hold tournaments at integrated clubs. (See https://tinyurl.com/SIMazzolini).

Joan received a bachelor's degree in finance from The Ohio State University and a master's degree in journalism from Northwestern University.

Joan is an author and co-editor of this book. She is married to co-editor Dave Davis.

Bob McAuley and his wife, Trudy.

Robert "Bob" McAuley is part of a three newspaper family.

His father, Regis, was sports writer and the sports editor of the Cleveland News. Regis McAuley went on to the Cleveland Press, where he was baseball beat writer and executive sports editor.

Bob McAuley is a 43-year veteran of The Plain Dealer, working in circulation sales and as a newsroom copy boy, and a reporter covering cops, news, and investigations. He spent the last 25 years of his PD career as an executive in the newsroom, starting with city editor in 1981 and ending in 2006 when he was Washington and medical editor.

He is currently Chair of the Board at Rose-Mary Center, a Catholic Charities nonprofit that cares for children and adults with developmental disabilities in group homes in Cuyahoga County. (See: http://www.rose-marycenter.com).

Michael O'Malley is an award-winning journalist who began his career in 1979 at the Lorain Journal in Lorain, Ohio, where (as a rookie) he received a first-place statewide Associated Press award for reporting on asbestos hazards in industrial work places.

After two years at the Journal, Mike moved to Youngstown to write for the Youngstown Vindicator. In 1984, he joined United Press International, working in Cleveland and then in Albany, New York, where he covered the New York statehouse and the Gov. Mario Cuomo administration.

Michael O'Malley.

In 1990, Mike was hired by The Plain Dealer where he worked for 23 years covering various beats, writing on politics, crime, urban issues and slice-of-life features. Many of his stories focused on social justice issues, earning him the first ever award for "Social Justice Reporting" given by Greater Cleveland Community Shares, a nonprofit group that supports social justice causes.

Mike has received a number of awards from the Society of Professional Journalists and the Press

Club of Cleveland. Mike left The Plain Dealer in 2013 in a mass layoff. His last assignment at the paper was religion writer.

Today, Mike is director of media relations for Cleveland City Council. He is a graduate of St. Edward High School in Lakewood and Cleveland State University, where he received a Bachelor of Arts degree in English.

Michael D. Roberts is a longtime Cleveland journalist and member of the Cleveland Press Club Hall of Fame. He worked as a reporter for The Plain Dealer, then as an editor, before leaving in 1973 and to become editor of Cleveland Magazine, a position he held for 17 years. In one capacity or another, he has worked with many of Cleveland's best – and most colorful – journalists, including Joe Eszterhas, Brent Larkin, Terry Sheridan, Jim Parker, Jim Neff, John Tidyman, Evelyn Theiss and Dick Feagler, the "best journalist of his time," he says. "He had a sense of the city like nobody else."

Mike also has written many important stories.

He learned the craft of journalism at The Plain Dealer in the 1960s, covering civil rights violence, the Tet Offensive in Vietnam, the agony of the Middle East, and the shootings at Kent State. His upcoming book, "Hot Type, Cold Beer and Bad News," is about those times and how they "tormented the soul of a newspaper." It is scheduled to be published later this year by Gray & Company. (See https://www.grayco.com).

Louis B. Seltzer (1897-1980) was the 38-year editor and the force behind The Press from 1928 until his retirement in 1966. "They called him 'Mr. Cleveland.' Dick Feagler, who worked for Seltzer, said in "Stop the presses." "We didn't. They did. They, the mayors, the governor, the President. To us, he was Louie. He did not strut the office in regal splendor. He popped in and threw a string of firecrackers on the floor of the city room. He hit reporters in the belly." Seltzer wrote about his years at The Press in his autobiography, "The Years Were Good: The Autobiography of Louis B. Seltzer." (See the e-book edition at https://tinyurl.com/CSULouisSeltzer).

Mary Anne Sharkey is a veteran journalist who works as a communications and public affairs consultant in Cleveland and Columbus. She began her newspaper career at The (Dayton) Journal Herald while attending the University of Dayton, where she graduated with a degree in English. After working in the combined Dayton Daily News and The Journal Herald Statehouse Bureau, she joined The Plain Dealer's Statehouse Bureau. She was the first woman president of the Ohio Legislative Correspondents Association, was promoted to statehouse bureau chief and became editorial director in Cleveland. Mary Anne also was the politics editor and assistant managing editor at the PD.

Her post-newspaper career included working on campaigns for Governor, Mayor of Cleveland, Ohio Supreme Court, Congress, and statewide and local campaigns including two successful ones for Cleveland Metropolitan Schools and the statewide casino issue. She has also worked for Governor Bob Taft, Mayor Frank Jackson, Cleveland City Council, Cuyahoga County Council,

JobsOhio, JACK Ohio casino, Cleveland State University, Ohio Board of Regents, Cuyahoga County Community College, and the Cuyahoga County Land Bank.

Mary Anne was a fellow at Harvard University's Institute of Politics, a board member of the International Women's Media Foundation, and inducted into the Cleveland Press Club Hall of Fame. She continues to do commentary work, most recently for Public TV and WKYC-TV. She has written stories for People Magazine, George Magazine, Cleveland Magazine, and Ohio Magazine. She co-edited "Ohio Politics," published by Kent State University Press.

Terence Sheridan is a former newspaper reporter, private investigator and freelance writer. He presently lives in Belgrade, Serbia, where he grows flowers and ties trout flies.

Harlan Spector worked for 23 years at The Plain Dealer, as an assistant metro editor and a reporter. He covered health and medicine, higher education and county issues. His reporting brought about changes at the The Alcohol, Drug Addiction and Mental Health Services Board of Cuyahoga County, the county Department of Children and Family Services, the Ohio Department of Health and other agencies. Today, Harlan teaches journalism at Cleveland State University and continues to write about health and medicine and other topics.

Journalist Terence Sheridan at the Sarajevo airport in 1993. Photograph by Elizabeth Sullivan.

Kaye Spector is a recovering newspaper reporter. She began her 30-year news career as an editorial assistant at the former Columbus Citizen-Journal while a journalism student at The Ohio State University. Kaye worked for several newspapers in Northeast Ohio, including the Sun Newspapers, the Medina Gazette and the Elyria Chronicle-Telegram, before coming to The Plain Dealer in 2000.

At the Plain Dealer, Kaye most recently covered health and medicine. Her other beats included local news, disability issues, suburban life and nightside general assignment. Kaye also was an assistant metro editor for several years, managing teams of reporters covering suburban news and police and courts.

She earned her master's degree in journalism in 2012, and is a member of the Society of Professional Journalists, serving on the Cleveland chapter's board and as chapter president. Kaye now works in marketing for a Cleveland-based hospital system. She and her husband, Harlan, also a longtime PD journalist, live in Shaker Heights with their son.

Scott Stephens has been a journalist and communications professional for more than 40 years.

He has worked at newspapers and publications in Pennsylvania, Florida and Ohio, including 18 years at The Plain Dealer.

In 2009, he won the National Headliner Award for education reporting. In 2010, the Education Writers Association awarded him second-place in national beat reporting. He has twice been nominated for a Pulitzer Prize.

He is currently executive director of communications and public relations for the Shaker Heights City School District in Ohio. Previously, he worked at the Chicago Public Schools as executive director for strategic communications. He came to Chicago after serving on the public affairs staff of the American Federation of Teachers in Washington, D.C.

While at The Plain Dealer, he served six years on the International Executive Council of The Newspaper Guild/Communications Workers of America, the largest media union in North America. He and his wife, photographer Christine "Chris" Stephens, have three adult sons and two grandsons.

Gail Stuehr is a journalist and public relations practitioner with specialties in media relations, publications, science, technology, medicine and education. She attended the University of Michigan School of Journalism and Kent State University, where she was a member and president of Theta Sigma Phi, a national honorary fraternity for women in journalism. After graduation and marriage, she joined the Cleveland professional chapter of TSP, later Association for Women in Communications, Inc., and served in several positions, including as president in 1975 and 1976.

After a decade of freelancing, for Cleveland Magazine, The Plain Dealer and the Southeast Sun, among others, she joined Case Western Reserve University in 1979, covering science and technology before beginning an 16-year career as director of public relations at the CWRU School of Medicine. She also served as communication coordinator of Cleveland-Heights – University Heights City Schools and marketing manager of United Way Services. Currently, she is a reporter with the Lake County Tribune.

Gail is a member of the Press Club of Cleveland and past member of Society of Professional Journalists.

Evelyn Theiss has been a journalist and writer for more than two decades. She spent 23 years as a reporter at The Plain Dealer, where her beats included being the politics writer, covering the national conventions and the presidential race of 1996; reporting on the Cleveland city schools and Mayor Michael R. White and being a feature writer. She also was the fashion editor from 2000 to 2005 and was covering the New York fashion shows on 9/11. She filed her first story from Manhattan within a few hours of the planes hitting the Twin Towers. In her last three years at the PD, Evelyn was a medical reporter.

She is now a writer and senior communications strategist at University Hospitals.

Evelyn Theiss.

While at The Plain Dealer, she was the first reporter in 40 years to get an interview with Ron Haeberle, the reclusive photographer who exposed Vietnam's My Lai massacre with his photos. This spring, Evelyn wrote a news feature for FOTO, the new Getty/Life Images website, on the 50th anniversary of the My Lai massacre and Haeberle, whose photos changed history. New information she discovered this year about that infamous day in 1968 made the story even more poignant. (See https://tinyurl.com/FOTOmylai).

For the last 10 years, she has been a correspondent for the national magazine Organic Spa, writing features on health and wellness, and travel. She received her bachelor's degree in journalism from Kent State University and, last December, her master's degree in urban studies from the Levin College of Urban Affairs at Cleveland State University.

Stuart Warner.

Stuart Warner has developed a national reputation as an editor and teacher of literary journalism. He has lectured on writing at Harvard, Duke, Columbia, The Poynter Institute, the National Writers Conference and many other venues. He taught full-time at Case Western Reserve University in Cleveland.

He has written, edited or supervised three Pulitzer Prize-winning projects and edited three other Pulitzer finalists. He was the lead writer of the 20,000-word narrative, "The Goodyear War," which was the centerpiece of the Akron Beacon Journal's 1987 Pulitzer-winning effort. He edited and supervised the Beacon Journal's 1994 Pulitzer Gold Medal winning project, "A Question of Color." At the Plain Dealer, he edited Connie Schultz's columns that won the 2005 Pulitzer for commentary and he edited Schultz's 25,000-word series "Burden of Innocence," which won the Robert F. Kennedy Award for social justice reporting and was a finalist for the Pulitzer in feature writing. He also edited the columns of Regina Brett, who was a Pulitzer Prize finalist in 2008 and 2009.

Overall, he has edited stories that won more than 70 national awards and regional awards, including a 2018 Polk Award for revealing that Motel 6 was handing over its guest lists to ICE in Phoenix. He has four times been named best columnist or essayist in Ohio by the Press Club of Cleveland.

Warner's 49-year career has included stops at the Lexington Herald-Leader, Rocky Mountain News, Seattle Post-Intelligencer, The Plain Dealer, AOL News, Huffington Post and the Arizona Republic. He is currently is editor in chief of Phoenix New Times. He was inducted into the Cleveland Journalism Hall of Fame in 2012.

William "Bill" Wynne.

William "Bill" Wynne is an award-winning photographer and photojournalist. Born in Scranton, Pennsylvania, and raised in Cleveland, Ohio, Bill was a student at West Technical High School, studying horticulture and photography. After graduating, he served as an aerial photographer, lab technician, and camera operator as part of the photo reconnaissance squadron of the U.S. Air Force during World War II, which included stints in the Southwest Pacific and the Far East.

Bill also worked as a photographer for the National Aeronautics and Space Administration.

He worked as a photographer for The Plain Dealer for about 31 years, capturing moving images of political and social significance, as well as nature and ordinary moments in daily life. A social justice advocate, he won numerous awards for his work, including the National Conference of Christians and Jews Brotherhood Prize. Bill also was part of the Plain Dealer investigative team that exposed the deplorable conditions and abuses at Lima State Hospital for the Criminally Insane in the 1970s, inspiring then Governor John Gilligan to open an investigation into abuses of patients at the institution. Nearly 30 employees ended up going to prison, and Bill and his partners received the Heywood Broun Award for their work, among other honors.

Bill married Margaret Roberts Wynne in 1946, raising nine children and sharing over 57 years together until her death in 2004. He recently celebrated his 96th birthday.

Resources

Resources related to our contributors and their essays.

Allard, Sam, Cleveland Scene magazine, "Roldo's Point of View: The legacy of a Cleveland hell-raiser," April 2018, profile of Roldo Bartimole. (See https://tinyurl.com/CLESceneRoldo).

Andrzejewski, Tom and Kay, Leslie, The Plain Dealer, "Justice in the Seventies: The System on Trial," December 1978, one of the nation's first computer-assisted reporting projects. (See https://tinyurl.com/SystemOnTrial1978).

Ashbolt, William, The Plain Dealer, photograph archive, The Cleveland Memory Project, Special Collections, Cleveland State University. (See https://tinyurl.com/WilliamAshbolt).

Barnett, David C. and **Wu, Annie,** Ideastream, "Dick Feagler Remembered As A Role Model & Inspiration," July 2, 2018. (See https://tinyurl.com/IdeastreamFeagler).

Bartimole, Roldo, The Cleveland Memory Project, archive with every issue of "Point Of View" published, more than 700 of them in 32 years. (See http://www.clevelandmemory.org/roldo).

Bartimole, Roldo, Teaching Cleveland, "One man can make a difference," story on Plain Dealer reporter Bob Holden, CEI and Muny Light. (See https://tinyurl.com/HoldenMuniLight).

Buchanan, Carrie, "Plain Dealing: Cleveland Journalists Tell Their Stories," 2018, interview with Cleveland-area journalist Gail Stuehr. To read a transcript of the interview, click here.

 An interactive or media element has been excluded from this version of the text. You can view it online here: https://pressbooks.ulib.csuohio.edu/plain-dealing/?p=1514

Clark, Anna, The Columbia Journalism Review, "I am alive at the Plain Dealer," July 31, 2013, story on the layoff of one-third of the newspaper's editorial staff. (See https://tinyurl.com/JCR-AnnaClark.).

Condon, George E., The Cleveland Memory Project, "Cleveland: the Best Kept Secret," 1967, republished as an e-book. (See https://tinyurl.com/CLEBestKeptSecret).

Davis, Dave, "Plain Dealing: Cleveland Journalists Tell Their Stories," 2018, interview with William "Bill" Wynne about photography, The Plain Dealer, his days in World War II and at the National Aeronautics and Space Administration. Bill Barrow of Cleveland State University joined the conversation. To read a transcript of the interview, click here.

An interactive or media element has been excluded from this version of the text. You can view it online here: https://pressbooks.ulib.csuohio.edu/plain-dealing/?p=1514

Davis, Dave, YSU Journalism Fellow, The Plain Dealer, "Transplanting Life," February 1997, a five-day series of stories with Ted Wendling and Joan Mazzolini on inequities in the nation's organ transplant system. (See https://tinyurl.com/TransplantSeries).

Diedrichs, Gary W., Cleveland Magazine, "What They Didn't Tell You About The Newspaper Strike," Jan. 1, 1975. (See https://tinyurl.com/CLEmag1974strike).

Flint, Jerry M., New York Times, "31 Ex-Employes at Ohio Hospital Appear in Court," Nov. 27, 1971, story on court appearance by 31 former workers at the Lima State Hospital for the Criminally Insane whose abusive treatment of patients was revealed by The Plain Dealer. (See https://tinyurl.com/LimaStateHospital).

French, Janet Beighle, Cleveland Memory Project, archive of mostly paper documents of the longtime Plain Dealer food editor, including articles, recipes, scrapbooks, and photographs from the PD's Food Section. (See https://tinyurl.com/JanetFrench).

Frankel, Rebecca, National Geographic, "Dogs at War: Smoky a Healing Presence for Wounded WWII soldiers, May 22, 2014, story about William "Bill" Wynne and his dog, Smoky, one of the first therapy dogs. (See https://tinyurl.com/SmokyNatGeo).

Haeberle, Ronald, The Plain Dealer, November 1969, photographs of the My Lai massacre that were first published by The Plain Dealer. (See https://tinyurl.com/PD-MyLai-Photos).

Jorgensen, Bill, The Cleveland Memory Project, WEWS-TV 5, television story on Plain Dealer copy editor Robert Manry during his 1965 Atlantic Ocean crossing, footage provide by the Northeast Ohio Broadcaset Archives, John Carroll University. (See https://tinyurl.com/ManryWEWS).

Manry, Robert, Cleveland Memory Project, "Tinkerbelle Sails the Atlantic," a 1965 documentary of the PD copy editor's adventure crossing the Atlantic Ocean in a 13 1/2-foot sail boat. (See https://tinyurl.com/TinkerbelleSails).

Manry, Robert, The Cleveland Memory Project, "Tinkerbelle: The story of the smallest boat ever to cross the Atlantic nonstop," e-book. (See https://tinyurl.com/ManryBook).

Neff, James, "Mobbed Up: Jackie Presser's High-Wire Life in the Teamsters, the Mafia, and the FBI," 1990, Dell Publishing, available as an e-book from Open Road Integrated Media, 2015. (See https://tinyurl.com/Neff-MobbedUp).

Osrin, Ray, The Plain Dealer, The Cleveland Memory Project, archive of The Plain Dealer's longtime editorial cartoonist's work. (See https://tinyurl.com/CSURayOsrin).

Roberts, Mike, Gray & Company, "Hot Type, Cold Beer and Bad News," a colorful book on

Cleveland journalism in the 60s expected out later this year by former Plain Dealer reporter and editor who went on to become editor of Cleveland Magazine. (See https://www.grayco.com).

Seltzer, Louis B., The Cleveland Memory Project, "The Years Were Good: The Autobiography of Louis B. Seltzer," 1956. (See e-book at https://tinyurl.com/CSULouisSeltzer).

The City Club of Cleveland, Doris O'Donnell and J. Michael Murry, 1991 forum on the Sam Sheppard case and the public's right to know versus the right of a defendant to a fair trail unprejudiced by excessive publicity. (See https://tinyurl.com/CityClubSheppard).

The Cleveland Press Collection, The Cleveland Memory Project, hundreds of thousands of clippings and photographs from The Press, Special Collections, Cleveland State University Library. (See http://www.clevelandmemory.org/press).

Theiss, Evelyn, The Plain Dealer, 2009 profile of Army combat photographer Ron Haeberle on the 40th anniversary of the newspaper publishing the My Lia massacre photographs. The piece includes an interview with former reporter turned Hollywood screen writer Joe Eszterhas. (See https://tinyurl.com/RonHaeberle).

Theiss, Evelyn, FOTO, "At My Lai: The Photographer Who Captured the Massacre," March 27, 2018, profile of Army combat photographer Ron Haeberle for the online Getty Images magazine. (See https://tinyurl.com/FOTOmylai).

Tricky, Eric, Columbia Journalism Review, "Roldo Bartimole, Cleveland's original alt-journalist," July 26, 2018, story on Roldo Bartimole and his newsletter, Point of View. (See https://tinyurl.com/CJRRoldo).

Vacha, John, Cleveland historian, original research, a Cleveland newspaper timeline and circulation numbers dating to 1875. (See https://tinyurl.com/CLENewspapers).

Webster, Don, WEWS-TV5, Oct. 10, 1982, coverage of a controversy between The Plain Dealer and union boss Jackie Presser. At issue was an a story that day in The Plain Dealer that appeared to be a "retraction" of earlier reporting identifying Presser as a federal informant. The unbylined story prompted an immediate picket of the newspaper by PD reporters. Presser held a press conference later that afternoon, declaring that the story vindicated him. Years later, Presser's crime associates testified before Congress that the story had been arranged by the mob to help Presser in his attempt to become president of the International Brotherhood of Teamsters. Our thanks to Lisa Lewis and the Northeast Ohio Broadcast Archives at John Carroll University for making the footage available. (See https://tinyurl.com/JCU-NOBA). Click the video player below to watch it.

 An interactive or media element has been excluded from this version of the text. You can view it online here: https://pressbooks.ulib.csuohio.edu/plain-dealing/?p=1514

Wynne, William "Bill," National Aeronautics and Space Administration, June 3, 2014, Oral History Project, interviewed by Sandra Johnson. (See: https://tinyurl.com/WynneNASA).

Wynne, William "Bill," The Plain Dealer, photograph archive, The Cleveland Memory Project, Special Collections, Cleveland State University. (See https://tinyurl.com/WilliamWynneCSU).

www.ingramcontent.com/pod-product-compliance
Lightning Source LLC
Chambersburg PA
CBHW081833170426
43199CB00017B/2713